To: J

From: Dr. Bob

Teach the Children
well because
they have only only
child hood

Robert J Wall
4/15/16

Racism Learned at an Early Age Through Racial Scripting

Racism at an Early Age

Robert L. Williams, Ph.D.

Professor Emeritus,
Washington University-St. Louis

Bloomington, IN      Milton Keynes, UK

authorHOUSE®

AuthorHouse™
1663 Liberty Drive, Suite 200
Bloomington, IN 47403
www.authorhouse.com
Phone: 1-800-839-8640

AuthorHouse™ UK Ltd.
500 Avebury Boulevard
Central Milton Keynes, MK9 2BE
www.authorhouse.co.uk
Phone: 08001974150

First published by AuthorHouse   1/25/2007

ISBN: 978-1-4259-2595-6 (sc)

Library of Congress Control Number: 2006902859

Printed in the United States of America
Bloomington, Indiana

This book is printed on acid-free paper.

TABLE OF CONTENTS

SECTION I
RACISM: ITS ORIGINS

SECTION II:
WILLIAMS RACIAL SCRIPT THEORY (WRST)

SECTION III
RACISM: ITS DEVELOPMENT

CHAPTER VI: THE COUNTERSCRIPTING PROCESS ..135

CHAPTER VII: MODES OF INTERRACIAL INTERACTION: IMMERSION-AVOIDANCE 161

SECTION IV
RACISM: ITS VARIOUS FORMS
AND EXPRESSIONS

INTRODUCTION — RACISM101: HOME GROWN AND HOME TAUGHT

Slavery has been destroyed in this country, but not racism.
Henry Steele Commander

1) What This Book is About

This book is about the acquisition of white *racial attitudes*, how they are taught, how they are learned, and how they are activated. More specifically, it is a book about what white parents teach their children about Black folks; about what white relatives teach children about Black folks; about what the media teaches children about Blacks and about what schools and religious organizations teach children about African Americans. Finally, this book is about seeing the acquisition and development of racism through the eyes of children.

The main thesis of this book is that white racism is taught (and learned) at an early age through a process known as "racial scripting". **A racial script is a series of programmed messages (e.g. stereotypes and myths) about a particular ethnic group and transmitted to children by parents, relatives, teachers, media, religious groups and significant others.** White racism is a family legacy passed down from generation to generation through racial scripts. The most significant point is that a racial script is taproot of racism. It is the main foundation from which other racial attitudinal developments spring. The book concludes with suggestions of ways to eliminate racism: 1) by stopping the teaching of negative racial scripts 2) by preventing the scripts from developing 3) by extracting their roots and 4) by replacing the teaching of racial hatred with themes of respect for all racial groups through the development of anti-racist models for parents.

Dr. Harry X. Davidson (1987) in his book, **Somebody's Trying to Kill You,** makes the critical point about the elimination of racism in the following metaphor. He recommends a process of deracination or removing racism by the roots. Davidson says:

> To kill weeds in your lawn, you must destroy their roots and not merely chop off the tops. A doctor who attempts to cure a disease by just treating the fever is very limited and not likely to be too successful. The fever merely indicates a deeper problem. P.9

Some evidence exists to support the manner in which racial hatred is taught. Allport and Kramer (1946) reported 69 percent of 437 undergraduates students indicated their racial attitudes were heavily influenced by their parents' attitudes toward minority groups. The more prejudiced students indicated they had taken over their parents' prejudicial attitudes more or less unchanged. Radke-Yarrow and Miller (1952) argued that even though some parents may not deliberately indoctrinate their children with a particular racist view, the children's racial attitudes invariably might be indirectly influenced by parental example and beliefs. The family is the basic institution through which the basic socialization processes are formed.

Parents are the primary agents of socialization. They define the child's world. They teach such things as reading, writing, arithmetic cultural values and the facts of life. Surely, we do not expect children to learn how to read, write, count and acquire life skills all by themselves. Of course we do not. They are taught by parents and significant others. But, in addition to teaching children " the three R's" there is also another instructional system taught to young children; and this is called the fourth "**R**" or *RACISM.*

Very little has been reported on how "racial attitudes" develop. Goodman (1964) outlined three phases for the development of racial awareness and racial attitudes as follows:

> Phase 1: Awareness, the dawning and sharpening of consciousness of self and of others in terms of racial identity;
>
> Phase 2: Orientation (incipient attitude), the learning and synthesizing of race-related words, concepts, and values;
>
> Phase 3: True Attitude: the establishing of full-fledged race attitudes. (p. 252)

Goodman's concludes that children begin to acquire racial attitudes at an early age. However, she does not explain how these racial attitudes are acquired. Where and how do they originate? Very few, if any, explanations focus on the **acquisition** process. Because of this deficiency, I decided to concentrate primarily on the manner in which the children *acquire* racial attitudes rather than on the development of racial awareness. I began with the assumption that the home, the school, the streets, the church and the media bound the child's world. It is within these boundaries that the "Four R's": Readin'. Ritin', Rithmetic and Racism" are initially required.

In her book, *Black Child, White Child*: **the development of racial attitudes,** Porter (1971) briefly suggests that racial attitudes are acquired in the home, but, her research focuses primarily on the development of *racial awareness* in Black and White children and not on *racial attitude acquisition*. With regard to racial attitude acquisition, she explains:

> One of the most important agents of attitude transmission is the family. The child may accept the parents' norms, values, and behavior patterns as his own through such processes as

identification; since he is not born with social values and attitudes, topics beyond his comprehension leave him no alternative but to internalize the values of others. The parents may transmit these racial attitudes directly and explicitly. (p. 14)

My basic thesis is: *racism is homegrown and home taught through a process known as racial scripting.* Whether one is White, Black, Native American or Hispanic, one will be taught the values of that home and culture. If the home atmosphere is one of prejudice or bigotry, racist attitudes will either be "taught" to the child or "caught" by the child. Gordon Allport (1954) makes a distinction between **adopting** prejudice and **developing** prejudice. He says

> A child who adopts prejudice is taking over attitudes and stereotypes from his family or cultural environment...Parental words and gestures, along with their concomitant beliefs and antagonisms are transferred to the child.

> But there is a type of training that does not transfer ideas and attitudes directly to the child, but rather creates an atmosphere in which he develops prejudice as his style of life. P. 297

Nonetheless, whether the learning is adoptive or developmental, it seems clear that the origin of racism and racist attitudes begins in the home. Parents are the primary character builders and nurturers of the children. Parents may transmit racist messages deliberately and/or unintentionally to their children. These "messages" are what I have labeled *racial scripts* or the taproots of racist attitudes. Racial scripts are powerful phenomena. They influence the child's everyday behavior knowingly or unknowingly.

2) Why Study the White Racial Psyche?

A simple answer to this question is that it has not been intensively studied. Over the past 75 years much has been written about the impact of racism, bigotry and prejudice on African Americans whose psyches have been the main focus of study. The compelling need is not to fix the victims of racism but to prevent the perpetrators of racism from becoming racists in the first place. We must stop putting band-aids on the racial problem and get to the roots of racism.

Many volumes have been written on understanding the Black American's psyche and identity. However, not surprising very little information has appeared in the literature on the psychological makeup of White Americans' psyches, their racial identity, racist thinking and racist acts. This imbalance needs to be corrected to the point of understanding the White American's psychological makeup. Clearly, racism is not solely a black problem. Both blacks and whites need to have some understanding of the dynamics of racism and what accounts for racist attitudes acquisition.

Further, we need to examine closely the white racial psyche so that white people can understand how and why they became a racist in the first place, how they can divest themselves of their racist beliefs and how to prevent future racist children. Since their racial attitudes may have been learned so early in life, they may not be aware of their origin, their development and their upkeep. The more we learn about how racist attitudes get started, the better we will be able to eliminate racism.

A black reporter for the New York Times described a conversation that occurred between a German and an African American. The German asked the African-American if he were aware of how some White Americans denigrated and belittled Black Americans. The German pointed out that whites described Black Americans as "animals" who had tails. The black reporter stated that he was aware of that description: "They're (White Americans) a strange breed of people." The purpose of this book is to study this "strange breed of people" by looking into their psyches and investigating how they are developed, transmitted and maintained.

Black psychologist Lloyd Delaney (1968), in an article entitled The White American Psyche—Exploration on Racism, discussed certain characteristics of the White American's psyche. According to Delaney, to look and feel superior, White Americans have a psychological need to create an inferior being, the African American. Whites also have a psychological need to look down on Black Americans so that they can look and feel superior. Delaney (1968) states:

It is this need that reflects the basic sense of inferiority and inadequacy on the part of the white racist, masking often his admiration of the Black man. He needs an inferior and he projects his inadequacies, his failing, relying on the pathetic device of skin to establish his "superiority." p.161.

Black Psychologist, Dr. Bobby Wright (1975) further described the white racist as a "psychopathic racial personality." He gives the following definition of the white racist personality:

.... In their relationship with the Black race, Europeans (whites) are psychopaths and their behavior reflects an underlying biologically transmitted proclivity with roots deep in their evolutionary history...he is unable to experience guilt, is completely selfish and callous and has a total disregard for the rights of others. (Pg.3)

As I began to conceptualize the thesis for book in 1999 one of the most heinous hate crimes of the Twentieth Century happened: the vicious, brutal dragging murder of James Byrd of Jasper, Texas. I asked myself the question "Why did these three white men commit such a terrible act?" What was the content of their psyches? How did their racist psyches develop?

3) Why Do These Things Happen?

There are many unanswered questions concerning racist activities. For example:

1) Why did whites in Money, Mississippi lynch Emmett Till in 1955?

2) Why did the three white men drag and murder James Byrd in Jasper, Texas?

3) Why do white people lock their doors when approaching a Black community?

4) Why do white conservatives oppose Affirmation Action?

5) Why are white people so afraid of black people?

6) What is the nature of a racial psyche that would bomb a church in Birmingham, Alabama in 1963 and kill 3 young black girls?

7) What kind of racial psyche is it that led to the murder of Medgar Evers in 1963?

8) Why did James Earl Ray assassinate Dr. Martin Luther King, Jr. in 1968?

9) Why did a former white New York patrolman torture the Haitian immigrant, Abner Louima with a broken broomstick?

10) Why was Sherrice Iverson raped and murdered by 19-year old white Jeremy Strohmeyer in a Las Vegas Bathroom in 1998?

11) Why did a white man slash Jason Johnson's throat in Joplin, Missouri in October 1998?

13) Why was Raynard Johnson hanged from a tree in Kokomo, Mississippi, June 16, 2000? Was it because he dated two 17-year old white girls?

14) Why were two unarmed black men shot and killed in St. Louis, Missouri June 2004, by police on a busy Jack -in -the-box Restaurant parking lot?

15) Why was J. R. Warren, a black and gay man, of West Virginia, savagely beaten and murdered on July 4, 2000 by two 17-year old white boys?

These questions caused me to investigate the structure of the White American racial psyche and its acquisition. Not much is known about this part of the white psyche. The answers to these questions reside in the racial psyche of white people, a gravely under studied group.

4) Black Invisibility or Black Hyper visibility

People do not wish to express racial feelings openly, especially when they tend to be negative. One's racial thoughts and experiences are very private. In general, whites tend to deny being racist. In fact, to call a white person "racist" is very threatening and demeaning. To understand how this is threatening to whites, we must understand that there is no real way they can defend themselves, except through their positive behavioral actions.

How can one tell whether a white person is a racist or not? I conducted a little experiment by sitting in one place where dozens of whites pass through every hour. I wanted to know if any of them would admit to being a racist. As they passed, I smiled, and a few smiled back, some turned their heads while others remained expressionless. It was as if I did not exist, invisible I suppose. I said surely some of these people would recognize me and speak. But that did not happen. One white man rolled past me in a wheelchair. I certainly expected him to speak or return my smile. But he did not.

As Ralph Ellison noted in the **Invisible Man**:

> I am an invisible man. No, I am not a spook like those who haunted Edgar Allen Poe; nor am I one of your Hollywood movie ectoplasms. I am a man of substance, of flesh and bone, fiber and liquids—and I might even be said to possess a mind. I am invisible, understand, simply because people refuse to see me...when they approach me they see only my surroundings, themselves or figments of their imagination indeed, everything and anything except me. (P 10)

To document further this invisibility or racism, I went into an upscale restaurant to have lunch. There were two white couples ahead of me. The white host came and asked each of the white patrons for their names and arranged to have them seated. I stood silently waiting for him to ask me. He looked straight at me for a long period of time, but said nothing. I just stood there. Finally, I said to him, "I'd like to sign up for a table too." He looked befuddled. When I asked him why he did not ask me, " He responded, "I didn't see you."

Now I am 6'4' tall, weighing 215 pounds and very black. How could he have not seen me? I deduced it was his "Blinders to Blackness". Many whites either see you in negative stereotypes or they don't see you at all. It is either hyper visibility or invisibility", both of which are false perceptions.

Now there are some whites that will relate to Blacks on a realistic level. For example, after eating at the same upscale restaurant, I stood outside for a while. A white gentleman asked me why was I standing outside. I replied that it was such a beautiful day; I wanted to get some fresh air. Then he asked me where I was from and what kind of work I was into. The gentleman proceeded to get to know me rather than assume certain things about me. Consequently, he was able to get a realistic appraisal of me.

5) Qualitative Research Method

Since I discovered that whites would not admit to being racist, I had to develop another way of finding out how racist attitudes are acquired. Thus, instead of asking white adults about their current racial attitudes (which I knew they would deny) I decided to ask their children. To do this study, I developed a *qualitative research technique* that I used to identify how racist attitudes are acquired. I did not want to know whether the children were racist. Rather, I wanted to know what their parents *taught* them about Black Americans. Consequently, I had the "children" to go back into the early stages of their lives and discuss how their attitudes towards black people developed in the first place.

This book contains material about the racial instructions, which their parents gave to them.

To get at racial attitude acquisition, I asked individuals to write and describe what their parents told them about Blacks.

The individuals were given the following instructions:

> You are asked to write a racial script paper. The construct, racial script, is a life plan or attitude learned involuntarily from significant others (e.g. parents, grandparents, uncles aunts, the media, peers, etc.) outlining how to feel, think and behave in response to Black people. Individuals adopt various forms and degrees of racial scripts for survival through socialization. Some racial scripts are functional; some are dysfunctional, i.e., they may be positive, negative, neutral/avoidance or mixed.

I began collecting racial scripts in the early 1990's and continued into the 21st Century. During that period, approximately 50% of the individuals reported negative racial scripting, 30% reported positive racial scripting and 20% reported mixed scripting, i.e., one parent gave positive scripts whereas the other gave negative scripts.

The basic idea for writing this book occurred during the time that I taught a course entitled "Black Psychology". It was a very popular class. Usually the classes averaged 150 students with white students comprising approximately 60% and African-Americans comprising 30 percent and Asians, Hispanic and Native Americans comprising the remaining 10%.

White students indicated that they took the Black Psychology course to gain a better understanding of black culture, as well as to have some interaction with black students. Many of them complained about the racial separation on the college campus. They sought to develop accurate perceptions about black people through this course.

Many students wrote "Thank You" notes to me. Following is just one of the notes written by a white student:

Dr. Robert L. Williams:

Thank you so much for enlightening me over the last semester. You have blessed me above my expectations and you are an excellent teacher and facilitator. This class has taken of blinders and dug down deep into the many layers of stereotypes and misconceptions. I wish every student enrolled at this university could take this class. This should be a general education course. My faith propelled me to take this course and I learned a great deal about how this world is really constructed. I see life with far more society than ever before and pray that reality will continue to slap me in the face. Than you for teaching me what I need to know. I have been privileged.

For ten years, I gathered information on the formation and development of racial attitudes in Caucasians, Blacks, Hispanics and, Asians and Native Americans. Most of the studies of racism focus on the black psyche (i.e. the victims of racism) and not on the main perpetrators of racism: **Whites**. In this book however, I will focus exclusively on whites and their acquisition of racial scripts. In a later text, I will discuss the racial script acquisition in blacks and other ethnic groups.

One of the requirements for the course involved the students writing a "racial script" paper explaining how and what they learned about African Americans early in life. This book will describe the experiences reported from interviews and written reports. I will emphasize the formation, development and maintenance of the racial psyche, primarily in Caucasians through this indirect qualitative, research method. Some references to blacks will also be mentioned. I will describe the methods by which "racial scripts" become embedded in the psyche of the white child and the process by which they are activated.

Thus, this is a retrospective account of their childhood. They were asked to look back into their childhood, to rewind the tape recorder and to recall what their parents taught them about black people. The most disturbing finding, but not surprising, was that many of the white students reported that they were virtually indoctrinated into fearing and hating black people. The majority of the white students grew up in racially isolated communities, attended predominately white schools, and churches and had little or no early experience with African-Americans.

6) Racial Isolation

Students discussed racial isolation by living in segregated communities as a major deterrent to their forming relationships and interacting with blacks. Many, many individuals describe their communities as follows:

- I spent my youth in a small rural town on the East Coast. The area was 100% white. Growing up, the racial issue was never dealt with directly by my family or by the community:

- Racial isolation was the name of the game in the community where I grew up in the Midwest. Isolation was due to the fact that not a single black person lived in the area when I was growing up, and only a few would venture into this total "whiteness" world to work."

- I was brought up in a little town that was 100% white. I knew that Black people existed, but never before had I talked to them. It was in High School that I had my first encounter with a Black person.

- I grew up in a small mid-western town with a population of 5600 White Catholic/Protestant people. Growing up, I never wondered why there were only white people in my neighborhood or for that matter in my entire town and the surrounding smaller towns. I never thought about African Americans.

- I grew up in an all-white town. I went to an all-white nursery school, an all-white elementary school, an all-white junior high school, an all-white high school and an all-white church. I had all-white teachers.

With the above racial composition of the communities where the children grew up, it is no wonder why so many of them are naïve about African-Americans. Nonetheless, these individuals "tell it like it is" whether they grew up in racially isolated areas or racially integrated areas of America. The excerpts to be presented in this collection contain a great range of thoughts and feelings from the very positive to the very negative. However, in all instances there is a great deal of honesty, sincerity and intense introspection in recounting their early experiences.

I often felt sadness in the collection of this material, because a large number of the students basically wanted to interact and treat people of other races equally. But they had been taught differently. As a society and probably as a human race, we have not been going about creating a just or fair society because we have been going about it in the wrong ways.

Significant changes in racial relations have taken place in the last thirty to forty years. Some of the walls of prejudice and racism have been torn down, but still some remain. Blacks no longer have to sit on the back of the bus; blacks can now vote freely in every state; blacks can now eat in all restaurants without fear of rejection; black and white children are now attending school together. Why, then, is this nation still divided racially? Why is it still racially polarized? It is my opinion that the answers lie in the racial psyche of each white individual.

Do we really understand the roots of racism and hate? It is clear, at least to me, that the roots are embedded in the psyche of individuals. The seeds of racial prejudice, hatred and racism have been planted and cultivated in the psyche. "If you plant a lemon seed, you will get a lemon tree." If you teach negative scripts, you will reap negative behavior. To be sure, if you teach racist or White Supremacy scripts you will get racist or White Supremacy beliefs and behaviors. Parents must feed their children values of love, obedience, faith, integrity and proper racial attitudes. Teachers must feed children values of honesty, the Golden Rule, love and respect.

Teaching a course in Black Psychology at a predominately white institution can create an emotionally charged atmosphere, particularly where the class is racially heterogeneous. The one and one-half hours that I spent in front of those mixed racial groups, (about 60% white and 30% Black and 10% other at one major mid-western University and 80% Black and 20% white at a second major University), at times, proved very taxing. Unbeknownst to many professors, dealing with race relations in a classroom situation is not the easiest task, particularly when the composition of the class is mixed racially. Students come with differing worldviews that have been taught and internalized.

To show how tension builds up in a race-oriented classroom, take a look at the following example. At the end of the semester the students are required to read and share their racial script papers in small groups. I usually go around and sit in each of the groups and observe the discussion for five to ten minutes. I remember this situation quite well because it caused a lot of tension in the class. One white female student indicated that she wanted to teach in an inner-city school. As she read her racial script paper she came across a section in her racial script paper where she quoted her uncle who frequently used the racist term "nigger". The small group, composed of both black and white students, sat quietly and listened to her racial script until she finished. Then one of the black students in the group calmly said:

> I am going to say this to you as nicely as I can and I am really going to give you the benefit of the doubt. I hope you will understand what I am about to say. I do not appreciate your using the term Nigger in my presence. It really upsets me and I wish you would not use it again.

The white student became very defensive and indicated that she was just quoting something that her uncle had said. She asked me if the term upset me. I said no. But other black students in the room indicated that they too were upset when a white person used the term Nigger. One could feel the increase in tension in the class. The session ended and I returned to my office. As I approached my office, the white female student came into my office very upset, crying hysterically. She could not understand why the students were so upset with her. She cried for more than a half hour. My point to her was I wondered if there was a lesson learned in that classroom particularly since she planned to teach in a Black community. Her response finally was "yes" she did learn a lesson, but it was a very difficult one.

I point out this situation because teaching about racism frequently erupts in to heated discussions especially when such topics as affirmative action and interracial dating and marriage come up.

Chapter I raises some important questions concerning the nature and origins of racism. Such questions as: Is racism inherited or learned? Is racism permanent? Is there a resurgence of racism in this country? Can the color line be erased? .

Chapter II provides a discussion of the theoretical foundations of **Williams Racial Script Theory (WRST)** the processes by which racial scripts are acquired and identifies the sources of the scripts.

Chapter III provides the first phase of **WRST, The Pre-exposure Phase** and the types of scripts that may be acquired at this time. This period of life is called Pre-Exposure due to the fact that the child may not have had any contact with African Americans but may have had instructions from parents about them.

Chapter IV discusses **The Discovery/Exposure Phase**. Discovery may be in the form of passive exposure, active friendly contact, a hostile encounter or a phobic interaction

Chapter V **describes Racial Script Activation,** a process showing how racial scripts are automatically activated when confronted with an African American.

Chapter VI provides insight into **The Counter-scripting Phase** or a time when racial scripts may or may not undergo changes.

Chapter VII involves **The Immersion/Avoidance Phase** where the individuals may get more involved with members of the opposite race or avoid them altogether.

Chapter VIII discusses **Racial Maturity and Racial Immaturity** in the racial scripting process.

Chapter IX tackles the problem of defining **White Supremacy, Racism and Closet Racists.** It further deals with white denial and the effects of racism on the community.

Chapter X discusses **Racial Myths and Stereotypes** as the carriers of racial scripts. It also deconstructs or dismantles the many racial myths designed to keep racism alive.

Chapter XI discuses **Traditional Forms of Individual Racism and New Expressions of Racism.**

Chapter XII discusses **Institutional Racism** and its costs.

Chapter XIII discusses **Cultural and Scientific Racism and** their impact on African Americans.

Chapter XIV provides case studies for **Racial Solutions** to the racial problems.

SECTION I

Racism: Its Origins

CHAPTER I:
RACISM:
QUESTIONS AND ANSWERS

You've got to be taught to hate and fear
You've got to be taught from year to year.

(From "South Pacific" by Rogers and Hammerstein)

1) Racism: Learned or Inherited?

Is racism inherited or is it learned? How is it acquired? How does it develop? How is it maintained? Can it be eliminated? These are compelling questions for which we must provide answers and solutions during this twenty-first century. My basic thesis is racism is learned, primarily in the home. Racism is a family legacy handed down from generation to generation. No child, black, brown, yellow, red or white enters the world as a racist. If racist attitudes are not inborn, where, when and how do they originate? Racist attitudes are initially formed and developed, primarily, in the intimate setting of the home. They are "home grown," "home taught" and shaped directly by parental instructions given to the child and indirectly by general racial attitudes and behavior displayed in the home. No, racism is not inherited; it is taught and modeled by parental figures and significant others. Powell (2001) clearly points to a teaching factor in the acquisition of racial attitudes. She states:

I believe that whites are socialized to be racist…That is whites are socialized to see "white" as "right"—to believe that white norms in terms of beauty, language, traditions and so on are superior to those of persons of color, and that everyone else wants to be like "us." (P. 26)

How do racist attitudes develop in the first place? Picture several newborn infants (Asian, African-American, Caucasian, Hispanic and Native-Americans) in multicultural, non-racist environments, or in families where all races are respected and their cultures are celebrated. The children would, in all likelihood, grow up to be non-prejudicial and free of racist attitudes. By contrast, now picture several newborns in families where racist attitudes and behaviors were prevalent. The children would most likely develop racist attitudes, reflecting what the environment models for the children. What the children's parents instruct, what the children hear their parents say and what the children see their parents do, all serve as basic instructional methods. One individual put the matter of racial-attitude-learning succinctly:

The racist attitude I learned in my life was essentially learned from my immediate family, my teachers and my close friends. These people were the "significant others" who outlined my behavioral responses to other races.

The structure of the home will determine whether or not the children will develop racist beliefs and practices. Initially, children do not learn racist attitudes from the community or sources outside of the home. The home is the primary source of racial attitudes.

In a similar fashion, attitudes for violence are taught in the home by parents. For instance, in March 1998, two boys from Jonesboro, Arkansas shot and killed four students, one teacher and injured 11 others. One of the boys, an 11-year-old came from a family of shooters. His father is the co-founder of a local gun club devoted to practical pistol shooting, a sport in which the participants fire at mobile or pop-up targets to approximate better real-life conditions. The boy's grandfather taught him how to shoot early in life. This 11-year-old child learned about guns early in life and owned a personal arsenal, including 2 rifles, a shotgun, crossbow and arrow.

A Caucasian killed Bill and Camille Crosby's son, Ennis, during a hate crime. His mother, Dr. Camille Cosby (1998) vividly described the "learned racist aspects" regarding the murder of her son in a USA Today article:

> I believe America taught our son's killer to hate African-Americans.... After Mikail Markhasev killed Ennis William Cosby on January 16, 1997, he said to his friends "I shot a 'Nigger.' It's all over the news." This was not the first time Markhasev had attacked a black person. In 1995, he served time in a juvenile center for stabbing a black man who was standing at a gas station. Presumably, Markhasev did not learn to hate black people in his native country, the Ukraine, where the black population is near zero. Nor was he likely to see America's intolerable, stereotyped movies and television programs about blacks, which were not shown in the Soviet Union before the killer and his family moved to America in the late 1980's. (p. 15a)

Dr. Cosby's point is well taken. Following the basic teaching of racial hatred in the home, the children may later be exposed to further reinforcements of this theme in the broader society, such as the media, schools and other social systems.

Further, there is not a gene for racial hatred or racial fear. While genetic factors determine whether an individual is male or female, black or white, the color of one's eyes and the pigmentation of one's skin, genes do not determine hatred or fear. Parents, relatives, teachers, friends, the media and the broader society teach racial hatred and racial fear. Consequently, racist attitudes may be socialized into children at an early age in their homes. Some parents are blatantly overt in their instructional methods concerning race relations; however, some are more subtle and covert and others feel insecure and avoid teaching racist attitudes altogether. Moreover, some parents teach positive racial attitudes while others teach and model strictly negative attitudes. Although they were found widely in our collection, it would be incorrect to conclude that the majority of parents teach pro-racist attitudes.

The Phil Donohue Show (circa 1990) aired a program depicting White-Americans who deliberately and blatantly taught their children to hate Black-Americans. Moreover, this program clearly revealed what some white families may be teaching their children about Black-Americans. The young children were being strongly indoctrinated at an early age in the principles of white supremacy. They were taught to believe that the white race is the best race because whites are smarter than blacks. They were also taught that whites are something special, and whites should be very rejecting, indeed, hostile to the idea of establishing interracial relationships.

A member of the Donohue audience asked one of the racist panelists whether or not she would let her sick child receive a blood transfusion from an African-American if her child desperately needed blood. The white racist panel member's response was "No, I would rather let my child die than to have his blood mixed with a 'colored' person." The program disclosed how the children are taken to Ku Klux Klan (KKK) rallies where racial superiority is drilled into their heads and the "N-word" is used frequently in the home. From these teachings, the parents strongly indoctrinated these children with racial hatred.

Similarly, on a Jenny Jones TV talk Show (10-31-96) entitled " I Want To Confront Former Racist Guests" one of her white guests was asked, "If you were in a life-threatening situation would you let a black physician perform surgery?" The guest's answer was "No, I wouldn't; I'd rather die."

2) Victim Analysis or Victimizer Analysis

Some white scholars analyze the victims of racism (African-Americans) and lay the cause of racism on the victims. One clear example of the "blame the victim" game is found in D'Souza's (1995) book, **The End of Racism**, when he argues it is a dysfunctional way of thinking to say that racism is responsible for the black problem.

D'Souza asserts slavery is not a racist institution and most racial discrimination today is not racism but a rational response to accurate generalizations of black people. D' Souza argues that "deficiencies in black culture," (not racism) are mainly to blame for racial inequalities. According to him, if black people are to become competitive, they must stop complaining and blaming their problems on racism and adopt the American cultural strategies that make for success, i.e. pull oneself up by one's bootstrap.

In his book, **Hating Whitey: and Other Progressive Causes**, David Horowitz (1999) makes a similar point by stating that black people blame white people too much for racial problems. Horowitz calls institutional racism a "radical fantasy." He chastises blacks for anti-white racism and tells the black community to look to itself for the solution to its problems.

The irony of D'Souza and Horowitz's arguments is that the oppressed cannot end oppression except, perhaps, as Frantz Fanon (1967) suggests through armed struggle. No we cannot let white racism completely off the hook. We must look at both sides of the equation.

Victim analysis is an inaccurate and inappropriate procedure to provide a realistic analysis of the causes of racism in the USA. We must examine the racist minds and look at their composition. We cannot understand the causes of racism by solely studying its effects, i.e. the Black-American or the victims. We must study the sources, the roots of racism (the white racial psyches) rather than their branches.

Examining the consequences of racism reminds me of a story about the man who was bending on his knees at a curbside under a streetlight. A policeman came by and asked the man what he was doing there at that time of night on his knees under the streetlight. The man answered that he was looking for his wallet. The policeman asked, "Where did you lose the wallet?" The man replied, "up in the alley." The policeman asked why then was he looking down there under the light. "Because" the man replied, "there is more light here." Obviously, the man was not going to find the wallet at the curbside where he had more light, just as we are not going to find the causes of racism nor ways to eliminate it in the psyche or behavior of the victims (blacks) just because they are more visible.

Moreover, we do not blame rape victims for being raped. We do not go to the rape victim and ask, "Why were you raped?" "What effect did that rape have on you"? That would be nonsense! We must locate the rapist to find out why that individual raped the victim. The rapist has a rapist mentality or a rapist psyche and an urge to rape women and that is why he raped the victim. The same is true for racism. We must go to the racist mind and examine the racist psyche in order to find the answers to white racism.

William Ryan (1976) clearly articulated how and what happens to victims of blame in his book, "Blaming the Victim." He says,

> Consider some victims. One is the mis-educated child in the slum school. He is blamed for his own mis-education. He is said to contain within himself the causes of his inability to read and write well. The shorthand phrase is "cultural deprivation".... What is wrong with the victim? In pursuing this logic, no one remembers to ask the questions about the collapsing buildings and torn textbooks; the frightened, insensitive teacher; the six additional desks in the room; the blustering, frightened principals; the relentless segregation; the callous administrator; the bigoted or cowardly members of the school board; the insulting history books; the stingy taxpayers. We are encouraged to confine our attention to the child and to dwell on all his alleged defects. Cultural deprivation becomes an omnibus explanation for the educational disaster known as the inner city child. This is blaming the victim." (Pp. 3-5)

Lani Guinier and David Torres (2002) in their book, **The Miner's Canary**, used an appropriate metaphor that refutes the arguments of all those who see the victims as responsible for their plight. These authors contend that:

Race, for us, is like the miner's canary. Miners often carried a canary into the mine alongside them. The canary's more fragile respiratory system would cause it to collapse from noxious gases long before humans were affected, thus alerting the miners to danger. The canary's distress signaled that it was time to get out of the mine because the air was becoming too poisonous to breathe. Those who are racially marginalized are like the miner's canary: their distress is the first sign of a danger that threatens us all. (P. 11)

Professor Guinier warns further:

We pathologize the canary. We act as though the solution is to fix the canary, to fit it with a tiny gas mask, so that it can withstand the toxic atmosphere. (Raspberry, 1998, p. B3)

Guinier maintains that we must cease arguing about what is wrong with the canary and seek to remedy the environmental conditions under which it exists and make changes in those circumstances. We must use the canary's distress signal as a need to fix the racial atmosphere of this country in order to eliminate the toxic effects of white racism.

3) Is There a Resurgence of White Racism in the USA?

Is racism dead or is there a resurgence of white racism in America? Is racism getting worse? Is it worse today than 25 years ago? Racism is not dead; it is alive. Racism has not left us. Leonard Pitts (2004) states:

It [racism] has only become a hide-and-seek thing, a did-you-see-it-or-did you-just-imagine it game…our confusion is not hard to understand in an era when racism wears three-piece suits and racists speak fluent PC. More to the point, an era where racist beliefs are hidden in policy, concealed in practice, their effects visible in statistics and studies but never in anything as crude as a sign that says 'Whites Only.' (p. B 3)

Eleanor-Holmes Norton, former head of the Federal Equal Employment Opportunity Commission reported that 1989 would be "remembered as the worst year in memory for blacks." Norton cited numerous court decisions that would reverse many civil rights gains. In particular, a supreme court held that white firefighters were not bound by affirmative agreements to end discrimination in Birmingham, Alabama. (Freivogel, 1989). This decision jeopardizes many minority job programs because whites may sue to challenge job preferences held for minorities. Further, the court made it easier for white contractors to challenge minority set-aside programs. The court shifted the burden of proof in job discrimination suits from the employer to the employee. The bottom line is translated to mean that the Supreme Court has made it more difficult to prove racial bias. Congresswoman Maxine Waters reacted to the decisions by asserting a firestorm of racial hatred is spreading across this country. While the most virulent forms of racism (lynching, etc.) have virtually been stamped out, new and more persistent strains continue to emerge.

Psychologist Dr. Halford Fairchild (2000) contends that racism has not disappeared but it is still operating in the twentieth first century. He states:

> There are some who assert that racism is obsolete and not a contemporary problem. But racism is a current event; only its expression is more disguised and subtle." (P.7.)

The Fourth Annual American Renaissance Conference held in Reston, Virginia (April 2000) is also a grim reminder that the harsh rhetoric and extremist views that fuel racist doctrines are hardly things of the past. Conference speakers claimed science shows the races are intellectually and physically unequal, with whites being superior to blacks, and that embracing diversity is a mistake. Phillippe Rushton, Professor of Psychology at the University of Western Ontario, the leading spokesperson, preached that superior genes in whites have made them intellectually and culturally superior to blacks. Rushton reported that whites have, on the average, more neurons and cranial size than blacks. They are therefore intellectually superior. He added that brain size is a very good indicator of IQ. However, at a White House conference on the Human Genome Project (June 26, 2000), Dr. Craig Venter of Celera Genomics charged that the concept of race has no scientific basis. The fundamental genetic code--the instructional booklet-- is universal. Celera Genomics Corporation, a private company, mapped the genetic codes of three females and two males who were Caucasian, Asian, African-American and Hispanic. Scientists were unable to distinguish one group from another. They concluded that race differences are very subtle and are based solely on environmental adaptation. ("Decade long", 2000, pp.1a and 6a)

There is a sharp difference of opinion between blacks and whites on racial conditions in the U.S. Blacks are saying, "Racism is getting worse." In contrast, whites are saying, "overall, things (racial relationships) are getting better. With all the strides blacks have made, I would like to think that race relations are getting better." However, black writer Nathan McCall (1994) wrote: "[Racism] Makes Me Wanna Holler," a book that describes the excruciating pain blacks suffer from racist experiences. A Gallup Poll showed opinions about race relations between Black- and White-Americans to be diametrically opposed. Ninety-two percent of blacks say race relations are poor. Eighty-four percent of whites say racial relations are fair. Similarly the acquittal verdict in the O. J. Simpson murder trial was rejected by the white community but supported by the black community suggesting that blacks and whites do not share the same perception of racial reality. Black-Americans are much more pessimistic (but seemingly realistic) about race relations, whereas whites are considerably less pessimistic. Blacks still see major problems between the races. Whites see fewer problems. Blacks find it is extremely difficult to be optimistic about improved racial relations in this country because of the many instances of racist acts. As targets of racism blacks are more sensitive to racism than are whites.

Over 60 years ago Gunnar Myrdal (1944), the Swedish Sociologist warned of the American Dilemma that could lead to racial conflict.

Robert L. Williams, Ph.D.

Also, over 30 years ago, the Kerner Commission warned this nation was moving toward two societies: one black and one white; separate and unequal. The "Report of the National Advisory Commission on Civil Disorders" (1968) predicted a deepening divide in black and white America by stating:

> Our nation is moving toward two societies, one black and one white-separate and unequal....What white Americans have never fully understood--but what the Negro can never forget-- is that white society is deeply implicated in the ghetto. White institutions created it, white institutions maintain it, and white society condones it. (P.1-2)

To see if any significant changes occurred in the nation one year after the *National Advisory Commission on Civil Disorders -the "Kerner Riot Commission* **(1969)** two organizations (Urban America, Inc. and the Urban Coalition) conducted a dramatic study to determine America's progress in racial relations one year after the 1968 riots. The authors came to this conclusion: "A year later, we are a year closer to being two societies, black and white, increasingly separate and scarcely less unequal."(P.118)

Twenty-five years or more later, we must ask the same question: "is racism still driving America into a separate and unequal black and white America?" The latest follow-up study of race relations comes from the Milton S. Eisenhower Foundation ("25 Years Later," 1993). This organization reported the racial gap is not only real, but things have gotten worse. There is not only a wide racial gap between blacks and whites, but there is also a very large economic gap. Blacks are worse off economically today than thirty years ago. The rich get richer and the poor get poorer and minorities are suffering disproportionately. We are now closer to being two societies, one black and one white, more separate, more unequal, more hatred and racism.

28

4) White Privilege and White Benefits

White privilege, the legacy from slavery, is the primary reason for the social, economic and racial gap between blacks and whites. Slavery led to practices that created "cumulative disadvantages" for African-Americans whereas it provided whites with "cumulative advantages" or special benefits and privileges. Alderwoman Dorothy Tillman (2000) of Chicago, Illinois argues that the white community passed wealth down to their descendants whereas blacks were passed down poverty.

A January 10, 2000 editorial article in the Florida Times Union refuted the theory of the cumulative disadvantages of slavery. The article entitled "The Lingering Issue" questioned the need to continue affirmative action in Florida, and presumably anywhere else in the USA, because slavery existed only briefly in America and its effects were not permanent. One hundred years of slavery in this country is hardly a "brief period" to say the least.

On September 19, 1998, the President's Advisory Board on Race submitted its final report to President Bill Clinton. It urged the President to make Americans more aware of white privileges. The report stated very clearly:

> We as a nation need to understand that whites tend to benefit either unknowingly or consciously, from this country's history of White privilege ("Clinton suggests Americans," 1998, p.4).

Frequently, whites are heard to say, "I didn't have anything to do with creating your situation. "Whites did that many years ago. I'm not to Blame." Our (blacks) response is: There are five principal aspects or consequences of slavery. These are:

1) The perpetrators: ones who were responsible for slavery

2) The collaborators: ones who worked together
   with the perpetrators to achieve slavery (i.e.
   newspapers, railroads, banks, etc.)

3) The advocators: ones who supported,
   defended and spoke in favor of slavery

4) The supporters: ones who encouraged or gave
   assistance to the perpetrators of slavery.

5) The beneficiaries: ones who received an
   advantage or a benefit from slavery.

While present day whites may not be perpetrators, collaborators, advocators or supporters, they are certainly beneficiaries. Consequently, whites have benefited from the legacy of slavery: "white privilege" and "white opportunity."

What is "white privilege?" Does it exist? Peter and Ginger Breggin (1994) in their book, The War Against Children; How the Drugs, Programs and Theories of the Psychiatric Establishment are Threatening America's Children with a Medical 'Cure' for Violence," feel that most White Americans are beneficiaries of slavery. They state:

Nearly all White Americans benefit indirectly and often unwittingly from the violent legacy of slavery and ongoing racism. Because of the color of their skin, white people are born with an entitlement--to make the most of what the society had already developed over its several hundred years of history. They are born into or have arrived in this society as its chief benefactors. (p. 180-181)

"White Privilege" produces economic and social benefits for whites. For example,

It is no accident the following conditions exist:

The U.S. Supreme Court is 89 percent white
Of the nation's airline pilots, 98.3 percent are white
Of the nation's geologists, 95.9 percent are white
On the nation's dentists, 95.6 percent are white
Of the nation's authors, 93.9 percent are white
Of the nation's lawyers, 93.8 percent are white

Of the nation's economists, 91.9 are white
Of the nation's architects, 90.6 are white
Of the nation's aerospace engineers, 93.8 are white

What's my point? The point is that we live in a predominately white society with the white majority enjoying the privileges of having an overwhelming and disproportionate share of the wealth and comfort and an even greater share of the control over the most important institutions. It is no accident that these statistics exist in favor of White Americans. They result from the legacy of slavery and continue with the presence of racism and discrimination.

"White privilege" is used to describe the advantages that whites have enjoyed in this country. Peggy McIntosh (1989) states:

> ...a "white" skin in the United States opens many doors for whites whether or not we approve of the way dominance had been conferred on us." (P.12)

For McIntosh white privilege is "unearned entitlement," "unearned advantage" and "conferred dominance." She states further:

> I think whites are carefully taught not to recognize white privilege as males are taught not to recognize male privilege.... I have come to see white privilege as an invisible package of unearned assets, which I can count on cashing in on each day, but about which I was "meant" to remain oblivious. White privilege is like an invisible weightless knapsack of special provisions, maps, passports, codebooks, visas, clothes, tools and blank checks. (p. 10)

McIntosh lists a number of privileges that she says grants her favor because of her white skin rather than social class, religion, ethnic status, or geographical location.

Paul Kivel (1996) however, in his book "Uprooting Racism: How White People Can Work for Racial Justice," makes a distinction between "White privilege" and "White benefits." He points out:

Privileges are the economic "extras" that those of us who are middle-class and wealthy gain at the expense of poor and working class people of all races. Benefits, on the other hand, are the advantages that all white people gain at the expense of people of color regardless of economic position. (P. 28)

Kivel (1996) believes that these benefits have historical roots. He states that

We can generally count on police protection rather than harassment...we can choose where we want to live and choose neighborhoods that are safe and have decent schools. We are given more attention, respect and status in conversations than people of color. We see people who look like us in the media, history books, news and music in a positive light...We have more recourse to and credibility within the legal system...Nothing that we do is qualified, limited, discredited or acclaimed simply because of our racial background. We don't have to represent our race, and nothing we do is judged as credit to our race or as confirmation of its shortcomings or inferiority. .... All else being equal, it pays to be white." (P. 28-29)

Murray & Smith (1995) make the following points regarding "white privilege":

White males occupy the most powerful and privileged positions in American society. They are in positions to make decisions that have major consequences for society. They dominate the large corporations, public bureaucracies, and other organizations. They look upon the machinery of state and local governments as theirs to run as a matter of privilege on the one hand, and a matter of rights, on the other. In addition, they occupy the key command posts of the social and economic structures where resources and values are authoritatively allocated.

The irony of the privileged status of white males is that many of them are unaware that they occupy privileged positions. They feel they occupy these positions because of their abilities and other subscription to American traditional values such as hard work, individualism and internalization of the Protestant work ethic. (p. 138)

Professor Robert Jensen (1998), a University of Texas Journalist, discusses "White Privilege" from his personal experiences as a white man raised in North Dakota where the African-American population is very small. The article is titled White Privilege shapes the U.S. He writes:

White privilege, like any social phenomenon, is complex. In a white supremacist culture, all white people have privilege, whether or not they are overtly racist themselves...Rather than try to tell others how white privileges have played out in their lives, I talk about how it has affected me. I am as white as white gets in this country; I was raised in North Dakota, one of the whitest states in the country. I grew up in a virtually all-white world surrounded by racism, both personal and institutional.

Perhaps most importantly, when I seek admission to a university, apply for a job, or hunt an apartment, I don't look threatening. Almost all of the people evaluating me look like me; they are white. They see in me a reflection of themselves-and in a racist world, that is an advantage. I smile. I am white. I am not dangerous.

[White privilege]...means simply that all through my life, I have soaked up benefits for being white. I was accepted in graduate school by white people. And I was hired for a teaching position by the predominately white University of Texas, headed by a white president, in a college headed by a white Dean and in a Department with a white Chairman that at the time had one nonwhite tenured professor.

These benefits and privileges begin early in the life of white people and continue throughout their life. Such privileges operate to reinforce feelings of superiority in white people. (P. C 1)

In another sense "white privilege" leads to a sense of guilt and other negative emotions. Allison Bailey (1999), a white woman, states:

> Anger and discomfort with the costs of "white privilege," white guilt, frustration with white intolerance, or just plain boredom with whiteness had led many whites down a bizarre path of racial dis-identification. ...When we recognize how members of our so-called "race" have colonized the globe, taken the natural resources of others as our own, and imposed our languages, customs, and values on members of so-called "non-white" peoples, it is tempting to want to dissociate ourselves from whites by either looking for the lost nonwhite ancestor or opting to "become black" or "become Indian." (p. 89)

"White privilege" is not a myth but a reality; "cumulative disadvantage" is not a myth but a reality. These two realities are diametrically opposed to each other.

It is very difficult for Black-Americans to be optimistic about racial relations and racism elimination in this country especially in light of the numerous instances of daily racist acts, both institutional and individual. In fact, whites usually comment about the huge gains made by Black-Americans. In reply, I see black progress in the same manner that Malcolm X stated. Paraphrasing his words, by saying:

> If a man has a knife embedded six inches in your back, and he pulls it out three inches "some progress" has certainly been made. But the fact remains; he still has a knife embedded three inches in your back. You want the knife completely out of your back, the wound healed, the man punished and compensated for the injury.

5) Are Racial Hate Groups Growing?

Another indicator of worsening racism is an increase in the number of racial hate groups in the USA. Rock music and the Internet touting white power and advocating violence against minorities have significantly aided the growth of hate groups. Hate groups are rapidly gaining strength nationwide. According to a report released by The Southern Poverty Law Center (SPLC), (2000), there are 474 hate groups in the U.S that represent an increase of 20 percent in 1997. According to Morris Dees, Director of SPLC, there are 300-500 hate Internet websites that make it easier to preach hate and to recruit new members. The SPLC warned parents to be concerned about their children's access to package hate propaganda. For example, SPLC relates that one group's site has a section called "creativity for children" which aims "to help the younger members of the white race understand our fight." These hate groups are a strong factor in influencing racial attitudes.

The new hate groups are actually chapters in organizations such as the Ku Klux Klan (KKK) and churches in the Christian Identity movement whose members cite the Bible as the source for racist views. Others consist of a sect of young white supremacists known because of their shaven heads, as "skinheads." The stereotypical skinhead has a close crew cut, swastika tattoo and wears heavy leather boots. Their goal is to create an all-white, Christian "perfect" society. The skinheads attempt to terrorize all non-WASPS, "Jews," African-Americans and homosexuals--by combining violence and vandalism to intimidate the so-called "inferior" races and persons of different ethnic groups and sexual orientation.

David Duke, former Grand Wizard for the KKK, heads a group called NO FEAR, which stands for "National Organization For European-American Rights." This group has decals on automobile windows and bumpers. Matthew Hale formed a white supremacist group, called the World Church of the Creator (WCOTC). Hale is a law school graduate who cannot practice because a state bar panel ruled that his racist beliefs make him morally unfit. On July 2, 1999, one of Hale's followers Benjamin Smith shot a total of 11 Asian- Americans, African-Americans and Jews, killing two before committing suicide July 4th in Southern Illinois. It is reported that since Benjamin Smith went on his two-state campaign of racial violence, Hale's organization has gained membership. Hale, the leader of WCOTC says the increase has more to do with the philosophy of his organization than with Smith's rampage. WCOTC has become a magnet for young, volatile white supremacists. Hale says he will use public access television to teach "racism" to white children and attract young misunderstood people like Benjamin Smith to his organization (Robertson, 2000).

A recent Harris Poll asked whether the media exposure of racial hate groups informed the public or gave more exposure to the hate groups. Twenty-six percent, or approximately 8,000, said it helped the public; sixty four percent, or approximately 20,000 said the coverage only served to give the hate groups more exposure; nine percent or approximately 3,000 reported "Don't know." The coverage most likely does both: it informs the public and it gives the hate groups more exposure. We cannot pretend a tumor will go away simply by ignoring it. To be informed is to be armed.

Racism in the St. Louis area is alive and resurging in the form of cross burning, increase membership of skinheads and Klan. "The folks don't all wear sheets anymore either" according to William Whitcomb a Justice Department official. He cited reports of skinheads, racists white youths, in Springfield, Mo. and the White Knights of Kansas in the Kansas City area. (Uhlenbrock, 1989)

6) The Color Line: Can It Be Erased?

DuBois (1903) put the matter of the continued presence of racism succinctly when he asserted: the problem of the twentieth century is the problem of the color line-the relation of the darker to the lighter races...(P. 5) The color problem continues to haunt us daily. In the twentieth-first century, it still is "the problem of the color line." At the 2000 Republican convention in Philadelphia that:

General Colin Powell, former Secretary of State,

The issue of race still casts a shadow over our society... We have much more work to do and a long way to go to bring the promise of America to every American.

The "color line" and its shadow are now more covert and manifest themselves in new ways: racial profiling, shopping while black, red lining, predatory lending and environmental racism. These are just some of the new ways in which the "color line " operates in the everyday life of African-Americans.

Can the "color line" be completely eradicated? I doubt it. Erasing the "color line" will be one of the most challenging tasks of the twentieth-first and other centuries because racism is so deeply embedded in the fabric and the infrastructure of American society. Like the weather, racism will always be with us in some form. Was Derrick Bell (1992) correct when he stated, "...racism is an integrated, permanent and indestructible component of this [American] society." (p. ix)

Bell (1992) states further

> Black people will never gain full equality in this country. Even those Herculean efforts we hail as successful will produce no more than temporary "peaks of progress," short-lived victories that slide into irrelevance as racial patterns adapt in ways that maintain white dominance. This is a hard-to-accept fact that all history verifies. We must acknowledge it, not as a sign of submission, but as an act of ultimate defiance. (P.12)

Essentially, Bell makes the point that the "color line" has been "broken" many times but has never been erased and according to him and will never be erased. It is true that many examples of the broken "color line" exist:

> On April 15, 1947, Jackie Robinson "broke" the color barrier in Major League Baseball when he signed with the Brooklyn Dodgers.

> Linda Brown, et. al. "broke" the color line in public education on May 17, 1954 when the U.S. Supreme Court issued a decision in the Brown vs. Topeka Board of Education.

In 1955, Mrs. Rosa Parks "broke" the color line in public transportation in Montgomery, Alabama when she refused to rise and give her seat to a white man.

In September 1957, the Little Rock Nine "broke" the color barrier in secondary education when they integrated Central High school.

In 1960, Charlie Sifford "broke" the color line in the Professional Golf Association.

The specter of the color lines still pervades the lives of Black-Americans in the twenty-first century. We have seen changes in racial relations in the U.S. over the 35 plus years following the death of Dr. Martin Luther King, Jr, but in many ways racial harmony and healing seem more distant today than in 1968. King's message was clear. He wanted people to be judged by the content of their character, rather than by the color of their skin, but this has not occurred. Skin color is still a major factor in the development of racist attitudes in this country.

7) Is Racism Permanent In The US?

Will racism ever end? Is this nation losing its fight against racism? Is there a fight at all? An examination of recent racial incidents would lead a prudent person to conclude that racism is increasing in this country and there is not a program in place to contain or to eliminate it. I strongly disagree with black Sociologist Julius Wilson's analysis of racism and classism. In Wilson's book, **The Declining Significance of Race**, he states today, class barriers are more significant discriminating agents against blacks than racial barriers. Wilson (1978) states:

Race relations in the United States have undergone fundamental changes in recent years, so much so that now, the life chances of individual blacks have more to do with their economic class position than with their day-to-day encounters with whites. In earlier years the systematic efforts of whites to suppress blacks were obvious to even the most insensitive observer. Blacks were denied access to valued ingenious schemes of racial exploitation, discrimination and segregation, schemes that were reinforced by elaborate ideologies... However in the economic sphere class has become more important than race in determining black access to privilege and power. (p. 125)

My disagreement with Wilson rests on the fact that black people do not encounter racism because they are poor but because they are black. Although class is a major factor, it is secondary to racism. The KKK did not attack blacks because they were poor, but because they were black. Dr. Martin Luther King, Jr. was not assassinated because he was poor, but because he was black; James Byrd of Jasper, Texas was not dragged behind a pickup truck and murdered because he was poor, but because he was black; Abner Louima of New York City was not brutally sodomized with a broomstick up his rectum by New York police because he was poor, but because he was black; Amadou Diallo of New York City was not shot at 41 times and hit 19 times by New York police because he was poor, but because he was black; Raynard Johnson, a 17-year-old black honor student in Kokomo, Mississippi was not hanged in his yard because he was poor, but because he was a black youth seen with two white girls. I could go on with these refutations of Wilson's class-based assertions, but let us re-raise the question: why do we need to study the white mind and the source of white racism?

The next chapter will describe several building blocks of racial scripts, the process by which racial scripts are acquired and some sources of racial scripts.

SECTION II:

Williams Racial Script Theory (WRST)

CHAPTER II:
RACISM:
ITS ACQUISITION AND
TRANSMISSION THROUGH
RACIAL SCRIPTS

1) Definition of Racial Script

A racial script contains detailed instructions in our lives about ways we are supposed to view other races, and how we are supposed to feel about them. Racial scripts are an integral component of one's life script. Babcock & Keepers (1976) define a life script as "A life plan based on a decision made in childhood, reinforced by the parents, justified by subsequent events and ending according to plan." P. 276.

Racial scripts however, are more specific and play a major role in the continuance or discontinuance of racism, bigotry, prejudice and stereotypes in the USA. Racial scripts are initially formed in young children as a derivation of their parent's beliefs and racial behavior, which are imparted through their instruction and modeling. Positive or negative racial scripts tended to be "handed down" from one generation to the next and so on and on. In its simplest form a racial script is the process by which racist attitudes are learned, maintained and expressed. After a racial script is learned, it can now be activated upon the appearance of race-specific stimuli in the environment. By definition,

A racial script is a series of programmed messages (e.g. stereotypes and myths) about a particular ethnic group and transmitted to children by parents, relatives, teachers, media, religious groups and significant others.

The messages may be positive, negative, neutral or mixed. A racial script represents a shorthand way information about a group of people is given. Racial scripts cause people to focus on certain attributes within a racial group and ignore others. The specific characteristics focused on are called the "salient attributes" i.e. black skin is the feature that stands out. Generalizations are based on these salient attributes, for example, that the group to which certain persons belong is homogeneous with regard to a wide range of traits. Although racial scripts are not set in granite, they do resist change. Even if the individual meets someone who does not fit the script, opinions resist change. The individual might miss-perceive or forget counter examples.

One individual explained her frustration:

- I had black friends in school, but their relationship struck a dissonant chord with me. My heart told me that prejudice is stupid and immature, but my head was still filled with everything that my parents and society had taught me. I was not ready to cross the line to think for myself, that is, to base my thoughts on my own beliefs and experiences.

When internalized by the child, the script will serve to determine how he/she will perceive race and react to a particular group of people. A script results from an early identification process by the immature child in which he/she adopts the parents' behaviors (scripts) and aligns his/her behavior with the realities of the home situation. The age at which this identification occurs varies from child to child.

Negative racial scripting robs the child of his/her autonomy to make decisions about races and prevents the development of independent thinking. The more thorough the scripting process, the less control the child has over his/her perceptions and reactions to members of different racial groups. Scripting develops "mind sets" or predispositions to respond according to the racial instruction recorded. Thus racial scripts are little pictures, images or messages carried around in the minds of the young child. Racial scripting is similar to dropping instructions into the letterbox of the human subconscious. One is aware when these ideas are posted, but one is not aware when they will be expressed.

Racial scripts are usually stereotypes or myths of a particular reference group. The stereotype of the African-American is typically a distortion or caricature of the person. The African-American stereotypes are likely to be ones of low intelligence, dangerous, lazy, impulsive, drug addicted and criminal. Stereotyping creates thinking in terms of "allness" rather than looking for differences to explain and understand the behavior and the culture of a particular group.

2) Building Blocks For Racial Script Theory

The basic building blocks for RACIAL SCRIPT THEORY are drawn from three theoretical models:

a) Francis Cress Welsing:
   COLOR CONFRONTATION THEORY

b) Janet Helm: **WHITE IDENTITY MODEL**

c) Eric Berne: **TRANSACTIONAL ANALYSIS**

a) Francis Cress Welsing: White Supremacy Model

Dr. Francis Cress Welsing (1991), a noted African American Psychiatrist, developed a theory of White Supremacy which states:

> White or color-deficient Europeans responded psychologically, with a profound sense of numerical inadequacy and color inferiority, in their confrontations with the majority of the world's people-all of whom possessed varying degrees of color-producing capacity. This psychological response, whether conscious or unconscious, revealed an inadequacy based on the most obvious

and fundamental part of their being, their external appearance. As might be anticipated in terms of modern psychological theories, whites defensively developed an uncontrollable sense of hostility and aggression. .... However, the most profound aggressions have been directed towards black people, who have the greatest color potential and, therefore, are the most envied and feared in genetic color competition."(Pg.4-5)

Welsing further suggests that because Whites are aware of their genetic inability to produce color, they built the myth of White genetic superiority. To support this myth, Whites then developed an elaborate social, political and economic structure to support the myth of the inferiority of African Americans. To paraphrase Welsing, Whites have to tear down black people in order to make themselves look good or to build themselves up. Their identity is based on having a race to look down on so they can feel superior. In Ebonics, we would say, "They have to make their s--t look good so that our s--t will look bad."

b)   Janet Helms: White Identity Formation

Janet Helms (1984), a very creative black Psychologist, was perhaps the first person to develop a White Racial Identity Model to explain the manner in which Whites identify (or not identify) with other Whites or develop a non-racist identity. The evolution of a White racial identity requires two considerations 1) the rejection of racism and 2) the development of a non-racist White identity. To accomplish these goals Helms hypothesized that White racial identity formation occurs via a six-stage process:

> 1) CONTACT: These persons are unaware of racial issues. They approach the world in a color-blind fashion and show a general unsophisticated understanding of the impact of racism. Generally, these persons view African-Americans with curiosity and/or fear.

2) DISINTEGRATION: Persons at this level are aware of racial issues on a personal level, but do not want to assume any responsibility for discrimination. This stage may activate moral dilemmas and emotional discomfort.

3) REINTEGRATION: Persons at this stage are likely to idealize everything White and denigrate everything African American. They accept the belief in White supremacy and black inferiority

4) PSEUDO-INDEPENDENT: This stage is one of intellectualization in which the persons question the notion of White Supremacy and begin to acknowledge their responsibility for racism. They are no longer comfortable with a racist identity and begin searching for new ways to redefine their identity.

5) IMMERSION/EMERSION: Persons at this stage will begin to search for answers by immersing themselves into reading autobiographies of Whites, participating in White conscious raising groups and focusing on changing White people rather than African-Americans.

6) AUTONOMY: This stage represents the highest level of white racial identity formation and may be considered as racial maturity or self-actualization.

c)   Eric Berne: Transactional Analysis (TA)

Eric Berne (1964, 1972) developed a theory of Transactional Analysis (TA) that employs three forms of ego functions: parent, adult and child. The parent ego is composed of behavior copied from parents or authority figures. A person in the parent state is a direct playback of a videotape recording of his/her parents of authority figures.

Thus, the parental racial script is essentially a blueprint for a lifestyle of interacting with a particular racial group. The parental racial script is a life plan that guides the person's behavior from childhood through adolescence and even into adulthood, by determining how his/her interaction with African-Americans will be. The parent script is a huge recording in the child's memory bank. The data in the parent was taken in, as a rule, and recorded "as is" without editing. The mother and father become internalized in the parent ego, as recordings of what the child observed what they say and do. The child's recorder is on all the time. In his/her set of recordings are the thousand sets of "do's," "don'ts," "Yeses" "no's, "Never trust a man," "Never trust a woman," "Do unto others as you would have them do unto you."

While external events are being recorded in what is called parent, there is another recording being made of internal events that influence the responses of the little person to what he sees and hears. It is the seeing, hearing, feeling and understanding of this body of data that Berne called the child.

The adult is a data-processing computer, which grinds out decisions after evaluating the information gained from the parent, the child and the data the adult is gathering. Two of the main functions of the adult are 1) to examine parental data to determine if it is true and applicable today, and then to accept it or reject it and 2) to examine the child to determine whether they are appropriate or inappropriate.

The problem of the persuasiveness of racism (white Supremacy) in the USA needs to be addressed at a deeper, more personal level: in the conscious and unconscious Psyche of White Americans. Assuming that group forms of racism continue to exist as a function of individual racist beliefs, there is a compelling need to discover how the individual acquires his/her racist beliefs and how these beliefs may be modified and/or prevented. I believe if we understand how racist beliefs are acquired, we may then be able to discover how to eliminate them. Former President Bill Clinton suggests that Americans can overcome racism by learning about how it developed.

Within the past few years, I have been working on a new Theory of WHITE RACISM and how it is developed. This theory provides new tools and methods for understanding how RACISM originates, how it is perpetuated and how it can be prevented or erased. The details of racial script theory have been shaped by my personal experiences, experimentation, clinical observation and psychological studies. As we shall see, the concept of racial script theory as a learned response is crucial to understanding racist foundations.

I refer to this new theory as RACIAL SCRIPTING. Racial scripting provides a system for changing racist behavior. Racial scripting allows us to look at RACISM as it is acquired and in its developmental stages. By changing child-rearing practices, we can change racist attitudinal development.

It is my contention that racial scripts play a major role in the continuance or discontinuance of RACISM and STEREOTYPES in the USA. Racial scripts, like many other types of scripts, are formed in children initially as a derivation of their parent beliefs and instruction. Racial scripts are "handed down" from one generation to the next and so on. In this way "generational continuity" of racism is maintained.

3) The Racial Script Acquisition Process

Children acquire racial scripts initially from their parents. Allport (1954) found that children learn bigotry or racism in three ways: 1) by adopting the prejudice or bigotry of their parents and other family members 2) from the cultural environment or 3) by being raised in such a way that they acquire suspicions, fears and hatreds of certain groups. What Allport identified as the "learning of prejudice," I labeled the "Racial Scripting Process." When internalized or adopted by the child, the script will serve to determine how he/she will perceive and react, for example, to African-Americans.

A racial script results from an early identification process by the immature child in which he/she adopts the parents' (the primary group) behaviors (scripts) and align his/her behavior with the realities of the home situation.

Racial script acquisition occurs in several ways: **a) identification b) injunctions and c) attributions.**

a) Identification

Identification refers to the process that influences the child to think, feel and behave in a fashion similar to another person, and in this case, the parent. In script acquisition, the child identifies with the parent, authority figures or a model. This is the only world the child knows. The age at which this identification occurs varies from child to child. The critical years are, however, from ages two to five. However, several conditions are necessary to facilitate identification with the parent model. First, the child must want to possess some of the parent's characteristics (and usually does) because the parents are seen as the powerful people who give rewards. Second, the child must believe that he/she and the parent or models are similar in some way. Children generally want to please their parents. So when racist scripts are presented, the child is then likely to accept the script at its face value. The child is not likely to be critical or to question the validity of the script. More than likely the child will say, "My parents told me to do this, to believe this, so I must do what they say, especially if I am to be loved by them."

Negative scripting robs the child of his/her autonomy and prevents the development of independent thinking. The more thorough the scripting, the less control the child will have over his/her reactions and interactions to and with members of the African-American community. Racial scripting develops "mind sets" or predispositions to respond according to the racial messages recorded. Thus, racial scripts are little pictures or messages carried around in the minds of the young child. These scripts are usually stereotypes and/or myths of African-Americans.

The stereotypes of the African-American are typically caricatures of the truth. They are usually ones that create low thinking in terms of "allness" rather than looking at single individuals to determine their particular personality and behavior. A myth is worth a thousand words and is used to implant racial stereotypes in the minds of these White children. For these reasons, racial scripts remain virtually unchanged from generation to generation.

The following will illustrate how the child identifies with or adopt the racial scripts from parents:

- My mother, unlike my father, had no prejudiced comments to make. She was an idealist who believed in equality for everyone and she was, for the most part, "color blind." I was very close to my mother and as a result I adopted most of her beliefs as my own. For the most part she caused me to be open to all races.

  I worked in a bookstore, which had a staff that was mostly black. I became close with my co-workers; they trusted me and I trusted them.

b) Injunctions

Script acquisition, also, occurs through a process called **injunctions** or the parents telling the child what not to do, e.g., "don't get dirty" "don't play in the streets." "Don't play with black kids," Injunctions are loaded with negatives as "don'ts." The injunctions contain the fears and anxieties of the child's scripts. In his book **Race Attitudes in Children** Lasker (1929) describes an example of script injunctions. Injunctive scripts vary in intensity, ranging from mild to very intense.

He relates the confession of a student from a midwestern university as follows:

Early in my life, as far back as I have any recollection, I was taught to hate the Negro with all the force my childish impulses could muster. To me Negroes were fiends and intent upon killing me…While still pretty much a child, I never saw a Negro but I would tremble at the thought of one.

The first words I remember having heard my father tell me were to keep away from Negroes because they would harm me. Whenever my mother would instill discipline in me she would threaten that: "A big black man would get me" if I didn't behave.

- My parents spoke badly of black people. They indirectly conditioned within me some of their racial attitudes. My most vivid memory is of driving in downtown. We had stopped at a stoplight and a black man began to cross the street and immediately my mother told my brother to lock our doors. I found it weird when in our own city, my mother never asked us to lock our doors.

Ten years later I brought this up to my mother and it was explained to me that it was done because of the area we were in, not the particular person. I can understand that, but that was not the message I got when I was 8- years old. I saw it as specific to the black man because White men had crossed the street before and I was not told to lock the car door then.

The following will illustrate the manner in which the child adopts the parental instruction without knowing why:

- My sister dated a black boy. My Dad was surprised and upset. He strongly objected to this relationship. Dad's reason behind his objection was the Bible. He said that the Bible states we shouldn't mix the races. He stated that interracial dating is a sin. Consequently, I always thought that interracial dating and marriages were a sin. Now, why do I think that way? I really don't know, but I think it is because of what my Dad used to tell me.

The reason this child thinks "that way" is because her father pre-programmed her with an **INJUNCTION** to think "that way." Some parents will comment "I like blacks just as much as the next guy; it's the Niggers I don't like. There is a difference, you know."

Injunctive racial scripts as "Don't date or marry a black man" carry with them heavy baggage for White children. Many White adults fear that the end of racism and racial segregation will mean numerous marriages between blacks and Whites on a grand scale. This fear (the racial myth of miscegenation) is the **granddaddy** of all racial myths and fears. Underlying this myth is the fear that with the end of segregation, there will be the end of freedom of choice of marriage. These White parents believe that thousands of White women will be carried off into marriage with black men. It takes two to make a marriage and we all have the right to choose whom to marry.

Ironically, the same Whites who will fight to prevent a black American from living in their neighborhoods will not hesitate to employ a black maid to care for their children, or a black cook to prepare their food. If the White person believes that blacks are lacking in moral integrity, why do they permit a black maid to take care of their children? If whites believe that blacks are physically dirty, dangerous and ignorant, why do they permit blacks to prepare their food?

c) Attribution

Lastly, script acquisition occurs as a function of **attribution**, or the process of being told what to do, giving permission to do, the right thing to do, e.g., "It's O.K. to play with blacks," "Do unto others as you would have them do unto you," "You must share with others." This is a script of "giving permission" to behave in a certain way. In fact, children decide on their O.K. –ness early in life. They learn "I (a white person) am O.K.-You (a black person) are O.K." in homes where racist scripts are not taught. Children also learn "I (a White person) am O.K—"You (a black person) are not O.K." in homes which many racist themes are practiced.

- My parents were the main source of my script acquisition. They had a number of black friends and encouraged me to have them as well. Often my parents brought home a black couple they knew and they were as accepted and well treated as any of their other friends. Because my parents accepted black people, I felt that I too should feel the same way.

We moved to a small town where there was only one black family who was my mother's best friends. She loved the family as her own, which encouraged me to do the same.

4) Sources of Racial Scripts

Six sources/agents of racial script acquisition will be discussed in this section: **a) Parents b) Relatives c) Friends (peers) d) Media e) Schools and f) Churches or Religious Organizations.**

a)   Parental Racial Scripts

The primary racial script to the child is transmitted by the parents or significant others. These scripts are transmitted to the child through direct or indirect instructions. These are by far the most important, most enduring scripts and are usually deeply embedded. The scripts are very stable and resist extinction mainly because they represent an extension of and identification with the parents or the model. Adopting the scripts is similar to obeying a command of the parents. The feeling of the child is "I will be loved by my parents if I accept these instructions, but I will be rejected (not loved) if I do not," or "If I reject these instructions I will be rejecting my parents and not be loved." In a sense, the child is being a "good-boy" or " good-girl" by being obedient.

Parental love is a much desirable goal for the child and is translated to mean, "I love you" and is interpreted as a reward for the child who adopts a parental script. Parents praise children when the children show an internalization of a parental script. This reward strengthens the child's tendency to behave in a fashion similar to the parents in the future. For example, if the parental script is the golden rule, "Do unto others as you would have them do unto you" and as the child adopts this script, he/she is most likely to receive praise from the parents. If the child shows that he/she is not adopting the racial script, praise is withheld and the child may be scolded or punished in some way. In general, children want to please their parents. They are least likely to reject racist or any other script during the formative years of their lives.

At any rate, it is probable that children of strict parents are more afraid of violating parental scripts than are children of permissive parents. If the child does not show adoption of a parental script, the parent is likely to say something to the effect "I'm disappointed in you" conveying the idea that the parent has been hurt and praises are not forthcoming.

Harry Stack Sullivan (1953) describes three types of "ME's:" the "good me", the "bad me" and the "not me." The "good me" emerges when the child receives praise for identifying with the parental racial teachings. The "bad me" emerges when the child rejects parental racial teaching. The "not me" emerges because the child cannot grasp the meaning of racial scripting or racial experiences. Intense anxiety shatters their ability to comprehend what is happening. Intense confusion ensues and the child is overwhelmed and can't find words to express the confusion.

Although parental messages contain varying degrees of positive, negative and neutral content, some parents send blatantly destructive racial injunctions to their children: "don't trust niggers" "blacks are dangerous, watch them." Later in life these negative, destructive scripts can be triggered off or activated when confronted by an African-American. Injunctions tell the child what he/she must not do in order to remain in the parent's favor. Permissions, when followed, are rewarded; injunctions, when disobeyed, are punished.

b) Scripts Induced by Relatives

A racial script may also be passed down through several generations. Although parents are the primary providers of scripts, relatives may also play important roles in script building. Grandmothers and grandfathers, in particular, may be transmitters of scripts to the young child. Brothers, sisters, aunts, uncles and cousins may play similar roles in script acquisition. The child is caught in these interlocking scripts that have been passed down culturally for generations.

The following is an illustration of how racial scripts are obtained from relatives and the impact they have on the child:

- I had no racial script to follow from my parents. My father and mother never said much about races. To this day, I have no idea of their feelings on this mater. I do know however, how the rest of my family feels; the rest meaning aunts, uncles, cousins and grandparents. They've told their racist jokes and have made many racist comments in my presence.

- Until age ten, I had no real contact with blacks. Although my mother taught me that everyone was equal, most of my influence came from my four very racist cousins. Their influence led me to believe that blacks were lazy and to be feared due to their violent personalities. I was very scared of, and as a result, I had no desire to come into contact with these people. I saw blacks as inferior to Whites with their only redeeming qualities being they were simply athletic robots with no intellectual capacities.

- I have an older sister who was very much a "mother hen". Whenever I would watch TV shows, such as "Good Times" or "What's Happening," my sister would lecture to me that such shows were prejudicial and stereotypical against blacks. My brother and I were playing in the swimming pool. We decided to use words as "salt-pepper," all in innocence. My sister furiously told us not to use that language because a black family was at the poolside and we might possibly insult them. My sister made me self-conscious in what I said, thought and how I viewed blacks. She taught me to be keen and thoughtful in what I said.

- The most significant racists in my family were without a doubt my grandparents. 'Nigger" is how my grandparents referred to blacks, and the word was said by them in a tone of vicious hate. My grandfather wouldn't even watch basketball games on television because there were too many "niggers." In general, I believe he thought and still thinks of blacks as dirty and inferior.

- My parents tried very hard to counteract the negative images of black people my grandfathers projected. Both of my grandfathers had horrible attitudes toward black people, thinking they were inferior, good-for-nothings that took jobs away from more deserving whites. Often, one of my grandfathers, the more vocal of the two, would say something derogatory about "them damn niggers," and my parents would then try to explain his behavior to me. They would say, "Never mind Grandpa, he grew up during very hard times,' or 'Grandpa had a few bad experiences with black people at work." The bad part was by trying to explain/excuse his behavior they were rationalizing. My parents were condoning their racist remarks instead of putting a stop to it. If they would have angrily told him he was wrong, it would have made more of an impact on me than simply telling me to disregard his remarks.

- One day my grandmother and I started talking in the den about school and the friends I was making in my classes. I believe I must have mentioned someone's name that had an origin of black descent. My grandmother quickly hopped off the couch in pursuit of my mother. Not understanding what the nature of the problem was, I was quick to follow her footsteps into my mother's room. When I arrived in the doorway, I will never forget the anger on both of their faces and my grandmother's persistent use of the "N-word." They argued back and forth about black folks for almost a week.

Here is another example of how a script is passed down unintentionally to promote generational continuity:

- A mother was preparing to bake a ham for Christmas. She cut off both ends and put the ham in the baking pan. Her daughter asked why she cut the ends of the ham off. The mother said she really didn't know but would ask her mother who always cut the ends off. When the mother asked her mother why, her mother said she was really doing what she saw her mother do and that she really had no answer. So they decided to ask their grandmother who said that she always cut the ends off because the ham was too long to get into the pan.

c) Friends (Peers) Induced Scripts

Peers are quite influential in providing racial scripts. In order to be accepted into the group and to be one of the "crowd," children will conform or acquiesce to the prevailing racial attitudes through their association with their peer group. Several individuals pointed out how friends influenced their racial script development:

- I was extremely isolated from the larger culturally and racially integrated cities while growing up in a southern town. I was never actually aware that other races existed. The earliest racial incident I can recall occurred when I was about five years old. My family went to a restaurant for dinner with our neighbors. On my way to the restroom with my girlfriend, our neighbor's daughter, my attention was caught by a group of black waiters where they had dropped a tray of dishes. My girlfriend scolded me and told me not to stare at them because black men liked to kidnap and rape young White girls. Needless to say, I was terrified. My girlfriend then proceeded to leave me alone in the restroom. Naturally, I screamed and cried until finally my mother came and found me. After that incident I was terrified every time I came in contact with black males.

- Most of what I believed about blacks came from racial jokes that I heard from my friends and some of my family. My friends concerned themselves with the sexual myths, and my family made jokes about the slower intellect and superior athletic abilities of blacks. Accepting these myths was not difficult because the only blacks I knew were in the remedial classes and were by far the best athletes in school. My script was shaped by these myths and jokes, which were definitely negative, and I accepted them without question.

- I do acknowledge a distinct behavioral shift into a form of avoidance upon entering high school. I know this was caused by peer pressure. Up until this point racial difference in social groupings in school seemed irrelevant. However, this quickly changed in high school. There was a very high ratio of blacks in my high school and strong racial polarization occurred. There was occasional crossing of racial boundaries, but as a general rule, one went with ones' own group or paid severe consequences. Social punishment often came in the form of ostracizing, pejorative labeling and mocking.

My social situation and stance placed me in the avoidance out of fear of what my peers would think or say. For it was very difficult for me to cross racial barriers or even show interest in blacks without being offensive to my peers, or getting offended myself. I became immersed in and internalized my peers' norms.

d) Media-Induced Scripts

Media based racial scripts are those acquired mainly through the television, films, books, newspapers and magazines. Since many children watch television during the early formative years, media-induced racial scripts may develop during this critical formative period. It is especially important in locations where there are no blacks in the child's neighborhood. Between the ages of three to five, the average

American child is extremely susceptible to the influence of television. Children less than five years of age watch, on the average, over 23 hours of television each week. For many children television has become one of the major agents of socialization.

Although the effects of television on the development of racial scripts are not known at this time, it is presumed that it has a strong tendency to influence attitudes. For example, a great deal is known about the effects of television violence on children. Cater & Strickland (1975) suggest that a child who has watched a violent video is more likely to engage in subsequent aggressive acts than one who has not. The case of Nathaniel Tate, a young black male, is a clear example of how TV influences one's behavior. Tate killed a seven-year-old girl by practicing some wrestling techniques he watched on television. Initially, Tate was sentenced to life in prison without a chance for parole but after serving two years in prison he was released.

In addition to violence, television tends to promote the development of racial scripts that tend to stereotype African-Americans in negative ways. Media scripts may be positive, negative, neutral or mixed. They are, however, secondary in strength to parental scripts. Media information is likely to be acquired, accepted and followed. Greenberg (1972) studied children's reaction to black children on television using samples of black children from urban, suburban and rural settings. The study hypothesized that large numbers of White children given this early exposure to television and their limited exposure to real-life blacks, might be obtaining their earliest impressions about black people from TV. Many White children stated that TV was their main source of information for how blacks talked and dressed. Greenberg reported that TV exposure contributed more to a stronger belief than personal contacts, and that the TV blacks were more realistically portrayed than personal contacts. The bottom line is the cultural images and stereotypes of African-Americans, which have been presented by the mass media to the White American child, have created false and incorrect impressions. The TV serves as an alternative socializing agent.

The following excerpt shows how some children experience blacks especially when they live in a racially isolated area:

- I grew up in an all-White community. There were no blacks in my school. The first black man I ever saw was Gordon on the television show Sesame Street. I began watching that show at a very young age, and as I learned my numbers and alphabet, I subconsciously learned about black people. Although Gordon's skin was different from white actors, I knew he was a person like all the other actors. But Sesame Street, although it seems like a childish show also taught about racism. It often had skits that showed black and white children playing together and others that discussed racism and showed that all people, no matter what color of their skin, were still people like everyone else. So Sesame Street taught some valuable racial lessons.

The following illustration shows the influence of TV on the formation of racial attitudes, particularly where children live in segregated communities and do not get proper race related instruction:

- Before Dan met any African-Americans, his racial script was greatly influenced by television. He lived in a predominately White community and believed for some reason that most African-Americans were criminals and came from lower social-economical class. He was frightened (afrophobic) of African Americans. He didn't know why. This fear was heightened by what he saw on television, especially the news where African-Americans were portrayed primarily as criminals, gang members and drug dealers. Today, he is fighting to overcome his fear of blacks and is disappointed that his parents did not prepare him better.

- Television played a major part in my early development of racial scripts. The news was always showing negative images of African Americans. The news shows were always reporting on crime and drug problems in predominantly black neighborhoods. The reports presented such a negative view of those neighborhoods that it seemed like all the black people must be either criminals or victims.

- I suppose television helped me formed my racial script about blacks. At a young age, I started to watch the news and as we all know, the news never contains much positive material; it is filled with murder, murder, and more murder. Unfortunately, most of the times I watched TV, the murders and escaped convicts happened to be blacks. I found myself stereotyping blacks and all the while feeling guilty about it.

- My first awareness of racial differences occurred when I was old enough to watch the news and understand what the reporters were trying to get across to the public. I heard many different statistics, studies and observations that showed a difference between blacks and whites. These issues in the news showed me that in many cases, blacks have higher rates of criminality than Whites, higher rates of suicide, more instances of poverty and homelessness, less overall education and lower paying jobs. I also started watching television shows which portrayed blacks in occupations such as maids and car washers (such as "Good Times") and noticing that White people held the majority of political offices. I saw movies and comedy shows that had blacks talking a slightly different language with words that weren't familiar to me.

Another illustration of how the media influences are found is in the American Film institute recent ranking of *The Birth of a Nation*. This film, made in 1915, was ranked as one of the 100 best films ever made. *The Birth of a Nation* is clearly a racist film that demonized blacks and justified the black codes and Jim Crow policies that emerged. The movie portrayed blacks as being happy-go- lucky in slavery and emphasized the violation of southern white womanhood by black men. (USA Today June 29, 1998, p 13a)

Television was not the only medium inducing negative scripts of blacks. Films were produced that portrayed blacks as 1) the contented slave 2) wretched freedmen 3) comic Negro 4) brute Negro) 5) tragic mulatto 6) exotic savage and Aunt Jemima house maid and babysitter. These negative images have strong influences on the perceptions of the child.

Of these historical and contemporary stereotypes of blacks in films, the most damaging of the past and present, are the comic Negro and the exotic savage. The former portrayed in such shows as, "Amos N' Andy"and "The Little Rascals." "Amos N' Andy" displayed blacks as being slow, foot shuffling and very dishonest. *The Little Rascals* perpetuated racial stereotype characters as "Sunshine," "Buckwheat," "Farina" and "Stymie." Examples of the negative depictions are rolling the eyes and being so frightened that their hair would stand on end. Blaxploitation movies of the 1970s showed exotic primitive blacks in such movies as "Superfly." "Shaft" and "The Mack". These movies portrayed blacks as pimps, dope peddlers and prostitutes.

Patricia Raybon (1989) clearly states what many blacks feel about their depiction on television:

- Coverage [on TV] of blacks is worse than lazy journalism; it's inaccurate journalism. This is who I am not. I am not a crack addict. I am not a welfare mother. I am not illiterate. I am not a prostitute. I have never been in jail. My children are not in gangs. My husband doesn't beat me. My home is not a tenement. None of these things defines who I am, nor do they describe the other black people I've known and worked with and loved and befriended over these 40 years of my life. Nor does it describe most of black America, period.

  Yet in the eyes of the American news media, this is what black America is: poor, criminal, addicted and dysfunctional. Indeed, media coverage of black America is so one-sided and so imbalanced that the most victimized and hurting segment of the black community, a small segment at best, is presented not as the exception but as the norm. It is an insidious practice, all the uglier for its blatancy. p. 11

With the media's depiction of black Americans as sick, pathetic and deficient, it is no wonder that white children develop distorted images and racial scripts of black people. Why does the media continue to play this game? I think it is because it wants to play the sensation game. Without sensationalism in the news, the media feels no one would watch it. On one occasion I asked a local St. Louis TV reporter: "why the station did not present more positive pictures of the black community?" His reply was it is a competitive, moneymaking situation and if they did not present this negative image, other TV stations would.

To further show how African Americans feel about many of TV shows featuring blacks, Dr. Samella Abdullah, former President of the National Association of Black Psychologists issued a national press release on September 28, 1998 concerning a racist television program (The Secret Diary of Desmond Pfeffer) scheduled to be aired. The release stated the following:

> The Association of Black Psychologists is concerned about the public images of black people that are depicted in the media (print, television, and movies).
>
> Historically, citizens and institutions in the United States continually demean, dehumanize and depreciate the character and morals of the people of African descent who live in America. Certain acting roles have been defined and categorized as appropriate roles for Africans in America because the whites, who benefit socially, psychologically and economically, view these roles as acceptable. Blacks are often portrayed in character roles where they appear to exist solely to benefit and pleasure the "massa's" will and convenience (mammy, Uncle Tom, slick coon, sexual objects and clown/buffoon). For example many food-packaging companies have historically used pictures of blacks in servant roles. They have used these portrayals to market grits,

oatmeal, orange juice, pancake syrup, etc., inferring that blacks are happy to serve and that personal services by blacks remain in every kitchen.

Today, we are confronted with the plan of UPN/Paramount/ Blockbuster Entertainment, Inc.'s plan to air a television program "The Secret Diary of Desmond Pfeiffer," which is to be a situational comedy about an Englishman of Moorish descent. This black man is mistaken for a SLAVE and is brought to America where he works as kitchen staff in President Lincoln's kitchen. Whether the story of the black man becoming enslaved and providing free labor in Lincoln's kitchen is true, we do not know. What we do know is that this is not a situation to laugh at but to cry about. How can UPN/Paramount? Blockbuster/ Entertainment, Inc. be so callous in their treatment of black people during a painful and torturous period so slavery? We ask that if such a program is to be aired, that the program be a dramatic series of a horror series depicting the truth, torture and enslavement of black people. The claim that this program satirizes contemporary politics and current events is justification for updating the time frame of the program from the Civil War period to the transition into the 21st Century. Is that the message to Americans intended to be the same? Messages then and now continue to escalate mentally oppressive images and stereotypes to keep black people in "their places."

In order to understand the negative of stereotypes, UPN/ Paramount/Blockbuster, Inc. producers and employers will need training, because their "White Privilege" blinds them fostering misinformation and insensitivity. Marketing negative stereotypes about black people during the worst of times are no laughing matter. [1]

---

1 Note: UPN/Paramount/Blockbuster cancelled the showing of this HBO television production.

Just how does the television containing black movies psychologically affect White children? One participant wrote the following on how the media influenced the development of his racial script:

- My parents never discussed the issue of race with me. They tended to avoid volatile issues unless they were forced into the open. This was unfortunate for me because I grew up learning about race through the stereotypes of the media, the indirect socialization of my parents and the mis-education of my schooling.

  I grew up in the 70s and 80s when the media was ignorant of its racist portrayal. Shows in the 70s would generally only show blacks in roles as criminals. I would see a token black in a power position as an exception to the rule and the black criminal as the rule. The media built a firm stereotype in my mind of the black man as someone who wouldn't get far and would probably wind up in crime.

- My parents did not address the problem of interracial relations, but TV did. It was the major means of socialization for myself and most of my friends. The problem was that TV sent mixed messages. The same channel that had the kids from the "Brady Bunch" bridging the racial barriers to make friends of different races had the stereotypical black and Puerto Rican gang members and drug dealers. The message seemed confusing: we are all equal and should go out of our way to make interracial relations better. Blacks and Puerto Ricans are violent, untrustworthy and should be avoided if possible. Those who are foolish enough to encounter other races end up dead, robbed or on drugs.

Another individual gave this account of how TV affected the formation of her racial scripts. :

- When I was very young, I sang these words along with the TV.

"Come and play
Everything's okay
Friendly "Niggers" there
That's where we meet
Can you tell me how to
Get to Sesame Street?"

I lived in a nearly exclusively white, upper middle-class, conservative, small town. My parents never commented on my singing. It wasn't until much later that I realized that the word was "neighbor" and not "Nigger!"

Another individual reported that her first encounter with differences between blacks and whites occurred while watching television. According to her the news reporters showed her that blacks have higher crime rates than whites, higher suicide rates, more instances of poverty and homelessness, less overall education and lower paying jobs. Also, she stated that TV shows portrayed blacks in roles as maids and car washers while whites held majority of political offices.

e) School-Induced Scripts

School-induced racial scripts are acquired through classroom instruction, books and teachers. These scripts may be acquired during the pre-exposure and/or discovery phases. They may be positive, negative or neutral.

A good example of how teachers can effect children is provided in the film **"In the Eye of the Storm"** later renamed as a CBS documentary **"A Class Divided."** In the late 1960s a third grade teacher in the State of Iowa, Jane Elliot, wanted to show her students how prejudice operated. Initially, she concocted a myth that blue-eyed students were "superior" to brown-eyed children. Consequently, she claimed brown-eyed children, were "second-class citizens." She made the brown-eyed children sit at the back of the room, denied them second food helpings, made them stand at the end of the lunch line and did not allow them to use the drinking fountain. The "superior" blue-eyed children were given special privileges which included extra recess time. The "inferior" Brown-eyed children were forced to wear collars for easy identification.

The two groups' reactions to this mythical situation were strikingly different. The performance of the brown-eyed children deteriorated rapidly whereas the performance of the blue-eyed children soared above average. Brown-eyed children showed low self-esteem whereas blue-eyed children displayed high self-esteem. Brown-eyed children exhibited a depressive and angry mood whereas the blue-eyed children seemed happy and joyful.

On the second day, Ms. Elliot told the class that she had made a terrible mistake. She said that the brown-eyed children were "superior" and that the blue-eyed children were "inferior." The brown-eyed children were elated. They tore off their collars and put them on the blue-eyed children. Now the performance and behavior of the blue-eyed children deteriorated just as that of the brown-eyed children.

The point being made here is that Ms. Elliot created a myth, which caused the children's behavior to be affected negatively or positively depending on the way she phrased the myth. The same thing happens when African-Americans become the victims of unfair racial myths and racial scripts. African proverb states: "A myth is worth a thousand words."

At an early age, children recognize discriminatory practices in the classroom but they may not have a label for the activity. Following are four additional examples of school-induced scripts. The first example shows how the instructor can negatively influence a student's script. The second illustration shows how an individual expressed her awareness of an expression of covert individual racism. The third and fourth examples reflect how the curriculum can positively influence a student's script formation.

- In elementary school I hung around with a lot of black girls. It seemed only natural. My teacher, (a white man) however, thought this was wrong and told my mother that I should stop playing with these girls. I'll tell you that growing up these days is difficult. The mixed messages that children receive from their parents, teachers and friends are enough to cause major confusion. Then, when their own personal experiences also begin to conflict with the racial scripts that they have already formed, what is a child suppose to think?

- In elementary school, for reading lessons, the black children were all in a different group than the whites. I don't know exactly how, but all the children in the white group knew we were the superior readers to the black group. The whites were taught by a certified teacher and had the latest audio/visual and computer equipment. A teaching assistant who used old books and had no audio/visual equipment or computers taught the black students. At this age, I didn't think much of the self-fulfilling prophecy being created in this atmosphere for promoting the underachievement of blacks later on in life. All I was able to comprehend at this young age was that the black people were inferior to me and I wasn't expected to socialize or learn with them.

- In my American History class there was a section on the Civil Rights movement and I was finally introduced to Alice Walker, Richard Wright and James Baldwin (the writer whom I admire and love the most). We also watched a great deal of documentaries on the plight of minorities, which included a preview of the scary possibilities of a man named David Duke.

Richard Wright's "Black Boy" probably had the biggest effect on me. This book gave me a better understanding of the struggles minorities had to face. I read about the injustices and frustrations with which black people had to dread. It also made me realize I had much more to learn about people of other cultures. Thusly, I became more motivated in my pursuit of knowledge of their cultures. I chose to tap in to the resources I had available in my community such as magazine articles dealing with racial issues as well as the occasional movie or documentary. When I came to college I began to take classes in African-American studies so that I could be exposed to many writers of different cultures. My mind has been awakened to the institutionalized racism that I once had no awareness existed.

- In the fourth grade, I was assigned a famous African-American to give a presentation on. I was assigned George Washington Carver, but I had never heard of him. I found out a great deal about Carver. I learned about the problems that blacks face. I'd never learned about black scientist before in my classes. because racial issues rarely came up for discussion. I admired Carver for his achievements in the face of adversity. As other students presented on blacks, I gained a great deal of respect for black Americans through this class exercise.

Schools must provide courses in anti-racist education (or prejudice reduction) programs designed to help students develop non-racist attitudes. These procedures are also used to describe processes that teachers and other educators use to prevent and/or eliminate individual and institutional racism. When anti-racist educational practices are implemented in curriculum materials, hiring practices, teacher attitudes, expectations and school policies, steps are then being taken to eliminate racism from the school system.

f) Community Influence on Script Acquisition

The community is very influential in determining racial script acquisition. Some communities strive for racial awareness and fairness. These communities may be integrated and have a good mix of all races in the area. Oak park, Illinois is a good example. However, some communities are just the opposite and lead to a formation of some negative racial scripts. One student described her community's influence:

- Growing up in an all-white community did not facilitate my personal interaction between black and white people. My family lived in a growing and developing, upper-middle-class suburb. Not only is my neighborhood completely white, but also when a black family tries to buy a home there, they are refused. This was done because our parents wanted to keep the community free from any disturbances. The school district we belonged to had no blacks. The teachers were all white. A black person was rarely ever seen in my town. I was always told that I should avoid any contact with black people because they are known to cause problems. To me black people only lived in Harlem or in the ghettos. I was nine years old before I had any interaction with black people.

g) Church and Other Religious Organization- Induced Scripts

Many children learn their racial scripts in Sunday school or in religious settings. The next two individuals discussed how they were taught racial scripts in a religious setting in a positive manner

- I spent my youth in a small rural town in the northeast. The area was 100 percent white. Growing up there, the issue of race was never dealt with directly by my family or by the community. The golden rule was imprinted in my memory, and we sang songs that have found a niche in my mind. I still remember the words to one, which has become a cornerstone in my racial script.

  Jesus lover of the little children
  all the children of the world
  red and yellow, black and white
  they are precious in his sight.

  A painting accompanies these words in my mind. Sitting in the corridor, waiting for Sunday school class to begin, I would stare at this painting, which portrayed a bearded man with many children of various colors sitting around him as if listening to a story. Some sat on his lap while others sat legs crossed and open eyes gazing intently and innocently. In my naiveté I asked my teacher who the man was and why does he have so many children. She replied, "Why that's Jesus and he's telling those children a parable, a parable has a moral that shows how good little boys and girls act.

- As a child, I had little or no exposure to black people. I grew up in a city where the population was mainly white, Catholic people. Before I met a black person, very little was ever said or taught to me about people of different races. The only mention of other races came in my grade school education through the teachings of my religious classes. I attended private, Catholic schools all of my life and was always being taught that everyone is equal in the eyes of God, no matter what color or creed. Furthermore, I was always taught to treat others, as I would want them to treat me. I feel that these ideals have guided me and are present in the way I treat others- equally regardless of race and creed. My religious education influenced my early formation of my racial beliefs.

In the next vignette, this individual asks: Am I a Racist?

- I grew up in a racially isolated community. I had little or no contact with blacks. When I walked into my new college dorm room I was shocked. There lying on the bed was a black girl, a black roommate. I talked to my roommate while my mother unpacked. I picked up my ankle weights, which had been punctured. I said that they're leaking "gross black stuff all over me." I was immediately acutely conscious of the fact that I had used "gross" and "black" together in a sentence. I turned away embarrassed and distressed to think that they might perceive me as a bigot. Was I? I wondered. I hoped not, but I wasn't sure anymore. I had so many questions running through my mind. I liked my roommate a lot but I kept wondering if our racial mix would put other people off. I didn't want to jeopardize my future relationships with peers. At the same time my counter stream of conscious thought was berating me for being so self-critical and petty. Other conflicts nagged at me. Was it a mark of prejudice to tell people that my roommate was black when I was describing her? Was it deceitful or reverse discrimination not to? I just didn't know. I felt so bad and confused.

Clearly, this individual is confused about relating to blacks. She does not seem to know the proper thing to say or what defends blacks. Obviously, she has had very little contact with blacks and is afraid to interact out of fear that she will be wrong. On the other hand, the fact she has a black roommate worries her because she wonders if this will turn off her white friends.

The next chapters (3, 4, 5, 6, 7, and 8) will present the process or the manner in which racial attitudes (scripts) are acquired. Six phases of racial script acquisition are defined as follows:

1) **PRE-EXPOSURE**: the first phase of Racial Script Theory occurs prior to the child experiencing an African-American. This phase occurs between birth and approximately four to five years of age.

2) **Discovery/Exposure**: the second phase of WRST involves some form of exposure and/or contact with an African-American.

3) **Script Activation**: the third phase consists of a process of an automatic response to race-specific stimuli or "acting before you think."

4) **Counterscripting:** the fourth phase of WRST refers to a process of confirming or dis-confirming a racial script.

5) **Immersion/Avoidance:** the fifth phase involves the relationship the child establishes with African-Americans -either positive or negative.

6) **Racial Maturity/Immaturity:** the sixth phase refers to the level of inner security with members of the opposite race.

SECTION III

Racism: Its Development

CHAPTER III
THE PRE-EXPOSURE PHASE

To introduce the Pre-Exposure phase, I begin this section with a story written by a fourth-grade white student, whose pen name is Irshgrl13. She gave me permission to use the story.. It is based on a little town where she lived in the Deep South. She states, "My point in writing the story was to express my feelings of how racism hurts everyone." The following is an unedited version. The title of the story is:

ACROSS THE RAILROAD TRACKS

In the Deep South, there was a little town that was split in two by a set of shiny railroad tracks. On one side a proud, prominently white community lived and worked, prospered and played. And on the other side, a proud black community lived and worked, prospered and played.

The blood red sun rose and set each day on the town and the last ray touched the house of a little white girl named Marta. She was a curly topped blonde little girl with prominent ears and a beautiful set of clover-hued eyes. She was raised in a large family with many brothers and sisters. Every day her father would guide her protectively across the grand wide streets, through the orchard grove and to the side of the large railroad tracks. He would pick up things and explain them and the little 4-year old girl would point and ponder with her tall father.

One day little Marta pointed across the tracks at the black community and asked, "Daddy, who lives there?" Her father looked across and said, "Colored people." The girl didn't quite understand and asked, "Can I go over and see if there are any little girls for me to play with?"

"No" answered the father. "My daddy told me not to talk to Colored people and I will tell you not to." Marta frowned, but continued to walk the track.

The blood red sun rose and set each day on the town and the first ray touched the house of a little black girl named Lisa. She was a curly topped, brown-haired little girl with a prominent nose and a beautiful set of tan-hued eyes. She was raised in a large family with many brothers and sisters. Every day her father would guide her protectively across the mud ditch, through the flower field and to the side of the large railroad tracks. He would pick up things and explain them and the little 4-year old girl would point and ponder with her tall father.

One day little Lisa pointed across the tracks at the white community and asked, "Daddy, who lives there?" Her father looked across and said, "White people." The girl didn't quite understand and asked, "Can I go over and see if there are any little girls for me to play with?"

"No" answered the father. "My daddy told me not to talk to white people and I will tell you not to." Lisa frowned, but continued to walk the tracks.

On the following day, both little girls snuck out of bed, curious about the forbidden race on either side of the tracks. They both came face to face and soon became friends. They both agreed that they should get home before their parents awoke, but they agreed to meet at the same place every day at the same time.

And they did. But they played for a bit longer than expected and their parents both found them and scolded them and forbade their children to see each other again.

But Lisa and Marta were such good friends and they still snuck out to see each other. One day Marta came to the tracks with a can of black shoe polish. She began to rub it on her skin. Lisa stared at her bewildered. "What are you doing?" she asked.

"I'm making myself black, so your parents will like me." Lisa smiled and said, "Wait here." She soon came back with a tube of white face cream and rubbed it on herself. They hugged and agreed that they would now be friends forever.

But they once again stayed out too late and the parents came screaming and yelling. Marta and Lisa ran, afraid of what they would do to them, or even worse, if they would stop their friendship. They turned to the right and to the left, black side to white side, but they knew they were welcomed on neither side.

So they ran down the only neutral thing in town, that strip of silver tearing the town apart---the mascot of their forbidden friendship. The significance of them to the two small children was tremendous. So they ran down the tracks, perhaps looking for some rainbow of peace at the end. There had to be. But every day, at precisely 7:00 AM, the train chugged around the bend and down the tracks and as it struck 7:00 o'clock, Lisa and Marta ran down the railroad tracks, dark hand in white hand. And the train couldn't slow down enough to stop…and the two children were hit, from the back, and killed instantly.

Both parents realized how stupid they had been, and how precious their children were. The railroad tracks were torn down, and in its place, two little graves stood side by side-- the graves of the two little children who had died in the name of hatred. The blacks and whites were no longer separated, but mingled. Both races laid railroad spikes on their graves and cried for them.

Some say at exactly 7:00AM on a bright Sunday morn, you can hear a train whistle and giggling, and fewer see a faint train riding by, two children waving from outside the window…and the train fades into the radiant horizon of the land of peace.

I especially liked this story because it is so rich in symbolism. It is also true to what parents tell their children about other races. The story shows how traditions are passed on to children. For example both fathers were quoted as saying, "My daddy told me not to talk to blacks (whites)."

The story shows what racial isolation can do for the psyche of small children and what happens when they do come together and interact with each other. But more importantly, the story shows how the two little girls tried to literally transform themselves so that the parents would accept them. The inner transformation had already occurred. And lastly, the iron railroads were torn down, symbolizing that racism and prejudice were ready for destruction.

1) Introduction

The pre-exposure phase is defined as the early period in the child's life before he/she experiences an African-American. The white child, as do all other children, come into the world with a ***tabala rasa*** (i.e. a blank slate) regarding black people. It is during this pre-exposure phase the child receives racial scripts from parents, the television, relatives and friends.

During this phase of pre-exposure, pro- racist or anti-racist attitudes are transmitted to the child. As such these early attitudes and behaviors are not based upon direct experiences with blacks, but primarily from racial lessons. These lessons determine how white perceptions of African-Americans are learned mainly from parents, relatives, friends, teachers and the media.

The majority of the white participants reported that they had little or no contact with black people until they entered elementary school. Approximately 70 percent of the participants reported they grew up in racially isolated neighborhoods and did not have much opportunity to interact with members of other races. In fact, in many cases, they were forbidden to interact with black children.

2) Recurring Themes of Racial Isolation

Recurring themes reflecting racial isolation of whites is not uncommon in literary novels. Margaret Halsey's (1946) "Color Blind: A White Woman Looks at the Negro" states:

> There were no Negroes in the rather remote suburban neighborhood where I grew up and none in the grammar school I attended…. as a child I never saw Negroes except in the streets and stores and public utilities. I do not remember being instructed in any particular way of thinking or feeling about them. As I recall it nobody ever talked about them at all" (p. 3).

In many cities, suburban areas and rural communities, racial isolation is paramount. Many families literally strive to keep their white children separated from black children. The consequences of this racial isolation exact a heavy toll on the children. Some of the common themes of racial isolation and its effects are presented in the following vignettes:

- I had no exposure to African-Americans until I was ten years old. I lived in a neighborhood that consisted of all whites. I constantly found myself confused about what to think of "colored" folks.

- I was really never exposed to black people. I grew up in a neighborhood that was predominately white, so my parents and teachers formed my ideas about black people.

- During my childhood I lived in a totally white environment. I did not understand the concept of a black person.

- Growing up in an all-white suburb, I never really encountered black people until the seventh grade. I don't remember being taught anything positive or negative about blacks. They just did not exist to me.

- All of my life I have lived in white, middle-class neighborhoods. I went to elementary and high schools that were predominately white. It is safe to say that these situations were very segregated and offered little acceptance of blacks. This created a natural breeding ground for prejudice, which is so commonly accepted in areas similar to my town.

- The neighborhood in which I grew up in was exclusively white. I never had any interaction with black people until a black girl moved into my third grade class. Until this time the only things I knew about black people was what my parents told me: blacks are lazy, stupid and dangerous, especially the men. I was extremely afraid of black men when I saw them on the streets.

- I was brought up in a little town that was 100 percent white, so I had no contact with blacks. I knew that black people existed, but never before had I talked with them or interacted with them. I had a pre-conceived idea of what to expect and how to act that had been strongly influenced by my parents and partly by the environment I lived in. I distinctly remember a handful of adjectives that my father always spit out when referring to blacks. He described them as being lazy, crooked and stupid. My father would make derogatory remarks such as: "those black bums live on the streets begging for money. Why don't they get a job and stop living off welfare? That is the taxpayer's money that they are mooching off. Blacks are just plain criminals."

3) Recurring Themes of Early Interracial Interaction

In some instances individuals reported early positive relationships with black children. In addition, each individual had a positive racial script that was confirmed by experience.

- When I was about five, I had a very close black friend named Johnny. My parents thought the world of him, and like I said, he was one of my best friends. He used to sleep at my house over the weekends and if he wasn't at my house, I was at his. In grammar school, Johnny was not my only black friend. I had lots of black friends.

- While shopping with my mother I saw a little black boy in a shopping cart. I was confused and exclaimed this confusion to my mother. "What is that?" I asked. What she told me was that he was just like me, human, but his skin was a different color. My parents stressed that all people are human no matter what the color of their skin may be.

I became friendly with a black boy in the first grade. I performed as a soloist in the school orchestra. After the concert was over, he complimented my playing and proceeded to give me a gift. He gave me his favorite baseball card, Reggie Jackson. When you are a first grader, a Reggie Jackson baseball card means the world to you. It didn't matter what the color of his skin was; he became my friend.

The pre-exposure phase is the first step in the racial scripting process. It is the age period from birth to the first exposure, contact, interaction or encounter with a member or members of a different racial group. This period is the primary period during which the child is taught his/her basic racial scripts.

This period of training/socialization is similar to the pre-game sessions an athletic coach uses to prepare the players for a game. The coach devises a cognitive plan (i.e. a game plan) and strategies that will hopefully lead the team to victory. A team member learns the appropriate language of the plays necessary to execute when performing in the game. The team member knows what he/she is supposed to do when the game starts.

Similarly, in racial scripting the parents are usually the coaches and they prepare the child for the outside world and how to behave with African-Americans. In the process of socializing the child, they also provide scripts for moral, sexual, political and social issues. In addition, they consciously or unconsciously induce racial scripts. The racial scripts may be positive, negative, neutral or mixed.

4) Examples of Pre-Exposure Racial Scripts

There are eight (8) categories of Racial Scripts within the Pre-Exposure phase as follows:

a) Positive Racial Scripts: "Blacks are O.K.;"
b) Negative Racial Scripts: "Blacks are not O.K.;"
c) Non-verbal Negative Scripts;

d) Additional Negative Racial Scripts
e) Neutral Avoidance Racial Scripts:
f) Mixed Racial Scripts: "Who's right?":
g) Anchor Racial Scripts:
h) Maids As Anchor Scripts

a)   Positive Racial Scripts: "Blacks Are OK"

Positive racial scripts are ones which affirm the true qualities of a race's history and culture. The scripts are reported in an unbiased manner. Positive racial scripts are not "color blind" instructions to the child but are anti-racist messages that enable the child to accurately see black people realistically. Following are some examples of how positive racial scripting is done:

- My mother gave my racial script to me. Before I met a black person, my mother sat me down and told me that when I start school, I would be meeting many different types of people. She told me there would be different colored children and some children who spoke different languages. I accepted this belief and asked her what I should do when I see one of these children. She told me to just treat them like all the other friends you make.

- My parents taught me by the Golden Rule: "Do unto others as you would have them do unto you." This is a familiar adage. I often heard from my mother during my childhood. Before I started my schooling, my mother would make me repeat the Golden Rule to her and also another: "If you want someone to share with you, you must share with him or her also."

- My perspective about black people can be attributed to my immediate family. My parents instilled in me the way people should be treated. They taught me that each person is the same no matter what color or religion they are. They also taught me never to judge a person by what they look like on the outside. You should keep an open mind about people you do not know. People should be treated equally, regardless of the color of their skin.

- My parents displayed very liberal views; and therefore raised me in accordance with this attitude. I have always been taught to treat people as equals, and to treat them as I wish to be treated. Because of this philosophy, I tend to focus on people as individuals rather than parts of a particular race. This upbringing has left me with a positive attitude when dealing with people of another race. My parents instilled in me a strong set of values. They taught me respect and accept others for their differences. I am very thankful for their guidance and proud of their ideals. I feel lucky to have grown up in such an open-minded environment, especially when I see the opposite.

- My racial script tended to be of a positive nature. When I was very young, I attended Sunday school at church. Though there were no black children there, the idea of racial equality was strongly stressed. We were taught that God created all men and women equally regardless of their skin color. In fact, I remember one of the songs that we sang that described this. My parents supported these ideas of equality at home. We lived in a very white neighborhood, but my parents always taught me that blacks were no different than ourselves. Because the influence of the church and my parents my script toward blacks was very positive, I was not in the least bit afraid to interact with other races.

It was not until kindergarten when I had my first contact with blacks. Two kids in my class were black. Because I had a positive script, I was not hesitant in becoming friends with them. Over the course of the years, they became two of my best friends. We shared birthday parties and played together. I feel that my positive racial script was mainly responsible for the success of this relationship. If I had had a negative racial script, I might have acted very differently.

- My parents confirmed the script in my head that blacks are human beings like everyone else. My father and I saw a black man fall and hurt himself while riding a bike. We stopped and picked him up and brought him home. I saw for the first time that blacks bled red blood and feel pain just like white people.

In this last illustration, the fact that the father stopped and helped the black man who had fallen from his bike made a big impression on his son. That made an indelible impression on the formation of his racial script.

b) Negative Verbal Racial Scripts: "Blacks Are Not OK"

Acquired in the pre-exposure stage, negative racial scripts become powerful psychological phenomena. They form mindsets that determine one's perception of people and things not experienced. Negative racial scripts may even create anxiety and phobias about things unseen and unknown. Gordon Allport (1954) once told the story about the little girl who asked her mother, "Mother, what is the name of the children I am supposed to hate?" (p. 307) Allport explains the child was attempting to be obedient by integrating her racial scripts into her daily social interactions. The child wanted to hate the right people when she sees them. She does not know what a black person is; she has learned only the negative linguistic tag or racial script.

In the story described earlier, "Across the Railroad Tracks," the white parent told his daughter not to play with the little black child. Similarly, the black father instructed his daughter not to play with the white child.

Some individuals freely admit that they were negatively racially scripted in their environment as in the following examples:

- I am a racist. As much as my heart would wish otherwise; I can make no other claim because I was raised in a racist environment by family members who loved me, but taught me a view of the world that considers white people to be universally superior. I retain somewhere in my psyche an element of fear. I have been able to recognize a good portion of the stereotypes and racial myths that I have been taught. I attempt to eliminate them from my attitudes, but it is difficult to do so.

  I spent the majority of my childhood in the South, known to be quite proud of its cultural heritage, yet quite racist towards blacks at the same time. My first memory of racial consciousness was when I asked my mother if "Nigger" was a bad word.

- As a child, my parents regarding the black race gave me negative scripts. They felt that blacks should not be trusted; they commit the majority of the crimes; they are of a lower class status than whites and are generally dangerous people.

- "Never trust a 'Nigger.' They're all lazy and expect to be paid for lying around and reproducing. They're all on welfare." These are just a few of the racial stereotypes I was taught by my family as I was growing up.

- I grew up in a home completely surrounded by much prejudice. I was raised in a predominately white neighborhood. My father owned a store in an area that was entirely black. Naturally his customers were all black. For many years, my father would come home from work complaining about his black customers. I began to think all blacks were thieves, cheaters or welfare recipients. My experience at my father's store plus his complaints led me to a very negative opinion of blacks.

- As a small child, I had relatively no contact with blacks. The small town that I lived in had rather segregated neighborhoods. My parents are racists and I was scripted accordingly. "Nigger" was a household word. "Nigger" became a common word in my vocabulary and I formed a negative script. I was taught that blacks were all lazy, dumb, mean and to be avoided. Although, I had not had any real contact with a black person, I avoided them whenever in public since they were not to be trusted. I believed they were inferior and should be treated accordingly and that they had been brought over from the jungle. My parents, as well as many of my relatives who were similarly racist, reinforced all these views.

c) Negative Non-Verbal Racial Scripts

Not all negative scripts are verbal. Some are given in a nonverbal fashion:

- "Dad squeezed my hand a little harder around blacks signifying that they are dangerous.

- Just a little girl of about three or four, I remember hating to hold my dad's hand while walking down the street. There was ferociousness in his grip that quite frankly scared me. It is only now that I know why Dad was gripping so hard. He was trying to protect me from what he regarded as a dangerous world. So influenced with fear from his childhood experiences, he transmitted the message to me as "always be on the lookout around blacks." Thus my early experiences with black people were first triggered by my Dad squeezing my hand a little bit harder around people who "looked suspicious," unfortunately signaling me that Blacks and Hispanics were dangerous."

- I remember once my mother and I were on an elevator when a black man entered. She quickly pulled me closer to her. I was afraid that something was wrong. This made me afraid of the black man who came onto the elevator. I was glad when we got off.

d) Additional Negative Racial Scripts

There were numerous other negative racial themes. Some of the more common ones are summarize in the following:

1. Don't trust a "Nigger."
2. Don't play with blacks.
3. Don't date blacks.
4. Don't get close to 'them.'
5. Don't you know that all "Niggers" are liars?
6. Blacks are thieves.
7. Blacks are lazy.
8. Blacks are ignorant.
9. Blacks are dangerous.

e) Neutral /Avoidance Scripts

Many parents avoided discussing racial issues with their children and put it off by using the excuse "they will find out later when they are mature and be better able to understand." These parents are very insecure about racial issues. They may harbor prejudices themselves or simply are naive about racial issues. Nonetheless, this avoidance situation leaves the child in the position of discovering how he/she should interact with persons of a different race. Essence Magazine (1996) reports that 80 percent of white parents and 70 percent of black parents state that they have discussed racial relations with their children. The remaining 20 to 30 percent of the parents do not bother to discuss racial relations with their children. When parents do not bother to discuss racial issues, a great deal of naiveté sets in. There are numerous dangers inherent in the neutral/avoidance approach. It puts the child in a vulnerable position. Later, when the child faces a racial situation and mis-handles it, or becomes confused and mixed up, the parents realize that it was a mistake not to discuss racial issues with the child earlier. As one individual put it:

- My parents never really discussed the issue of race with me. They tended to avoid volatile issues unless they were forced out into the open. Fortunately for them, the race issue never surfaced. This was unfortunate for me because I grew up learning about race through the stereotypes of the media, the indirect socialization of my parents and the mis-education of my schooling.

Similarly a large number of individuals report they had no memories of any discussions centering on racial issues:

- I suppose I was raised with a neutral script. I grew up in a predominately white suburb. I don't remember if my parents said anything positive or negative about black people. But I know by their actions they never told me to stay away from them and never tried to keep me from them.

- I was not exposed to many (if any) black individuals. I would, however, classify my early development as neutral. My parents avoided the subject and I was left to formulate my own opinions in regards to African-Americans. My first contact with a black person was a little girl in my swim class. The first day, I wondered if her color was going to come off in the water.

- My parents never sat down and told me anything about blacks. However, I do remember my first experience and how it shaped my attitude toward the black race. Our kitchen sink had not been working properly, so my mother called the plumber who happened to be a black man. I remember walking into our kitchen after a morning bath and seeing this big, muscular black man in our kitchen. I

asked him, "doesn't your Mommy make you take a bath?"
Being very good-natured, the man said "yes" his mommy
did, but he had black skin and was not dirty. He then let
me touch his skin so that I could see that the color did
not rub off. At that point, the inquisitive two-year old
in me took over and I proceeded to touch his hair and
teeth (which seemed so much brighter than mine). I also
remember asking him what color was his bottom (black or
pink), as his skin was black and his palms were pink. He
thought this was quite funny and went on to explain that
he was black all over, except his palms and the bottom of
his feet. That day after he left, I told my mom I wanted to
be black because they had dark skin and did not have to
take a bath as often as a white person.

These reactions were common among many individuals who
reported their parents either avoided discussions of racial issues or
remained neutral and did not take a position. Finally, this last story is
a classic example of what happens when racial discussions are avoided.
A young Caucasian woman named Ellen told this story:

- Ellen (a white female) and John (a black male) lived in the
South on a plantation owned by Ellen's parents. Ellen's
parents never really explained racism or racial relations to
her. She was only age five at the time when this incident
occurred.

  Everyday Ellen and John would run and play in the southern
  sun while their parents were working or busy doing chores.
  During this particular summer, heavy rains fell and flooded
  the farmlands. In one area, water filled the area and made a
  large water puddle. Ellen and John got together and began
  wading together in the puddle.

  Within a few minutes, Ellen's grandfather screamed at her
  to stop playing and come home immediately. He was quite
  upset and angry. Grandfather spanked little Ellen. She was
  confused and hurt. She did not know why she was being

punished: playing in the puddle of water or playing with a black boy? She could not figure it out.

Later in life she learned that black and white children should not play together and that a black person should not look at a white person with direct eye-to-eye contact. She was stunned because she really liked John. She was now afraid to play with him.

In this last story, Ellen had not received a racial script from her parents or grandparents. The action by her grandfather left her confused and perplexed. Such is the case when parents do not care to explain racial differences. The next vignette illustrates what happens to a child who receives little or no racial instructions:

- I had no concept of what being prejudice was, and unfortunately I learned the hard way. It is something I am still embarrassed about today. When I was in the second grade I forgot to bring something for "show-and-tell," so I decided to tell a joke my friend had told. I don't remember exactly what that joke was, but it had something to do with black people and watermelons. Not even half way thorough the first sentence, my teacher stopped me and told me to stay after class. I was completely stunned and started to cry. I could not figure out what I had done to make my teacher angry. My teacher called my parents and we had a long talk about what I said and why it was bad. I remember feeling sick to my stomach for a long time. It's the same feeling I get now whenever I think about it.

f) Mixed Racial Scripts: Who's Right?

An African proverb states: *"When two elephants fight, the grass suffers."*

In many cases, the child may receive a mixed script, one from the father and a different from the mother or grandparents. Two opposing scripts (one positive and one negative) are likely to create a state of discomfort and confusion in the child. According to Festinger (1957), when two or more of a person's cognitions (i.e., scripts, beliefs etc.,) are in opposition, an uncomfortable psychological state (dissonance) may result. Festinger further suggests the person will not only make efforts to reduce the dissonance, but may attempt to avoid situations that are likely to increase the dissonance. Several methods of reducing the dissonance are proposed:

1) Changing a particular behavior, e.g., the child may avoid contact with African-Americans altogether

2) Changing the belief of one of the parents, e.g., attempting to persuade one of the parents to give up the racist thinking, or

3) Seek new information to confirm one of the parental scripts and disconfirm the other, e.g., asking the parent to read certain anti-racist materials, racist materials, attend lectures, watch certain programs on television and so on.

Mixed racial scripts put the child in crossfire between the two parents. Such mixed messages may confuse the child about what parental script to follow. In some cases, the child will vacillate from one script to the other. In other cases, there will be script failure or the development of counterscripts.

Lucy Gibson's (2002) article, "It all Started With My Parents," discussed her mixed racial scripts and how it affected her:

> My Dad had contempt not only for women, but also for people he considered "lowered races," particularly black people....he believed that whites were mentally superior to other races...He particularly disliked and mistrusted black people. My mother, on the contrary, believed strongly in the equality of races, so this was one of the subjects they argued about (p. 83).

child, so his views still played a major role in my attitudes towards other races. As a child I knew I was supposed to consider black people as equals, but I was skeptical considering that my own father lived by different beliefs.

Some children have parents who practice "do as I say" but "not as I do." Wrote one individual:

- I feel my racial script from my parents was more preached than practiced. For example, my mother held my hand a little tighter when a black man climbed on the bus. My sister once told my mother that she was interested in a black boy; my mother said that she would advise her not to see him because of the problems it might cause. Thus, although my parents were against racism and preached equality of the races, they never did much to back up their thoughts.

g) Anchor Racial Scripts:

Anchor scripts are memories that are held securely in place for long periods of time; anchors may be positive or negative. The anchor is a stabilizing memory of a racial event that occurred at an earlier period in life. Not realizing it, many children have early interracial experiences that serve as anchor scripts. These are experiences in the past that elicited a positive or negative interracial response and now serve as a stimulus to trigger a similar response in the present. As such an anchor script is a trigger mechanism.

Anchor:" I Remember Johnny!"

When I arrived at my summer camp my counselor greeted me with open arms. To my surprise, my counselor, Johnny, was black. I was very scared. I wasn't sure why I was scared. I do know that I wasn't scared of the other counselor who was white. I never shared my view with anyone.

I don't remember the day I began to look at the black counselor as my friend. I do remember filling out the camp questionnaire at the end of the summer. In the blank next to whom I would like as my counselor the next summer, I indicated Johnny, the black counselor.

Right up until this day, that summer experience has meant something very special to me. It may not seem important, yet to an 11- year- old it was very important to know you have a good friend as a black person. Today, whenever I hear any racial stereotyping of blacks, I just think back and think of Johnny, my black counselor.

In this case the "memory of the black counselor" is the anchor script. It is the positive trigger that serves to prevent this person from buying into the negative images of African- Americans. This student discusses "Robert the doorman" who served as an anchor script for him:

Ever since I can remember, my parents have always taught me that all people were created equal no matter what color or race. From the time I was a little boy, there was no difference in my eyes between my black friends and my white friends.

As a child, everyone appeared equal to me although some people had darker skin than me. While waiting for the school bus everyday, Robert the doorman never hesitated to make me laugh or gave me a treat. I always looked forward to my morning meetings with Robert because he always started my day off with a smile. Robert always had something positive to say to start the day off, no matter how dreary the day seemed. Robert had two children of his own. On some weekends my parents, my brother and I would see Robert and his two sons playing ball in the park. They would always ask me to join them. We had a good time playing with them.

However one day Robert was not there to greet me off to school. I assumed that he was sick even though he had never been sick before. Robert never did return to his job. I can remember the sadness in my heart when I realized that I would probably never see Robert again. He had been transferred to another part of town; I will always remember him as my favorite person.

h) Maids as Anchor Racial Scripts

One of the most interesting findings was that a large number of white children do not experience the pre-exposure phase (i.e. an absence of blacks) because they have African-American maids or other domestic workers in their homes. Thus the child's earliest memories of African-Americans are of these significant caretakers and/or domestic workers. Approximately 15 percent of our sample reported having African-American maids, baby-sitters, nannies or domestic workers of some kind in their homes during their early formative years. In many cases, the children became extremely attached to the maids or baby-sitters and related to them as their surrogate mother.

Lillian Smith's (1961) ***"Killers of the Dream"*** discusses her awareness of this dual relationship that many white children developed with two Moms, one black and one white:

> …. This small white child learns to love both mother and nurse; he is never certain which he loves better. Sometimes, secretly, it is his "colored mother" who meets his infantile needs more completely, for his "white mother" is busy with her social life or her older children or perhaps a new one, and cannot give him the time and concern he hungers for…. But when he is miserable, he creeps away and crawls up in old black arms, every curve of which he has known by heart since babyhood, and snuggles against a cotton dress…. Sometimes he wants to stay in her lap forever (Pp. 127-128).

These kids develop strong attachments to their maids to the extent that many relate to them as parental figures. In home situations where maids are present, the pre-exposure period is different than in homes where there are no black employees. As a rule, children with maids in the home usually develop very positive racial scripts.

Below are several examples that characterize the quality of the experience the children had with their maids and how their racial scripts were formed:

- I cannot remember a time when I wasn't interacting with races other than my own. Our house sitter, Rosie was a true grandmother. And Bessie, our cleaning lady and nanny, kept me entertained and happy. Both of these black women played a crucial role in my life since the age of two. This resulted in my development of positive racial attitudes.

- My first exposure to a black person occurred when I was brought home from the hospital as an infant. My nurse was a black woman. She served as a second mother to me throughout my childhood years. She was considered a part of the family. I really cared for her a lot and still keep in contact with her.

- I don't remember what happened the first time I met a black person; however, I have the feeling that all I did was cry, eat and throw up. This is because my baby nurse was a black woman. My parents loved Brenda, the baby nurse. "Bren" was what we called her. She was the most energetic and extraordinary woman of fifty years that I ever met. My greatest moments with Bren were immediately at breakfast time. On my birthday, she would always have several presents waiting for me—all of which a lot of thought had obviously been put into this choosing. She always chose the present that little girls and boys drool over when they are advertised. The best gift of all though was a key chain with plastic dollar bills that fan out. I carried that key chain around for years though I never had any keys. I realized, not too long ago, how much these presents meant to us, how much Bren cared for us and how much we cared for her. Although Bren no longer works for my family, we still talk, usually on birthdays. I look back and see the love that was shared between her and my family.

- My earliest recollection of primary contact with a black person is a black woman, Dianna; we affectionately called "Di." She was in charge of us when my parents were at work and basically raised us. We referred to her as our black Mom. My mother and Di used to say, "You have one white Mom and one black Mom."

- My grandmother had a terminal illness that required her to hire a twenty-four-hour registered nurse; an older black woman named Joanna. I grew to have the greatest respect for Joanna. My scripting occurred by watching my mother hug and hold long conversations with Joanna every time we visited. This woman who gave so much of her time and attention became my grandmother more so than my true one. She spent a lot of time with me by talking to me and making me a part of her time and attention.

- Yvonne played an important role in my childhood years. She helped raise me from the day I was born until I was 13 years old. She was a black woman in her sixties who not only fed and played with me, but she taught me values, morals and the beliefs of her culture. She came everyday and got us ready for school, walked us to the bus stop and waited for us upon our return home. Some of my favorite memories were the times when my parents went away and Yvonne stayed with my sisters and me. When we were little, Yvonne used to bring the roll-a-way bed into our room and as we drifted off to sleep she would say her prayers to us and make us say them too: "Now I lay me down to sleep. I pray to the Lord my soul will keep; if I die before I wake; I pray to the Lord my soul will take." I had such a deep respect and admiration for Yvonne throughout my childhood, and that special love continues to this day. Not only did I love Yvonne as a mother; I respected her as a friend.

In the majority of cases where the families had maids, the parents taught their children positive scripts about African-Americans. The children reported that the maids were admired and highly respected by family members, thus serving as role models for them to acquire positive racial scripts. The maids fed, entertained, dressed and disciplined the children. As one individual reported: "my maid didn't take no stuff" and that she was a strict disciplinarian. Another individual reported her maid was an elderly black woman who was "more like a grandmother while my biological grandmother was remote and cold."

- My mother hired a black housekeeper, Avery. She was dedicated to my family as we were to her. Throughout my early childhood years, Avery served as my second mother as she cared for me, bathed me and changed my diapers. In the daytime, we watched cartoons together while my parents were at work and when she put me down for my nap; her time was spent doing housework. But I was not blind to the fact that Avery was the housekeeper, yet she served as a source of love and respect. I accepted her blackness as I accepted my own whiteness. Avery was part of my family as each member was a part. She was present at all birthday parties and celebrated holidays with my family.

My first encounter with black children occurred during my elementary school years. Because of my early exposure to Avery, I did not find my few black peers to be a source of discomfort. They were students like I was, seeking an education.

I began watching news regularly on television throughout junior high school. As I sat in front of the TV set each evening, I would see many stories where black people were convicted of crimes. The black race as a whole was portrayed in my dominant society as the instigators of a robbery or a killing. They were depicted as an inferior race. But to me, Avery was my equal. Thus the media did not influence my views towards blacks.

- I never had a pre-exposure stage concerning my relations with blacks. The reason for this is that since before I can remember a black woman cared me for. When I say, "cared for" I don't mean watched until my parents got home. I mean watched, disciplined, directed, taught and everything that the mother is usually responsible for. The woman's name was Annie Smith. My parents worked long hours and were seldom home so there was a need for some one to take care of my twin brother and me. I thought of my parents as Dad and Mom and I knew they were important figures in my life, but Annie was certainly just as important and her authority was unchallengeable. Although she was paid, my brother and I did not think of her cares being her job, and I don't think she thought of it that way either. There was no mistaking the fact that my brother, Annie and I were family.

My brother and I went everywhere with Annie. We ate with her at home and out, we went to church with her and we went to the beauty parlor with her. Many times we would be the only white people amongst many black people. During these times I never felt alienated or different. Wherever we went, we were Annie's boys.

It is clear from the above vignettes that maids played a significant role in shaping the children's attitudes toward Black-Americans. Indeed, many of them felt extremely close to their maids, in fact, so close that some of them looked upon them as surrogate mothers.

Many white parents teach their children a "code" regarding the way in which they are to interact and to treat blacks. There is a training period through which the children pass. During that period their habits are groomed into their behavior, speech and thoughts. They learn, for example, "to talk down to blacks" and to expect blacks "to talk up to them." There are many explicit rules; some are given verbally and some are given non-verbally.

From the words of Sarah Patton Boyle (1962) **The Desegregated Heart**:

> My stereotype of the "typical Nigra" grew as a result of a type of indoctrination which was, I think, eighty percent pure implication, unvocalized on the part of my elders. For example, I can't recall ever being told that the Negro's mental endowments were basically inferior to those of whites, but I was surrounded by a whole pattern of behavior which implied it. I think I was told by my mother that the Negro lacked the capacity to appreciate attractive surroundings (p. 17).

One common finding was the individuals did not address the maids as adults, i.e. not as "Mrs.," "Miss," or by the maid's last name. The maid was addressed by her first name as "Mary," "Annie" or Rosie etc. The children were most likely imitating the parents who referred to the maids by their first names. Perhaps this is a cultural difference phenomenon, because in the black culture, children are carefully taught to address elders and adults as "Miss," "Mrs." or "Mr." to show respect for the elders. Maids and yardmen are all addressed as Mr. or Mrs. in the black culture. Adults are rarely addressed by their first name.

I recall as a graduate student, one of my professors discussed how he liked his maid and the relationship he had with her. He mentioned her first name, but when I asked him her last name, he was speechless. He did not know her last name! He had never been taught to refer to black maids by their last name. That was the invisibility and the lack of respect and recognition of the maid's adult status.

Several observations will illustrate the point of how whites tend not to address blacks, especially maids and servants, in an adult fashion. First, let us look at some of the literary characters and then at some of the examples that we have gathered.

Sarah Patton Boyle (1962) states:

> ....We had a maid named Coreen....[who] used to take me fishing on summer evenings when her work was done. With mutual satisfaction she taught me all she knew of the art....Our farm hands lasted longer than our cooks. We kept one of our monthly hands about six years. His name was Tobe. I regularly helped Tobe do all the interesting things done on farms (Pp. 17-18).

Note that Sarah Boyle did not address either of the black adults as "Mr." or Mrs." Now let us look at what happens when a black adult breaks the "code" and addresses a white person by the first name in a familiar tone. A Black woman attending Howard University in Washington D.C. worked part-time cleaning rooms where Sarah Boyle lived. The two of them talked quite a bit and discovered they had some common interests in Art. One day the black woman called Sarah Patton Boyle "Patty" instead of "Miss Patton" as she had been customarily addressing her. Here is Sarah Patton Boyle's (1962) reaction to a black person not addressing her as "Miss:"

> I felt my entire interior congeal. A Negro had failed to call me "Miss".... I experienced a terrible wave of depression...for I must have somewhere let our relationship become an equality one, thus inviting 'this kind of thing' (P.40).

While giving a lecture to a group of social workers and psychologists, one of the psychologists related a story that supports this notion of the lack of respect that whites have for Black-Americans. The psychologist stated that while growing up his parents had a black maid named "Eula" who taught him how to print certain letters of the alphabet. His teacher, a white woman named "Mrs. Jones," also taught him how to print letters. He was confused and could not figure out why the maid was simply referred to as "Eula" who taught him to print, while the teacher had to be called "Mrs. Jones." As a child he was puzzled and confused over this double standard.

I explained to him that traditionally there is a "culture of disrespect" where whites devalued blacks and did not address them as "Mr." or "Mrs." for two reasons: 1) the "three-fifths doctrine" that stated blacks are not fully a man or woman and 2) many whites who believe that blacks longitudinal development skips adulthood and follows two stages:

a) Boy becomes uncle
b) Girl becomes auntie

One of the individuals in my study reported a similar story regarding this "culture of disrespect:"

> When I moved to a private, all-white school, I first encountered racism. But it was not the kind of racism I had seen on television when I was watching "Roots." This was a new, or refined and hidden kind of racism. In fact, I really didn't understand it to be racism until later when I attempted to write an article for the school newspaper.
>
> You see there were no black faculty members at the school. The only blacks were the janitors and the food service workers. The students referred to the blacks by their first names. The two white workers were referred to as Mrs. Logan and Mr. Billy. All the teachers were called Mrs., Miss or Mr.
>
> I asked why shouldn't the blacks be addressed as "Mr." and "Mrs."? I wrote an article addressing this question and was surprised by the negative reaction I received. My article was eventually printed but in a watered-down fashion, in a small box at the bottom of the page.

I clearly remember while living in the South (Little Rock, Arkansas) playing with a little white girl named Mary Lou. We both were about ten or eleven years old. I always called her by her first name, "Mary Lou" and she responded. One day her father told me that Mary Lou would soon be twelve years old and that I would have to begin calling her "Miss Mary Lou," because on her birthday she would be a young woman. I never played with Mary Lou again, because I was not about to call this child "Miss." The irony of this story is my mother worked for this family as a domestic worker. Mary Lou called my mother by her first name: Rosie, but I had to call Mary Lou's mother "Miss Ann."

Sarah Patton Boyle (1962) tells a similar story:

> On my twelfth birthday I was told I was a big girl now and that my relations with Negroes from now on must be formal. The current cook, the farm hand and all the colored children were ordered to stop calling me Patty and call me "Miss Patty" (P. 30).

CHAPTER IV:
THE DISCOVERY /
EXPOSURE PHASE

The second phase of racial script formation involves some form of discovery or contact with persons of different racial groups. The discovery phase is comprised of four levels:

1) Passive Exposure: Sight Only
2) Active Contact/ Interaction
3) Encounter/Hostile Interaction
4) Phobic Discovery: Afrophobia

1) Passive Exposure: Sight Only

The first level of Discovery is that of "Passive Exposure." At this level the child is merely exposed, but has no contact, to a person or persons of a difference race. Passive exposure is merely a "sight seeing" experience that may incite the child's curiosity about certain individuals of different groups. The exposure may be accidental, spontaneous or a planned experience for the child. It may take place within the home, on television, outside (as in the park), a store or on the streets. However, passive exposure does not involve direct contact, only observation by the child. This is merely "sight only" or passive observation. "Sight seeing" exposure may or may not have any impact on the formation of racial attitudes. Several examples of passive exposure are shown in the following vignettes:

- I was brought up in a rural, segregated, all-white," bed-room" community. The first time I actually encountered an African-American person was one day I asked my mother at the grocery store why that lady had dark colored skin. "Don't point dear," my mother replied, "It's impolite." But later my mother told me that God made people in all different colors: white, black, red, yellow, etc. But he loves them all equally.

- Child: "Grandmother, who are those people over there?" referring to some African-Americans on the opposite side of the street.

  Grandmother: "Oh! They are just some new people that God just made."

- The neighborhood in which I grew up was exclusively white. I never had any exposure to black people until two young black girls enrolled in my school. I saw them in the school but never had any direct contact with them.

- When I was a youngster I asked my grandfather, why people had a skin color different from mine. He said that when God made people, he first molded them. He made blacks darker because they had been left in the oven a little longer than the other races. Mexicans and Chinese were baked less than blacks but not more than whites. We (whites) were taken out of the oven a little before all of the other races and that is why we have a lighter pigmentation.

- I was born into and grew up in a strictly white neighborhood. There were no black children or teachers in the elementary schools. As such, up until my first contact with a black person my scripts were blank. My earliest memory of seeing a black person is a very vivid one. I was 7 or 8 years old and had gone to Atlanta with my parents to visit someone in the hospital. While they were inside, I waited in the car with my grandmother. I remember seeing two black girls pass on the sidewalk. I stared at them for a long time before I asked my grandmother why they looked liked that. I remember very clearly what she said. She told me that they were a new kind of person that had just recently been "invented." God wanted to have all different kinds of people, so he decided to make some that were a different color. I really can't say whether this was a positive or negative experience, but I do know this idea of black people as a "new race" stayed with me for a long, long time.

In the above situations, the children were exposed to African-Americans but they did not have contact or interaction with them. However, they still gained some impressions of blacks, whether positive or negative.

2) Active Contact/Friendly Interaction

The second phase of Discovery is that of "Active Contact" and involves some form of friendly or cooperative interaction. This contact may be an interaction that involves developing a mutual or reciprocal relationship with each other. The contact (interaction) is of a friendly nature, one in which there may be play, cooperation, achievement of a joint goal and development of a friendship.

The advantages and disadvantages of early interracial experiences have been the focus of many research studies. The nature of the contact activity affects the outcome of the attitude. Amir (1969) extensively reviewed the literature on inter-group relations and concluded that "favorable" interracial conditions tend to reduce prejudice, whereas "unfavorable" conditions tend to increase racial prejudice. The underlying assumption is: positive racial contact will enable children to know each other better and this close contact will lead to the reduction of racial prejudice and inter-group tensions thereby improving interracial relations. Amir (1998) further adds that cooperative activities tend to improve racial attitudes while competitive activities may have a negative effect.

According to the "Contact Hypothesis," the more one gets to know individuals of a minority group, the less likely one is to be prejudiced against that minority group. Further, the hypothesis proposes that one dislikes blacks because one has been socialized into holding false and derogatory opinions about them. If such opinions are false, then positive experiences with blacks should tend to erase the negative perceptions.

Cook (1985) studied the "Contact Hypothesis" and found inter-group contact induces friendly interracial behavior when certain characteristics are present. The contact hypothesis predicts a favorable change in attitude and interpersonal attraction will result when there is personal contact with members of the disliked group, provided five conditions are present:

1) The status of the participants must be equal

2) Attributes of the disliked group that become apparent must dis-confirm the prevailing stereotyped beliefs (scripts)

3) The contact situation must encourage, or require, cooperation in the achievement of a joint goal

4) The contact situation must promote adequate associations between groups so that members will be seen as individuals rather than as persons with stereotyped group characteristics

5) There must be group equality

However, there is an "inverse contact hypothesis," found in studies (Butler, D. & Stokes, D. 1969; Chaples, E.A., Sedlacek, W.E., & Miyares, J. 1978; Ray, J.J 1980), conducted in Britain, Australia and South Africa According to this version of the Contact Hypothesis, the more one comes in contact with blacks, the more prejudiced one becomes. Negative contact leads to hostile relations and increases prejudice and tensions in inter-group relations.

However, my findings suggest that the earlier the racial interaction, the better as seen in the following reports. The following vignettes show the positive effects of early positive interaction with blacks.

- When I got to elementary school there were several black children who were part of my group of friends. We were on patrols, we went to the same parties and they were in some of my classes. Blacks and whites kissed each other when we played "Spin-the-Bottle" and "Two Minutes in Heaven." My most memorable encounter with a black person was when I entered college. I was dancing by myself and a black man who I had seen from a distance, asked me for a dance. The next weekend he asked me to have lunch with him. I had never been on a date with a black man before, but the idea excited me. We ended up going out to dinner a couple more times and became very close.

- I met Johnny when I was three years old, and until this very day, he has remained my very best friend. Because I met Johnny at such an early age issues such as racism and discrimination had no bearing in the relationship that Johnny and I shared. As I grew older, I realized that Johnny was black but this had no bearing on the friendship that we so dearly shared.

- Sue lived in an all-white community. She attended Sunday school and church where there were no black children. The idea of racial equality was stressed in school. In church, the children were taught that their parents supported racial equality at home. Her racial scripts were very positive. It was not until kindergarten that she had her first contact with blacks. Two kids in her class were black and because she had a positive racial script, she was not hesitant in becoming friends with them. Over the course of the year the two black kids became her best friends. They shared birthday parties and played together. Her positive racial script was mainly responsible for the success of this behavior. If she had a negative racial script, she might have acted very differently.

3) Encounter/Hostile Interaction

Not all-early racial contact is positive. The third form of discovery involves an "encounter" which in this context means to engage in a hostile manner or to pose some form of opposition. Encounter involves a conflict between individuals of some nature. Amir (1998) proposed prejudice might be strengthened by competitive contacts, unpleasant, involuntary or unwelcome contact, contact that disadvantages a participant or contact when the participant is frustrated. The following vignettes will illustrate the manner in which hostile encounters effect racial attitudes:

- In the middle of the third grade, I went to live with my mother and attended a new elementary school. Anxious to fit in and be accepted, I insisted on taking the bus to school on my first day. I awaited the bus and finally it stopped in front of my house. I got on and to my amazement the bus was filled with black children. I was the only white child on the bus. I was greeted on the bus with cruel jeers and scowls from almost every child. I took a seat next to a black child and she immediately made a face, got up and sat with another black girl. I felt lost; I felt stupid; and I felt shame that I was a white person as my eyes welled up with tears. At this point, I had very negative feelings toward blacks I could not bring myself to ride the bus anymore.

- My first contact with a black person was very negative. I was in the second grade and a black boy from the 3rd grade beat me up because I would not kiss him. He threw a chair at me, pushed me down and punched me after school. I disliked blacks from that day on. Maybe that was wrong, but that is how I felt.

- When I entered high school I had my first negative encounter with members of the black race. Black students were bussed from the city to my school in the suburbs. One afternoon while walking through the corridors six black girls approached me. There was no reason for them to feel any animosity toward me, since I never came in contact with them. They pushed me and harassed me. I was terrified as I reached the door to my classroom. I was shaking and laid my head upon my desk and began to cry.

  For a few months following this encounter I associated all black people with the six girls who had disturbed me that afternoon. At school I was scared to walk through the halls alone and I made certain I was accompanied by a friend at all times.

- One day we were outside playing ball and I caught this black boy's ball. It was really a big deal to catch his kicks because they were the highest of anyone else's. This black girl was so enraged that I had managed this feat, that after the act, she looked me square between the eyes, took a deep breath and beat the crap out of me. Once she had finished she said, "If you ever catch his ball again, you old white cracker, I'll beat you up again." After this incident I went home and looked up the word "white cracker" in the dictionary. After this, I began building armor to protect myself from black people.

This child is not the only one that does not know the meaning or the origin of the term "cracker." When a black calls a white a "cracker" it is natural to assume that this is a bad term. But when you know the origin of the term, as referred to white people, you may think differently.

During the slave period of American History, the white slave owners would watch over their workers out in the fields. When one got out of hand and had to be put back in place, so to speak, the white man would sometimes crack a whip to let them know he meant business. When the slaves would gather in their houses at night, they would talk about their day and refer to the white man as the "cracker," because of the whip he would use on them. Thus, the term "cracker" is essentially complimentary rather than derogatory.

4) Phobic Discovery: Afrophobia

In some instances, children, prior to entering school, may have developed a fear or hatred of African-Americans or what I call **Afrophobia**. It is a race-specific phobia that involves a varying degree of unrealistic fear. Dr. Cornell West, Professor of Afro-American Studies and Philosophy of Religion at Princeton University, stated in a speech given at the Sorbonne in Paris, France, "A discussion about racism is a discussion about white fear" (Reep, J. (2000, p. 1). Sixty-one percent of whites interviewed say they fear a group of black men whereas only 40 percent of blacks say they fear a group of white men (Essence 9-19-96) Those persons who experience **Afrophobia** will go to great lengths to avoid African-Americans. This fear is irrational, illogical and is not based on any reality-based information. FEAR stands for False-Evidence-Appearing –Real!

The development of **Afrophobia** is not necessarily intentional. It may be accidental, as in the following example:

- This little girl visited the hospital with her father as he made rounds. While her Dad was checking the patients, she sat and played with the nurses. Her father introduced her to an African-American man in the hospital. The man stuck out his hand and offered to shake hers, but she withdrew saying that she couldn't shake his hands until he washed them. This little child stated she never saw an African-American prior to this experience. She had no idea that people looked differently than she did. She assumed that he was just dirty. Her father tried to explain, but she was scared and began to cry. She developed a fear of blacks.

In addition, **Afrophobia** may be based on the negative racial scripts ingrained in the psyche by parents. There is an axiom that states, "You fear that which you do not know." The less knowledge one has about a group or person, the more fear and prejudice that person is likely to possess. Conversely, the more information one has about an individual or group, the less likely that person is to rely on stereotypes and the less likely the person will fear blacks.

Racism cannot be eliminated in this country as long as we are fearful of each other, or show fear of talking to each other as mature adults. Racism is a form of immaturity that represents a stage of arrested (fixed) development. It is still the child script that was learned early.

Studies have suggested that perceptual differences among groups may account for the development of fear and hostile racial attitudes. Allport (1954) discussed the potential role of "fear of the strange" for young children, i.e. people who look different from them. Allport suggests two things 1) that visible differences between people may imply real differences to the child and 2) that when interracial contacts occur at an early age strangeness and fear are decreased. Cantor (1972) using the "mere exposure" hypothesis of Zajonc et al (1971) reports that familiarity with other race faces may be positively related to children's racial attitudes. What is suggested here is early interracial contact is very beneficial to the child in developing positive attitudes towards a particular race.

Fear makes the racial problem much bigger than it should be. It magnifies the problem, freezes the mind and makes it virtually impossible to register new and valid information. Fear clouds opportunities for growth, erases and eliminates possibilities for solutions and limits one's ability to move beyond the place at which one's mind is stuck.

Imagine for a moment that if we blindfold someone who is Afrophobic and then present him/her with two persons one black and one white. There probably would be no fear because the visual stimulus that creates the fear is absent. The link between the automatic thought (the racial script) and the visual stimulus (the black person) has been interrupted.

Fear is at the heart of all hatred. It is the fear of the unknown, and fear of those who are different, that is projected on others as racial hatred. Whites are not always aware they are afraid of blacks. They think they are protecting themselves from real danger or a dangerous group of people. Fear breeds delusions (false beliefs) particularly when stereotypes are used.

Marshall O Lee (1993), a black psychologist at City University of New York observed how white fear operates or is activated in the presence of blacks. He observes:

> I have found that no matter how I dress...there will always be purse clutching. Some whites can't see that I'm wearing a Brooks Brothers suit or a cashmere coat. All they see is chocolate skin, and that elicits fear. Purse clutching is not the only subtle racism I experience. There are the elevator-escape artists-whites who duck out of the elevators after noticing a lone black male (Essence April, 1993, p. 46).

In his book, **Man in the Mirror**, Robert Bonazzi (1997) presents an excellent account of how **Afrophobia** originates. He states:

> Society did a terrible thing to us. Society told us that the time had come when we must stop playing with black children. We were made to understand that we had to change, in subtle ways, our attitudes toward the black lady who cared for us...Society would embarrass us that black people preferred it that way and I would embarrass them if we did not change the behavior and draw away from them...We saw them as 'other,' 'different,' and 'not like U" and always implied they were inferior to us" (P. 7).

Fear of African-Americans causes whites to avoid them (blacks) and this avoidance increases the fear. This process leads to a **"Cycle of Afrophobia"** that spreads to other African-Americans.

An Afrophobic reaction is automatically activated when confronted by a black person as the following person relates:

There have been many times when a black person will bump into me and I will reflexively reach for my wallet. It could be the wealthiest-looking black man, yet I cannot overcome this blind spot of fear. There are also many times when I will walk past a group of black teenagers and automatically assume that I am "in for trouble." However, there has never been any trouble. I just subconsciously assume there will be.

What this person is demonstrating is the automatic activation of the racial script in the presence of a race-specific stimulus, namely a black person. It is not the subconscious but the automatic nature of the response. What happens is the negative racial scripts (stereotypes) are automatically triggered when the person encounters a black individual. Levine (1995) labeled this reaction as the "default response" or an automatic, unthinking, instant response, e.g. a "knee-jerk" reaction.

The following illustrates how this individual was scripted into racial fear and avoidance of blacks. What was needed for him to overcome his fear was an experience with a black rather than the "second hand information" that he had received from others.

- I grew up in a small town in the Midwest, one which was secluded from many realities of the world. The ethnic makeup is 99 percent white, a figure that only allows one view when it comes to racism. I heard plenty of people talking down Blacks, Hispanics and Orientals with jokes and negative comments. They never thought anything about it, because there was no other racial view to contend with. I even found myself expressing the same thing and feeling no guilt.

  I can remember going out in the public and seeing blacks. I always tried to avoid them because of a certain FEAR that was placed in me from my childhood. My childhood environment forced this fear in me. The FEAR was that blacks were violent and untrustworthy. They would not feel guilty about what they had done because blacks had no conscience when it came to violence.

Misguided FEARS of blacks created a wall between blacks and the people of my small town. I finally challenged this fear, and in turn, I learned a valuable lesson about others as well about myself. My first real exposure with a black man was through basketball. Before the game, I felt real scared and intimidated to play blacks, but as the start of the game neared, I got a burning desire to win. I had to prove that I was better than a black because of what I had been taught. As the game progressed, I realized we were just young kids trying our best to win for ourselves and for our schools. We had similar goals during the game that night. I became more open to ideas and I realized that I never had any experience with blacks to create my own views; it was all from other people's views and experiences which I have based my ideas and views.

I realized that if I gave a black guy blood, he would not turn white; if he gave me blood, I would not turn black. I would still be the same. Ultimately, we must never lose sight of the fact that we are all human beings, regardless of the package we come in.

Afrophobia is very common in white children especially those who are not properly instructed by their parents. Children are very much aware of their parents' racial attitudes and internalize these attitudes.

- My mother was very afraid of black people. She used to tell me that "a black man is going to come and get you if you don't do this or don't do that." I used to have nightmares about black men raping me. Once a black man gave me what I thought was a dirty look, I panicked.

- My first encounter with a black person occurred when I entered the first grade. My best friend had bought me a leather purse and I couldn't resist taking it to school. As I left for school, my Dad gave me a dollar and warned me "to be careful with it and not to lose it." One of my classmates, Anthea, a black girl, complimented me about the purse after I had walked into the room that morning. I put the bag inside my desk, but when I returned from lunch, I was shocked to find my dollar was missing.

My heart thumped and I grew dizzy. I ran to my teacher and screamed. "Someone stole my dollar." No one admitted finding or taking it.

The next morning the teacher was talking to Anthea because she suspected she took the dollar. When I returned from recess, I found a crumpled dollar on my desk. Later, Anthea choked out an apology. I was petrified; I thought she would hate me even more and I was terrified to come to school the next day. I was happy that Anthea ignored me for the rest of the year. However, I had developed a phobia against black people.

In the third grade, there was an assembly put on by a group of men and women from Kenya. They played drums, danced, sang, wore colorful costumes and ran through the aisles of the auditorium. I was terrified. I tugged on my teacher's arm and told her how frightened I was. She had to take me out of the auditorium to alleviate my fears.

Before I entered middle school I didn't ever plan to use the girl's bathroom, because I heard rumors about how the black girls smoked cigarettes in there and would beat you up. That thought made me shake.

Before high school the same fears existed. Again, I had butterflies in my stomach every time I thought about the older black kids. I thought they would bother me. I had seen many television programs on rape and drugs.

In the tenth grade a very special occurrence altered my attitude. I was in the girls' bathroom and Anthea walked in. I felt like jumping out the window. She stared at me. I thought she was going to kill me. I was shaking. She softly said, "Laura, I love your boots; they are very pretty." I thanked her and we started talking. We both remembered the dollar incident and laughed about it. Anthea and I became very friendly once the flame was rekindled. Since then I have outgrown most of the trembling and preconceptions. However, walking in Chicago at night and seeing a group of ten black teenagers is the only time my heart starts dancing. Otherwise I love to hang out with blacks and think they are a lot of fun

CHAPTER V:
RACIAL SCRIPT ACTIVATION

1) Definition: Racial Script Activation

Racial Script Activation is the automatic triggering of a racial response to a person of a difference race. The racial script behaves as a set of "micro instructions" that are activated by a single race specific stimulus. In this case, a black person serves as the race-specific stimulus. Racial scripts and stereotypes are automatically activated when confronted with the primary racial stimuli and provide immediate access to the stereotype. Because of their ingrained nature, the scripts are triggered when confronted with racial stimuli. Racial script activation is a process of "acting before you think." Acting without thinking is very similar to shooting without aiming.

Script activation is similar to the manner in which Mary Ellen Goodman (1964) describes the formation of racial attitudes. She explains:

> [Forming] an attitude means being "ready" and "set" to act in a particular way, when and if you meet a certain kind of situation. Acquiring an attitude is like cocking a gun --the person and the gun are thereafter poised for action. Triggering [activation] comes for the person when the appropriate situation is met" (P.47).

Similar to attitudes, the racial script enables the person to respond very quickly. The individual sees a black person and reacts with the ingrained racial script immediately without thinking. The racial script "bypasses' the thought processes. The appearance of a black person causes the racist mind to go into a state of "hyper activation," which leads to an overreaction to blacks. This hyperactive state, however, is related to the intensity of the racial script.

For instance the equations:

a). The script "Blacks are Dangerous" causes the person to respond immediately with fear or anxiety when perceiving a black person.

b) The script "Blacks are OK" enables the person to relate to blacks without fear or anxiety.

2) The Racial Script Activation Model

FIGURE I RACIAL SCRIPT ACTIVATION MODEL

1. a = Activating Event (The appearance of one or several blacks)
2. x = Racial script = Blacks are dangerous
3. y = Racial Script Activation ("Oh, oh there's danger ahead")
4. z = Feelings and Behavior (Fear/anxiety and/or hatred)
   (Grips child's hand hard or pull child closer to body)

3) Racial Script Activation Examples

Let us examine several clear examples of racial script activation. In these examples, the racial scripts were automatically activated as if there were a "readiness to respond." In the first example, this young woman is of mixed parentage (a Japanese mother and an Anglo-American father). Her grandfather and father scripted her negatively about black people early in life. Butcher (1996) describes her racial activation process as follows:

I recoil when I think about my American grandfather driving us home, instructing my brother and me to lock our doors because we were passing through the "colored" section; or my father insisting that blacks were genetically inferior to whites. I instinctively associate young black men with violence and blacks in general with poverty. I have a habit of saying hello to the black strangers I pass on the street more than to anyone else" (p. 17-18).

Why does this young woman say "hello" to black strangers? Presumably, her racial script is activated and generates anxiety and/or fear when she meets blacks. The "hello" is a racially activated anxiety response. Similarly, I have noticed that many whites are very polite and courteous when they meet blacks on the street. They will "smile" nervously or say, "excuse me" or "pardon me." I tested this out recently by standing in a path where dozens of whites had to pass. As they passed many smiled, some turned their heads, while others mumbled "excuse me."

In the next passage, a clear example of racial script activation is presented.

a) Lady at the Casino

On a recent visit to a casino a Caucasian woman won a bucketful of dollars at a slot machine. She took a break from the slot machines for dinner with her husband. But first she wanted to stash her dollars in her hotel bedroom. As she was about to walk into an elevator she noticed two black men (a= Activating Event) already aboard. Her racial script "x" kicked in ("These two black guys are dangerous.") The woman froze for a moment and thought, "These two black guys are going to rob me" (y= the Racial Script activation).

She stood and stared at the two men and felt afraid, anxious, flustered and ashamed (z= Feelings and Behavior). She hoped they didn't read her mind. She cautiously joined them on the elevator. Avoiding eye contact, she turned around stiffly and faced the elevator doors as they closed. A second passed. Another second passed, then another but the elevator didn't move. Panic consumed her and her racial script kicked in again: "Oh my God, I am about to be robbed."

One of the men said, "Hit the floor." Instinct told her to do what they tell you. The bucket of dollars flew upwards as she threw out her arms and collapsed on the elevator carpet. A shower of coins rained down on the floor. "Take my money but please don't hurt me" she cried.

She heard one of the men politely say, "Ma'am, if you will just tell us what floor you are going to, we'll push the button."

"But you said 'hit the floor,' the lady cried.

"When I told the man to 'hit the floor' I meant that he should select our floor. That's Ebonics."

She thought "Oh my God, what a fool I have made of myself and was too humiliated to speak. She wanted to blurt out an apology but words failed her. How do you apologize to two perfectly respectable gentlemen whom you falsely thought were behaving as though they were robbing you? The three of them gathered up the strewn coins. The men helped the woman to her room. They could hardly hold back their laughter. As her door closed she could hear them laughing.

The next morning she received a dozen roses. Attached to each rose was a one-dollar bill. A card said, "Thanks for the best laugh we have had in years." It was signed Eddie Murphy and his bodyguard!

b) Black Man Mistaken as a Porter

- My sister informed the family that she had a steady boyfriend. However, we were all shocked when she told us that he was black. I remember dropping the phone when she told me. I wasn't angry, just shocked, because I had never imagined that she would date a black man.

Later my sister, her boyfriend and I visited my Aunt who lived in the South. My aunt greeted my sister and me at the door and let us into the house. My sister's boyfriend was getting a few things out of the car and didn't enter the house at the same time as we did. When he came to the door with our bags, my aunt took the luggage from him and gave him a tip and proceeded to close the door on him. I almost died from embarrassment and shame. Clearly, she thought he was a porter or something, not my sister's boy friend. I suddenly realized how thousands of blacks must feel when they are mis-perceived because of stereotypes because of skin color.

c) Dr. Williams Mistaken as a Hotel Bellman

It is not uncommon for black professionals or non-professionals, for that matter, to be mistaken for workers in hotels, hospitals and/or restaurants. I had an experience of stereotype activation. I had just finished giving a lecture at the University of Minnesota and stood near the bellman's desk waiting for him to bring my bags that I had left earlier in the day. While standing there a young Caucasian lady approached me and asked: "Would you please get my bags for me?" I was somewhat taken aback by this request, but I calmly told her I did not work there, that I was waiting for my bags also. I was not wearing a bellman's suit or a bellman's cap. I wore a very nice dark three-piece blue suit, polished shoes, a tie and a hat. I certainly did not have the appearance of a bellman. At any rate the bellmen at that hotel clearly wore identifiable uniforms.

Now, why did she think I was a bellman or respond to me as a bellman? I concluded that her racial stereotype or racial script was activated when she saw me, a black man, standing near a bellman's desk. Without thinking her racial script "defaulted" to: "Black man standing there, he must be the bellman." My black skin color proved to be a salient, race-specific stimulus, which triggered or activated that specific response. When I confronted her with the fact that she had just stereotyped me, she became very defensive. I told her that I was a professor, a psychologist and I had just given a lecture at the University of Minnesota on Racial Script Activation. She was shocked and began denying that she had stereotyped me. I told her my black skin was the salient characteristic to which she responded. Similar situations have happened to other prominent African-Americans. The reverend Jesse Jackson reported he was standing outside a hotel when a white gentleman mistakenly approached him as a hotel doorman.

d) Dr. Williams Mistaken as a Security guard

On another occasion, I was standing in the doorway at the Stratosphere Hotel in Las Vegas when a Caucasian lady approached me and asked: "Do you work here?" to which I replied, "No." My wife heard her remark to her daughter: "Oh, I thought he was with security." Again, this lady's racial script was activated when she saw a black man standing in the doorway of a hotel. Obviously he must be employed here. It is unknown if she would have asked a white visitor the same question. Here we have another instance of racial script activation where the color of the skin triggers the script in an automatic or reflexive manner.

The last example of racial script activation relates to a child witnessing her mother's script being activated.

- Once when I was about eight, my mother was driving through a poor and mostly black neighborhood. Suddenly, she became very nervous when she had to stop for a traffic light with a pair of black men walking by on the sidewalk. She quickly locked her door and told me to do the same. I remember it well because she was so nervous, and I didn't understand. It seemed to me that no one was paying any attention to us. The two men just walked right by without even looking at our car. When I asked her about it, she said the door should be locked when I am in a car. That incident along with other comments seemed to say that black neighborhoods were a dangerous place.

4) Racial Slurs

The following racial slurs are not slips of the tongue (lapus lingus) in the Freudian sense. They are, however, racial scripts. Take for example some of the racial scripts uttered by some notables whites:

a) U. S. Senator Trent Lott

At Rep. Strom Thurmond's 100-birthday party, Meacham (2002) reports Rep. Trent Lott walked in with openers "Why aren't there any black people here"? (p. 27) When told that this was not a diverse party, Lott continued, " Not even behind the counter"? (p. 27) Then he added, "We'd be happy to send you up some if you need any" (P. 27).

Fineman (2002) writes about Lott's slur:

> Thinking he was only among friends—Lott buttered up the honoree [Thurmond] by proclaiming jovially that the country wouldn't have "all those problems" had the Dixiecrats won power in 1948 (P.25).

Rep. Lott apologized, but the apology did not calm the storm of criticisms from black leaders and top Democrats. They demanded that Lott to step down as Senate Majority Leader. He later stepped down.

b) Washington State Senator Alex Deccio

Racial slurs are frequently activated in the absence of blacks, and, also during conversations about blacks. A Washington State Senator blurted out a racial slur during a heated argument with another colleague. State Senator Alex Deccio called State Representative Tom Campbell "a nigger in the woodpile" ("Washington State Senator," 2004, p. 12). Deccio said he immediately realized his mistake and apologized. But apologies do not undo the damage caused by racial slurs.

c) Jimmy "The Greek" Snyder: Sports Commentator

On Martin Luther King's birthday in 1988, odds maker and sports commentator Jimmy "The Greek" Snyder ended his reign as football analyst for CBS Sports. Snyder, in an interview with Washington D.C. TV reporter Ed. Hotaling, discussed a racial myth regarding the superiority of blacks in professional sports. Snyder remarked:

> They've [blacks] got everything. If they take over coaching like everybody wants them to, there is not going to be anything left for white people. The black is a better athlete to begin with, because he's been bred to be that way. Because of his high thighs and big thighs that go up into his back. And they can jump higher and run faster because of their bigger thighs. This goes back to the Civil War, when during slave trading the slave owner would breed his big woman so that he would have a big black kid.

Snyder's comments made the national network news that night and national newspapers the next morning. Many commentators gave excuses for his racist remarks by claiming he was intoxicated and did not realize what he was saying. Snyder was fired but later apologized and stated that blacks are better than white athletes because they work harder.

d) Al Campanis: Ex-General Manager of the Los Angeles Dodgers

On the 40th anniversary of Jackie Robinson's participation in Major league baseball, Ted Koepel interviewed Al Campanis, the ex-general manager of the Los Angeles Dodgers. When asked about the small percentage of black coaches, Campanis reasoned because of heredity, black minds are inferior to those of whites. He compared black's mental inferiority to, another genetic myth: buoyancy in water. Campanis claimed that blacks are poor swimmers because of their lack of buoyancy and black coaches are not as effective as white coaches because of their mental deficiency. These racist comments caused Campanis to be greatly criticized and to lose his job. He later apologized for his racist comments.

e) Chairman: Adolph Coors

The Chairman of Coors Brewing Co. blurted out a racial slur when he reportedly told a group of 110-minority businesses that:

> It's not that the dedication among blacks is less. In fact, it's greater. They lack the intellectual capacity to succeed, and it's taking them down the tubes. In Rhodesia the economy was booming under white management. Now in Zimbabwe, under Black management, it's a disaster. One of the best things [slave traders] did for you was to drag your ancestors over in chains (Jet 3, 1998 p. 7).

Coors immediately came under attack by the NAACP and PUSH who called the statements ignorant and racist. Coors immediately responded by apologizing and saying his statements demonstrated a lack of sensitivity.

f) Texaco Oil Company Executives

Another case of negative racial activation involved Texaco Oil Company Executives who were electronically taped making racist remarks about its African-American employees whom they described as "Jelly Beans." The executives made racial jokes about their defiance of official corporate affirmative action commitments.

1. Texaco agreed to pay a 176.4 million-dollar settlement for institutional racist actions.
2. Create an Equality and Tolerance Task Force
3. Adopt and implement company-wide diversity and sensitivity programs
4. Consider nationwide job posting of more senior positions
5. Monitor its performance on the initiatives provided in the settlement ("Three years," 2000, p. 1).

g) Eric Kronfeld: CEO of Polygram Records

A top executive at Polygram Records left the company after he made some racist remarks. Eric Kronfeld, Chief Executive Officer, is reported to have said the record company would have a hard time finding black executives who did not have a criminal record. Kronfeld stated:

> If every African-American male in the United States were disqualified from pursuing a livelihood.... because of a criminal record, then there would be no, or virtually no, African-American employees in our society or in our industry ("White Polygram," 1998, p. 65).

h) Marge Schott: Owner of the Cincinnati Reds Baseball Team

In an interview on Primetime Live (2-11-93), Cincinnati Reds owner Marge Schott, repeated her belief that everyone uses the word "nigger." She argued that racism is an invention of the press. Schott had been suspended from baseball for allegedly declaring: "I'd rather have a trained monkey working for me than a nigger."

i)   Bob Grant: New York City Talk Show Host

Bob Grant, the most-listened to talk show host in New York City, promotes white supremacy on his WABC radio show. A sample of Grant's ranting and raving on WABC:

> We have in our nation, not hundreds of thousands but millions of sub-humanoids—savages, who really would feel more at home careening along the sands of the Kalahari, or the dry deserts of eastern Kenya—people who for whatever reason have not become civilized ("WABC," 1-6-92).

j)   James Phillip: Illinois State Senate President

Illinois Senate President James Phillip said the following of non-white Illinois State workers: "It's probably a terrible thing to say, but I'll say it: some of them do not have the work ethics we have." He also remarked that those workers "don't squeal on their fellow minorities" (St. Louis Post Dispatch, (10-9-94).

k)   Dan Peavy: Dallas, Texas School Board Member

Dallas school board member Dan Peavy was forced to resign his post after a tape surfaced which he complained that the Dallas schools are hard to manage because they contain "ignorant goddam little niggers and everything else and all these chicken-shit parents." (Dallas Morning News, 9-29-95).

l)   John Pike: CBS Executive

According to writer David Lipsky (Details, February 1996) John Pike, head of late-night programming at the CBS network told the cast members of a CBS late-night pilot:

> Research shows there are three reasons why African-Americans are an important part of the late-night demographic; first, they

have no place to go in the morning—no jobs—so they can stay up as late as they like; second, they can't follow hour-long drama shows—no attention span—so sketches are perfect for them; third, network TV is free. CBS fired Pike after conducting a review of the incident.

m) William Bennett

William Bennett former Secretary of Education and Drug Czar, created a firestorm of controversy when he offered a solution to the nation's increasing crime rate. Bennett stated

> I do know that it's true that if you wanted to reduce crime, you could-if that were your sole purpose-you could abort every black baby in this country, and your crime rate would go down. That would be an impossible, ridiculous, and morally reprehensible thing to do, but your crime rate would go down. (Goldberg, 2005, p. b9)

Bennett offered no apology but gave a strange response when asked by reporters if an apology was warranted. He replied:

> I don't think that I do. I think people who misrepresented my view owe me an apology. (Fletcher and Faler, 2005, P.A. 25).

CHAPTER VI:
THE COUNTERSCRIPTING
PROCESS

1) Counterscripting: A Definition

Counterscripting is a process of disconfirming an existing racial script. Some scripts are confirmed while others are disconfirmed. When a racial script is disconfirmed a change is likely to occur. When a racial script is confirmed, no change is expected.

The type of racial scripts a person has reflects one's cultural heritage, learnings and values; but no one is tied permanently to his/her scripts. People can bring in new scripts, discard old ones and nurture new ones that they like.

Racial scripts are not permanent structures. They are subject to change throughout life, contingent on the types of racial experiences the person engages in. Various experiences may confirm/disconfirm racial scripts throughout life. For example, a positive interracial experience may neutralize a previously negative racial script whereas, a traumatic interracial experience may activate negative scripts. Counterscripts are developed directly opposite to an existing script. For example, if the original script is negative, the counterscript will be positive and vice versa.

Throughout life, we examine and explore as we plan our lives. Some begin to question their racial scripts at various points in their lives. They may begin to ask questions about scripts especially when their reality and their scripts do not match: "Is my script accurate?" Do I have a good script or a bad racial script?" Various experiences may lead to a revision of scripts. Babcock & Keepers' (1976) **Raising Kids O. K.** stated the following on the script change:

> When re-doing a script we weed out aspects, which are no longer functional. Just as we give away old furniture we also invest less energy into aspects, which become lower on our priority list. We can re-invest energy in parts of ourselves that have lain dormant for years. We can look at our script from a new point of view and decide we already have permission to do something we wish to do. We can dispose of whole sections of our script, or throw out the whole thing and start from scratch. (P.214)

2) Disconfirmation of Scripts

There are some individuals who rebel against internalizing racial scripts and do the exact opposite of what the script directs them to do. For example, the script may say "Be like me, my son. Don't trust Blacks." These negative scripts may be turned into positive counterscripts through experiences with African-Americans:

- My father had strongly racist opinions about African-Americans. Though my father was present some of the time during by child hood, the anger I felt toward him prevented me from adopting the racial script he presented. The last thing I wanted to do was be like my racist father. I assigned a negative weight to almost every thing he said and compartmentalized the racial scripts he displayed.

- My parents impressed on me a negative racial script towards African-Americans. In particular, the attitude was "blacks are intellectually inferior to whites, and that I would remain superior and aloof to them." I began to think I should not associate with blacks and that I should treat them as inferiors.

I began to question the truth and reality of this script that I held towards African-Americans. My parents began to send confusing signals to me as to how I should treat and interact with blacks. There were a few blacks living in our neighborhood. My parents treated them as friends and equals and they did not make derogatory remarks about these particular individuals. However, at the same time while watching the news, my parents were likely to generalize about blacks' lack of intelligence based on the interviewer's speech pattern. I became confused as to how I was to act in future interracial situations.

To further confound my confusion on the subject, in the second grade I had a black teacher. I found her to be very intelligent and caring; my parents also had respect for my teacher. How could my parents allow someone who supposedly comes from an inferior race to teach me? I began to question my parent's attitudes because of the lack of consistency. At this point, I began to separate my parents' views from my own opinion on the controversial subject.

Consequently, I had many positive encounters with black people and I developed an individual set of views on African-Americans, which I basically hold today. I formed the belief that blacks are people too. I did not find them to be collectively intellectually inferior to my race or myself. I came to the conclusion that blacks were the same type of people with the exception of their darker skin tone.

Others speak about having a negative pre-exposure script but their discovery and interactive experiences with blacks enable them to change to a positive script. For example:

- The southern environment where I grew up, as well as the negative scripting from my parents forced me to view Blacks condescendingly. As a result of several disconfirming interactions, I have undergone an enlightening transition in which I have re- evaluated my personal views on racial scripts.

Both of my parents' ancestors were slave- owners. One of my grandfathers was the Mayor of a small southern city and was the Grand Dragon of the Ku Klux Klan. Many of my relatives were active in the KKK. Consequently, my parents raised me to believe that blacks were inferior to them and also very dangerous individuals. My parents subsequently made derogatory comments in front of me regarding blacks. I naturally accepted my parents' attitude since I was never exposed to different ethnic groups and I developed very racist ideas based only on the behavior I had seen.

After breaking away from my family and my sheltered environment, I experienced several positive experiences that have disconfirmed my initial racial scripts. Being away from the South and my family caused me to question my parent's views and remarks about blacks being irresponsible, illiterate and socially inferior and how they shaped my values.

When I entered college, I was with my parents on the first day. My resident advisor was black. I could feel the tension building in my parents. They were extremely uncomfortable leaving me under a black person's responsibility. I also had some doubt about my resident advisor's qualification. Throughout the year my perception changed. I saw the advisor was extremely intelligent, articulate, responsible and sensitive in all situations that arose concerning others and myself. As I learned about my advisor's positive qualities, my original stereotype was shattered. Consequently, I became interested in further understanding the black race as a whole.

- I grew up in a home surrounded by much prejudice. I am not implying that my parents are violent white supremacists, but in retrospect I can see that the subtle hints offered to me were truly racist remarks. I was raised in a predominately white middle-class environment not very conducive to a positive racial awareness. My father owned a store in an area that was entirely black; naturally his customers were black. I remember my father coming home from work, usually tired, often complaining of his customers--all of whom were black. I began to think all blacks were thieves, cheaters or welfare recipients. Many of the things my father described were things that I as a young boy could see. I saw black men hustling in the street, haggling for lower prices or trying to buy clothes with food stamps.

My experiences with my father led me to a negative script towards blacks, however there was another factor that greatly influenced my perception of black people. After I was born, my parents employed a black housekeeper. She raised my sister and me for the last twenty years. Although my mother was around, the housekeeper prepared my lunch, played childhood games with me and for many years formed a strong bond. She is one of the most considerate, caring and tender people that I have ever met. I consider her as a part of my family, for I know she loves and has always taken care of me. For obvious reasons, this relationship complicated my other negative influences that I had in my father's store. Because she has been such an important part of my life, I needed something to open my eyes to racial equality.

When I entered college, I met a black man and we instantly became very close. I have invited him to stay in my home. This experience has caused me to re-write my racial script. I now feel more secure about racial relationships.

The next two vignettes will illustrate how racial scripts lead to preconceived notions about blacks and how real-life experiences lead to a counterscripting process.

- Before I actually met a black person, I had a preconceived idea or racial script of what to expect and how to act which was strongly influenced by my parents and partly by the type of environment I had been living in. I grew up in a typical, small, affluent white suburb. There was only one black family residing in my town and I never had any contact with them since their children did not attend school with me. However, I distinctly remember a handful of adjectives that my father always spit out when referring to blacks. He described them as being "lazy, crooked and stupid." My father would make derogatory remarks as: "Those black bums live on the streets begging for money, why don't they get a job and stop living off welfare? That is the taxpayers they are mooching off; blacks are just plain criminals."

My mother would tell him to stop making those prejudiced remarks and he was setting a bad example for his children. But my mother didn't realize what a hypocritical attitude she had herself, and just how prejudiced she actually is. I remember my mother said on our shopping excursions, "Watch your pocketbook! Those damn 'Niggers' are going to snatch it right from under you!" I also remember her commenting on blacks when it was time to apply to colleges and to take the SAT's. She would say how easy it was for black students to be accepted into colleges because they were a minority. From that point on I developed a fear of black people and thought that most blacks were criminals.

The first time I had a personal encounter with a black person I was in my freshman year of college. I met two freshmen black guys who lived on my floor. I was apprehensive at first to be friendly, but they were nice and friendly. I began hanging out with them and had lots of fun. It was then that

I realized that I could no longer follow the negative scripts I had been used to and taught. As classes got underway I befriended many other black students. I realized that I had to modify my negative script into a fairly positive one.

- I had many pre-conceived notions about black people based on the way that I had been socialized. In college I had my first interaction with a black student who was assigned to be my lab partner in our chemistry class. I had expected him to be a bad lab partner solely on the basis of his skin color. I was taught that blacks in general were unintelligent, unmotivated and dis-honest troublemakers. I presumed my new lab partner was no different and I gave serious consideration to requesting a change of lab partners. I didn't do so however and I have been thankful ever since.

Working with this person was my first real contact with a black person. I was raised in a primarily white community where blacks were discriminated against. My only exposure to blacks was their image, which was cast by the media and television. This image was not a good one. The papers printed only bad things that black people do and the television constantly presented the image of blacks as thieves, murders or other kinds of criminals.

When I first met my lab partner, we were both tense and we said very little. However, after the first lab we began to feel very comfortable with each other and began to get down to work. In the following weeks my lab partner shattered every stereotype of black people that I had. He was one of the hardest working and most intelligent people that I have ever met. On many occasions I would ask his help with a particular problem and he would never hesitate to help me. I realized that he and I were really not different, only in our skin variation. I also realized that he was not different from other blacks just as I was not different from other whites and there should be no reason why we should not be able to work together and forget the color of our skin.

Other individuals may revise, update or erase their old script when a conflict arises or when there is a conflict between one's script and the peer group's script. The individual has several options 1) drop his or her own script and accept the peer group's script 2) cling to his/ her script and become out of place with the group or 3) look for another group whose script is compatible.

The basic cause for the child's development of a counterscript or to experience script failure or disconfirmation is when the racial experiences are substantially different from the script the child internalized. Different reality experiences may cause the child to ask, "Why did my parents mislead me about blacks? What else have they lied to me about?" Parents must not wait for others to describe other races to their children.

Butcher (2003) initially became nervous and anxious when meeting blacks. However, later in life she experienced a very positive relationship with a black woman who was very helpful and supportive. This experience enabled her to redesign her script and become more positive and erase the negative one.

Following are several other examples that explain how the counterscripting process works. Three variations of counterscripting are provided to:

1). Illustrate how one moves from a
   negative script to a positive script.
2). Illustrate how a person moves from a
   positive script to a negative script.
3). Illustrate how a re-cycling process, i.e. how
   one moves from a positive script to a negative
   script and back to a positive script.

3) **Moving from a negative to a positive script:**

- For many years I feared and disliked blacks. I felt justified since they were all out to get us and they were all bad. This is what my parents told me. As time passed, my feelings of fear and animosity towards blacks were reinforced because every time I would come in contact with a black person, I would either avoid him out of fear or have some type of negative experience. I am constantly subjected to black men making rude, vulgar and pornographic and suggestive comments to me when I jog in the park. These episodes ranged from creating a feeling of anxiety when a black man stood behind me in line at a movie or supermarket to the trauma of having a close friend shot by a black man.

In high school I had a new type of encounter with blacks, which led to a revision of my scripts. I was placed in situations where I was coming in contact with black individuals daily, but this time I was establishing friendships with them. Because of the positive experiences I was having with them, I realized that the racist beliefs that I had were wrong. I gradually changed my beliefs and allowed for a harmonious relationship between blacks and myself.

The summer of 1984 changed my life's racial script. I had an experience that not only exposed me to a true unbiased Black America, but also helped me to better understand myself. I went into the experience with a previously acquired negative set of racial scripts and left with an entirely new belief system.

The scripts I held about black people had been forming since I was a child. It is needless to say that scripts that are developed in childhood often become deeply engrained within our belief system and it almost always requires a real life experience to dispel stereotypical beliefs and myths from our minds. Somewhere along the line I mistakenly began believing that it was poor black men who were responsible for the crime that occurred in our cities. I found myself scared when I saw a young black man on the street after dark. Perhaps I formed this mistaken belief by watching television where most criminals are wrongfully depicted as black men. The worst thing about this belief was that I did not even realize that I was being stereotypical. People trying to teach me that my beliefs were mistaken did not help.

The job I accepted for the summer was exactly what I needed. I chose to work at a food distribution center unloading watermelons from trucks. I was one of a few white people working on this job; at first I was scared. Would I get mugged? Beaten up? As the summer grew, however I made friends with many poor black men. In particular an extremely poor 85-year-old black customer taught me the most about life and black people. Everyday this old man would sit me down and tell me stories about his neighborhood and about the racism he experienced while growing up. H also told me a story when he was robbed and stabbed by a black man. He concluded that it was not the color of their skin but what was inside of them that made them criminals. By the time I left that job I saw a fuller more truthful picture of black life in the city. I had also made friends with many blacks who previously would have frightened me. I realize now that it is not skin color that makes a person commit a crime but that person's immoral beliefs.

- My parents, mainly my father, are racists and I was scripted accordingly. "Nigger" became a household word. From modeling my parents, "Nigger" became a common word in my vocabulary. I was taught that blacks were all lazy, dumb, mean and to be avoided. Although I had no real contact with blacks, I avoided them whenever in public since they were not to be trusted. I believed they were inferior and they had been brought over from the jungle

Eventually, I got to meet a person who was black I was prepared to see someone who was a borderline imbecile, a typical "Nigger." This man was quite nice, intelligent, clean and friendly. I remember shaking his hand and wondering if the color would rub off onto my hand. But he was all of the things I expected not to be and I sort of felt sorry for him, having to be a "Nigger" and that was confusing to me. I thought this man was an exception and had once been white.

My later experiences with blacks further disconfirmed my negative racial script. I came to realize that I had been hideously misinformed about blacks. I learned that the negative things that my Dad taught me were ridiculous stereotypes. I questioned all of his stereotypes and gave examples, which contradicted them. His response was: "My son is a Nigger Lover."

The next story is about a young girl who was given the following parental injunction: "Do not go into black neighborhoods, because they are dangerous." This girl violated the injunction and did the opposite and moved from a negative racial script (avoidance) to a positive one (immersion).

- The environment I grew up in was a subtle racist one. My town was mostly white and upper middle-class. I was told by my parents not to go into (or drive through) the south part of the city because of the dangerous conditions and the hatred blacks in that area had for whites. But unbeknownst to my parents, during the winter and spring semesters of my junior year in high school, I spent one afternoon a week tutoring underprivileged children, of all places, at a neighborhood center deep in that area. The kids, mostly Black and Hispanic were wonderful and craved for one-on-one attention. The negative script I learned from my parents completely contradicted the experiences I had with those kids. I often wondered, "Why did my parents mislead me?"

Continuing with scripts moving from the negative to the positive is another process we call "The Cookie Jar" phenomenon. This occurs when the child is forbidden to do something, such as being told not to go into the cookie jar. The fact that the child is told not to do something makes it more attractive and he/she becomes more motivated to rebel. As soon as he/she gets the chance to get into the cookie jar, he/she would. In a similar fashion, many white parents tell their children that they must not date blacks and they are told to stay away from blacks. Remember the theme in the story "Across the Railroad Tracks." Once the children made contact with each other and experienced a positive relationship, they broke out of the parental script and developed a positive counterscript. The cookie jar phenomenon is very influential when children are told not to do a particular thing, and they rebel and do the forbidden thing all the more.

The following stories will illustrate the manner in which the Cookie Jar phenomenon operates as a counterscripting process:

- I rebelled against my parents. When they would tell me not to hang around with black guys so much, it would make me want to do it more. I suppose I wanted to find out what was wrong with them, if anything. I discovered that they were great people and I really liked them.

- As far as my parents were concerned there was no need to form racial scripts because it was probably assumed that my close friends would not be black and I definitely would not date a black man, but I learned differently when they discovered that I had a black boyfriend. One day when I came home from school, my mother was extremely distressed. She said to me, "I heard you raving about this boy you like so much, so I decided to look in your yearbook to see him. You can imagine how I felt when I discovered he's black." My mother didn't like him because he was black.

My parents turned into my enemies. The people who supposedly loved me so much were making life miserable by forbidding my relationship with my black friend. His family was completely the opposite. They accepted and adored me. They welcomed me with open arms and made me feel like a part of their family. I was treated with as much love and respect, as they would have treated his girlfriend if she were black.

Somehow I was able to disregard the scripts of my parents, which were given to me. I rejected them with every bone in my body. They would never make me understand why I was wrong and why they were right. I truly believe that I am right.

The following illustrates another instance of the Cookie Jar Phenomenon, because as a counterscript, it is a "spell breaker." Take the following report of this young girl whose racial script is an injunction: "Don't date black men." In her freshman year in college, she began dating a black man, perhaps out of rebellion or whatever. Her parents were very much opposed to this relationship and cut her off from the family. This young woman wrote:

- I had to make a decision. I chose my boyfriend. He and I are extremely happy and plan to get married. My parents have finally realized that I was not going to give up someone I loved just because he had a darker skin than I. Although my parents are racists and taught me to distrust black people, they have slowly started to accept our relationship.

Here we have a strong case of a young woman who re-scripted her attitudes towards blacks. Her experiences were opposite to the script directives she received from her parents. Thus, she developed a counterscript that gave her permission to date a black man regardless of her parents' reactions.

4) Positive to Negative Scripting

In the following example counterscripting occurs by moving from a positive racial script to a negative one:

- I was taught to treat all people as I would like to be treated. I have related to blacks without difficulty. One day I was sitting on the floor at school with two girls laughing and talking when two black girls walked past us. They mistook our laughter to mean we were laughing at them (which we were not). Soon after they passed us, they turned around, came back and asked me in a very rough voice asked, "Are you laughing at me?" When I told her I wasn't, she said, "You better not bitch." Then she proceeded to insult me and slap me.

  That incident had an adverse effect on me. I became timid around black girls, fearing they would take offense to something I said or did. This very negative encounter caused me to rewrite my racial script. I didn't really develop racist feelings or prejudice of all African-Americans, but I was very fearful of black girls and went through some stages of avoidance. Whenever I walked down the hall at school and passed a black girl, I would pretend that I didn't notice them or that I was minding my own business so they wouldn't do anything to me. I stuck with my white friends and never made any attempts to befriend a black girl. I was not rude but it was just too uncomfortable for me to interact with African-American girls.

- My parents taught me about racial differences in a positive manner. At an extremely young age, they taught me not to be concerned with the color of people. I was brought up to keep an open mind and nothing more. I do not remember regarding black people as any different than myself until I went to high school. In the tenth grade, my family moved South. I went to a school that was over fifty percent black. For the first time in my life I was exposed to a large number of blacks and it was a cultural shock. I was overwhelmed.

This brought on a tremendous conflict for me. I had many negative experiences with black classmates that changed my racial script. A black classmate, during gym, took my football and claimed it as his own. I was very intimidated by him for the remainder of the year. I had negative feelings towards him, as well as many of his black friends.

Now let us examine the process of counterscripting that moves through three phases 1) positive 2) negative and 3) positive.

- My mother taught me to live by the golden rule. I started out with a very positive racial script. However, my stepfather was racist. This didn't help me to adjust to having so many blacks around me. The more my stepfather made racist comments, the more I seemed to get annoyed with the blacks around me. I also got a job in a jewelry store and my supervisor taught me to look out for thieves and this was directed at black people. Even the security guard followed blacks around in the store more closely than he did whites. All these experiences caused me to re-define my racial opinions considerably. Slowly, my positive past with blacks was overshadowed with a new, negative outlook. I guess this entire time in my life was very confusing as far as racial issues went. I went from an attitude of complete immersion with black friends to a complete avoidance due to fear. By the time I graduated from high school I wanted nothing to do with blacks. The whole experience was overwhelming.

Coming to college was the best thing that ever happened to me especially in this area. First, I was removed from the negative inputs of my stepfather and boss. Secondly, I was exposed to blacks that I felt I could relate to me. I began to remember the earlier attitudes I had before high school, and I began to act according to them. I started seeing blacks once as equals again.

Racial scripts are not etched in granite. There may be a regression back to previous phases depending on the experiences of the individual.

Script modification and script flexibility are specific characteristics of these phenomena. In the following case, this young man went through several changes that influenced his script re-cycling.

- Every Sunday at around 5:00 p.m. my grandparents arrived at my house. My family and I piled into our four-door car on our way to dinner. Often on these Sundays we took a journey to a fancy restaurant in the downtown area. My grandfather often made racist jokes calling the people "Niggers" and everyone in the car would laugh. I was too young to understand the jokes were racist.

  My first encounter with a black person was my housekeeper, Ann. She was like a mother to me. She was home when I woke up in the morning and my mother was at work. She made me breakfast and lunch. She ate with me in front of the television and she played board games with me. Her presence was just like any other person. I was too young to differentiate between black and white. I was not able to form negative or positive scripts because she was simply Ann. As a result I viewed black people as caring and even maternal, because Ann was like my second mother. My pre-exposure stage was negative, but my discovery stage is positive so far.

  But one day when I was about six years old, Ann sent me off to school like any other day. After school I went to one of my friends' house, because he invited me over to play. I did call Ann and tell her that I would be late. I just assumed she knew that I went to my friends' house. Ann tried for three hours to track me down, She finally found me. She was furious. She ordered me to come home immediately. My friend's mother drove me home and Ann coldly met me at the front door.

"Get upstairs and into your room" she said. I ran upstairs, slammed my door and hid in the pillow on my bed. Ann did not speak to me for five minutes, but when she spoke she said, "If you ever do that again child, I am going to beat the devil out of you."

I cried until my mother came home. I told her the story. Two hours later Ann was gone and never returned. My mother fired Ann.

From that moment, I developed a strong fear and avoidance of black people. Many of my friends had black housekeepers but I would never speak to them. I felt betrayed and feared them. All the black people I knew were housekeepers working for white people. The school I attended had no black children and the neighborhood I lived in had no black people. Subconsciously, I must have viewed blacks as lower class.

Now I had a negative discovery of black people and it confirmed my pre-exposure script. Because of this I developed an avoidance mode by choosing not to make any contact with black people.

But, then I met Bobby. He was in my seventh grade class. He was the funniest person I had ever met. We sat next to each other every day in class. We became good friends. Soon my fear of black people began to subside. We became inseparable. We played during recess, after school and frequently talked on the phone. One day my brother was on the phone and the call waiting clicked. It was Bobby. Politely my brother told him I would call him back. Bobby said it was an emergency and he need to talk to me right away. My brother replied more vehemently "He will call you back" and hung up on Bobby. Five minutes later Bobby called back. My brother was very angry and I could hear him screaming, "He'll call you back. Shut up Nigger!" I was astounded. How could my brother say that to him? I was angry, frustrated and confused. I began to cry. Quickly I called Bobby back, but he would not talk to me. I pleaded, "Just because my brother is a racist, does not mean that I am one. You are my best friend."

"No way, birds of a feather flock together" he said and hung up. The next day at school, Bobby would not talk to me. It took us several months before we were finally friends again.

Bobby taught me many things about my family and racial relations. I realized my family had given me a negative script through their comments about "Niggers" and telling racist jokes. However, my friendship with Bobby was far too important to me to view blacks as my family viewed them. I realized that there are nice white people, nice black people, mean white people and mean black people. I learned not to view people by stereotypes people place on others, but by the individuals themselves.

Looking back I realize that I began with a negative pre-exposure and then had a confirming negative discovery. I then entered the avoidance stage but did not internalize what I experienced. Even though I was slightly afraid of blacks, my second racial encounter with Bobby was positive. It was so fulfilling that I was able to overcome my fears. Even though I have not gained a racial maturity I do feel I am aware of what I have to do in order to attain that level.

It is interesting to examine the process that whites take to resolve conflict in dealing with their racial scripts when they are not confirmed in reality. This is especially true when they have been taught one thing by parents/grandparents but experience something entirely different. Their racial scripts are disconfirmed. We must remember prejudice is an unfavorable script toward a group of people that may develop before the individual has contact with the group. It is a predisposition or pre-judgment. Many white children are taught to hate and distrust Black-Americans. Some of the scripts have been confirmed while others are disconfirmed. In many cases it is impossible to confirm because the black person does not fit the stereotype attributed to him or her.

The following is an example of how a Georgia State Legislator, because of his relationship with a black maid, changed his vote in the passage of a Hate Crime Bill.

5) Hate Crime Bill:
A Shift In Racial Consciousness?

> Recently, the State of Georgia passed a Hate Crime bill that provides enhanced criminal penalties for persons who commit a crime against someone based on prejudice or hatred against a minority group. This is an edited transcript by State Republican Representative Dan Ponder from South Georgia entitled "A Shift in Consciousness" delivered March 16, 2000

> "Thank you Mr. Speaker, ladies and Gentlemen of the House. I am probably the last person you would expect to be speaking about the Hate Crime Legislation…I want to talk about it a little more personally, about how I came to believe what I believe.

> I am a White Republican, who lives in the very Southwest corner of the most ultra-conservative part of this state. I grew up there….

> I was raised in a conservative Baptist church. I went to a large mostly white Southern University…. I don't have a single ancestor on all of my family lines that lived north of the Mason-Dixon Line going back to the Revolutionary War. And it is not something that I am terribly proud of, but it is just part of my heritage, that not one, but several of those lines actually owned slaves.

So you would guess by listening to my background that I am going to stand up here and talk against hate crime legislation. But you see, that's the problem when you start stereotyping people by who they are and where they came from, because I totally, totally support this bill.…

There was one woman in my life that made a huge difference… she began working for my family before I was born. She was a young black woman whose own grandmother raised my mother. (She) came every morning before I was awake to cook breakfast so it would be on the table. She cooked our lunch. She washed our clothes.

But she was much more than that. She read books to me. When I was playing little league she would go out and catch ball with me. She was never, ever afraid to discipline me or spank me. She expected the absolute best out of me, perhaps, and I am sure, even more than she did her own children. She would even travel with my family when we would go to our house in Florida during the summer, just as her own grandmother had done.

One day, when I was about 12 or 13 I was leaving for school. As I was walking out of the door she turned to kiss me goodbye. And for some reason, I turned my head. She stopped me and she looked into my eyes with a look that absolutely burns in my memory right now and she said, "You didn't kiss me because I am black." At that instant, I knew that she was right.

I denied it. I made some lame excuse about it. But I was forced at that age to confront a small dark part of myself. I don't even know where it came from. This lady, who was devoting her whole life to me and my brother and sister, who loved me unconditionally, who had changed my diapers and fed me, and who was truly my second mother, that somehow who wasn't worthy of a goodbye kiss simply because of the color of her skin.

I have lived with the shame and memory of my betrayal...I pledged to myself then and I re-pledged to myself the day I buried her that never, ever again would I look in the mirror and now that I had kept silent, and let hate or prejudice or indifference negatively impact a person's life even if I didn't know them. Likewise, my wife and I promised to each other on the day that our oldest daughter was born that we would raise our children to be tolerant, that we would raise them to accept diversity and to celebrate it. In our home, someone's difference would never be a reason for injustice....

Now my daughter is completing her first year at college. She informed me last week that she and her roommate, who happens to be black, they were thrown together just randomly last year as a first year student had decided they were going to room together again next year.

I asked her the reasons that they had decided to live together again. She said, "Well, we just get along so well together." She mentioned a couple of other reasons, but do you know what was absent" Color, she just didn't think about it."

At Washington University where I taught a course in Black Psychology, many students went through similar transformational processes. The students reported major transformation as a result of being in the Black Psychology class. Some started out with racist ideas but began to reexamine and re-design their racial attitudes over the semester.

Several examples are presented here:

6) Black Psychology Class

- I feel I have experienced a personal transformation in learning about and developing a genuine concern for black causes. Taking this course in Black Psychology has played a major role in this transformation and has helped me to develop a futuristic perspective.

- I would like to give my own quote to how I feel about taking Black Psychology. It was like "finding a rose while looking through the Tulips." I found that I have taken a class which was one of the most creative, original and most enlightening classes I have yet to take.

- For the first time in my life, I saw that a "difference" does not necessarily or imply the connotation of "good" or "bad, rather it is just "different." And that is a very important and relevant distinction for me, that is, a difference is not a deficiency. We must teach our children to stop associating negative images with practices that are unlike their own. In this way, as a society we may begin to move closer to one another and learn form one another and conquer the problems that face us all.

- I feel that I have gotten more out of this class (Black Psychology) than any other class that I have taken at this university. This class has assisted me in becoming more aware and alert as a person in regards to all aspects of my life. I have become more involved in racial relations.

My opinions and attitudes concerning blacks have changed greatly especially after taking this class. I now feel I am more open-minded and knowledgeable about blacks. This class has made me aware of all the problems going on. I never knew about unfair biased testing or all the stereotyped and problems that blacks encounter and all the prejudices they face. I would never really consider myself prejudiced, but obviously I had prejudices against blacks that I was not aware of. I had pre-conceived notions and negative scripts of blacks I would not have called prejudices. I now feel that I can be more impartial, fair and open-minded in my dealing with blacks and I know that I have gotten past the stereotypes held by many people out of ignorance. It was necessary for me to re-write my racial scripts.

Counterscripting, i.e. changing one's racial script) is not an easy process, because change is against family beliefs. Primary parental scripts strongly resist change.

Abandoning parental scripts means turning one's back on family. Frequently it causes confusion and ambivalence when one experiences contradictory experiences to the primary support group. The following vignettes will illustrate the strong resistance to changing a racial script:

- I never encountered with a person of a different race until I was in the fourth grade. I lived in a very small town where the entire population was white. I had heard negative racial comments from my parents and grandparents. "Never trust a 'Nigger'; they're all lazy and expect to be paid for laying around and reproducing, and they're all on welfare. These are just a few of the racial myths I heard from my family, friends and peers as I was growing up.

  In elementary school I had several black friends. We played together and I liked them a lot, but I could not trust them for some strange reason. I have masked my feelings and not projected the way that I feel. I just could not trust the black children.

- As a child my parents gave me negative racial scripts regarding the black race. My parents feel that blacks should not be trusted, they commit the majority of the crimes, they are of a "lower" status than whites and they are generally dangerous people. My parents used to bother me about watching black shows such as "What's Happening" and "Sanford and Son" and would be angry upon hearing that a black family would be moving in next door.

  I am trying to understand black culture by taking African-American courses and I am hoping that it will refute my parents' negative racial views and prove the black race to be a wonderful, interesting culture. Unlike the actions of others, I am not avoiding the black race, but I do admit on a late night when a group of black people are walking toward me I will cross the street. Part of this fear is related to a negative experience I had on a field trip. A few friends and I were walking back to the buses. We were engaging in a normal conversation, giggling and gossiping. A young black couple walked toward us and smacked me in the face. She then said "You F---ing honky," then they ran away. I was hit so hard that a handprint remained on my cheek for ten minutes. I was in shock. What did I do to warrant this violent act? My parents' negative racial scripts had been confirmed by this unfortunate incident. The isolated incident caused me to be afraid of blacks.

The next series shows a full complete process ranging from neutral/avoidance to a negative script to a positive counter script.

- I did not acquire my current racial views until later in life. My parents did not discuss racial issues around me. I grew up in a predominately white suburb; thus there was no reason to question a race difference because I was never confronted with it as a child. My mother told me to be "colorblind," which seemed at the time to be the right way. I think now it is better to be color and culture conscious rather than ignore the whole differences. I do not mean that I treat people differently. This consciousness means to be aware of the difference and be conscious of the other person's culture. I believe that being brought up this way is much better than being brought up to be ignorant.

My first encounter with a black person had embarrassment and discomfort written all over it. I was a three or four year old. My father invited a black fellow worker to our house for dinner. This partner was a very tall, big black man. He was sitting at the dining room table and I stood up in the chair next to him. After a couple of minutes of looking at him, I reached out and touched his hand and said, "Your hand is dirty." He just laughed and said, "Honey I'm dark all over, not dirty." I did not say anything more on the subject.

Later I developed a negative racial script. I visited my grandparents who lived in a predominately black neighborhood. Most of the houses adjacent to my Grandparents' house were basically a wreck. I made a connection between African-Americans and this disorderly way of living. This obviously, was a very negative, let alone ignorant, script in my mind. It was not until middle school that I began to analyze my views. I became aware of my own racial prejudices and scripts. I realized how absolutely absurd my scripts really were. I made a conscious effort to change these scripts.

I noticed another change within myself after this so-called "thought search" I put myself through. I took note when people made sexist, racist, and homophobic or any other discriminatory remarks. I used to laugh at a good racial joke or a "fag" joke. I took offense to all of the jokes. I did not like to hear a racial joke.

This new awareness led me to a higher level of racial consciousness. I played soccer with a group and I remember being at the airport waiting to board our team's airplane. People were telling jokes to pass the time. One girl started a joke something to the effect of "This one black guy walks into a bar..." I cut her off and asked, "Is this a racial joke? Because if it is, I don't want to hear it." I could not deal with these people any longer, so I quit the team a month later. I felt good about sticking up for what I believed in and disregarding the peer pressure put upon me.

CHAPTER VII:
MODES OF INTERRACIAL INTERACTION: IMMERSION-AVOIDANCE

The next phase of racial script development, Immersion-Avoidance, is an either/or situation. One is either attracted to blacks and becomes immersed in their culture or one is repelled by blacks and avoids contact or interaction with them altogether. The racial script that one has internalized will determine which of these "modes of operation" prevails. Scripts determine the valence potential of the stimulus, i.e. the attractiveness or repulsion strength an African-American will possess for any given white individual. Racial scripts therefore contain positive, negative and mixed valences.

1) Positive Racial Script: Immersion/Attraction

Interracial involvement is determined by one's racial script. As such, racial attraction simply means a preference for a culture in addition to one's own culture. This preference is no different from preferring a Cadillac to a Lexus, or if one prefers "the blues" to "rock music." Preferences stem from racial scripts and become the first steps toward developing healthy racial attitudes.

Within this framework, a person with a positive racial script will tend to have positive valence and will be able to connect, associate or be involved with African-Americans. One individual whose parents taught him positive racial scripts explained that his positive interaction with a black individual enabled him to immerse himself in the black experience.

- My parents taught me to live by the "golden rule" to treat others as I would like to be treated. As I grew into adolescence, I developed several close friendships with blacks. One of my black friends went so far as to tell me about his racial upbringing. He told me of several incidents, both verbal and physical, assaults upon himself and his family by bigots in his southern hometown. He even influenced me to take an Introductory African American Studies course with him. I enjoyed the course so much that I decided to enroll in Black Psychology the next semester. I developed such an interest in racial affairs that I declared myself an African-American Studies major. I attended black theatre presentations and cultural workshops. I became immersed in the black culture.

Clearly one-on-one interracial interaction promotes, in many instances, positive feelings and reduces racial tension. The following examples illustrate this:

- Following my high school graduation I was hired in a small factory. The person assigned to train me was a black person. As first he seemed hesitant. I figured it was because I was new at the job. Later, I realized his distrust had nothing to do with me personally. He thought because I was white I was going to speak to him in some prejudicial manner. Once I understood his reluctance to associate with me, I did my best to open up and let him know I was not prejudice and he and I became close friends and spent many hours together. He tried to teach me black dances and rhythm, while I showed him a white guy could beat him in basketball. But more importantly we taught each other the senselessness of racism.

He remains a friend today and a constant positive confirmation of my racial awareness. This friendship changed my racial script.

2) Early Interracial Interaction

Early positive interracial interactions pre-dispose individuals to immersion. Individuals who have early exposure to a different race seem to develop healthier racial attitudes than those who do not. However, the home and the community must provide the primary spaces for this interaction to occur.

- I first met a black person, Andre, when I was three years old and until this day he has remained my very best friend. Because I met Andre at such an early age, issues such as racism and discrimination had no bearing on the relationship that Andre and I had developed. As I grew older, I realized Andre was black, however this had no bearing on the friendship we so dearly shared. He is still my beloved friend and will always be.

- I met John, a black boy, in the second or third grade. This boy was not the first black person I saw, but he was the first black person I would interact and engage in conversations. He was well known and well liked. On the first day of recess I was chosen as Captain of one of two teams. I didn't know many people so I relied on my racial script to pull me through. I picked John to play on my team. He was fantastic; he was an excellent athlete.

Over the years John and I became extremely good friends. We would choose each other for partners when doing projects for school, and would often go to the movies on weekends. John and I remained close friends all through high school and we still meet on vacations. We remain close friends to this day. Since my racial encounters with the black race were on a positive note, I did not form negative racial attitudes as a young child.

3) Community Diversity

Whereas early interracial racial contact is extremely important in the development of positive racial scripts, community support is also important. A good example of high community diversity is that of Oak Park, Illinois a western Chicago suburb that has been cited as a model of successful integration. In the 60s Oak Park enacted an open-housing law before the federal government passed one. Then the community developed programs to embrace diversity. Another example of high community diversity is University City, Missouri. There is a good mixture of Whites, Blacks, Jews and other ethnic groups in this community.

High community diversity tends to lead to racial immersion as reflected in the following anecdotes:

- Growing up in a racially integrated neighborhood was possibly the best learning experience I have ever had. It allowed me to become secure about myself and my own race, as well as other races and their respective cultures. Because of my experiences, I developed a desire to get involved in the black experience. I believe the immersion phase to be a crucial stage on the road to racial maturity. I have attended black professional meetings. I feel very comfortable relating to blacks and I am secure about my racial encounters. I feel confident that I am on the road to racial maturity and one day will be able to teach my children the same positive racial scripts that were embedded in me.

- "Do unto others as you would have done unto you," was the basis for the racial script given to me by my parents. My city has been nationally recognized in its efforts towards fair housing and my mother was a part of that effort. As an employee of the Housing Center, she worked toward racial unity rather than racial polarization in the community. My elementary school is the most racially diverse in our city. It is currently close to 50 percent black and 50 percent Caucasian. I was taught that the person matters, not the race.

I believe in order for people to feel more comfortable around people of other races, they must be around them in positive settings as children so they will grow up feeling more natural around them. Even if you are influenced by positive attitudes from your parents or television, you need the experiences of personal contact as confirmation to those attitudes. Therefore, I think all children must be involved with other children of all races on a day-to-day basis, starting at a very young age so they can acquire their own experiences with members of different races.

Black and white teenagers who live in integrated neighborhoods and attend integrated schools tend to have more liberal attitudes since there is more mixing and socializing among the races. These teenagers have moved beyond their parents' views on race. This next vignette is entitled "Racial Script Acquisition and the Influence of an Integrated Community."

- An architect named James Rouse developed a utopia in which people of all races and cultural backgrounds could live together in harmony. Rouse created this utopia in the form of Columbia Maryland—a progressive suburb of Washington, District of Columbia. Columbia differs from most suburbs because its residents represent members of almost every background and race intermixed on the same residential streets and in the same classrooms. My parents worked to instill a positive racial script in me at an early age and were encouraged by the atmosphere of racial and religious tolerance.

My family was close to one black family that lived across the street from us. The family always treated me as if I was a part of their family.

My classrooms were integrated with Blacks, Whites, Asians, Indians and Hispanics. I had many interracial relationships. In fact, I dated a few black guys from my high school, which was not considered unusual in Columbia. Thus Columbia has its positive influences and it formed a "protective "bubble" around its residents—protecting them form the ugliness of the outside world.

4) Negative Racial Scripts: Prejudice/Avoidance

A prejudice is an attitude or script in a closed mind ("Don't bother me with the facts. I've already made up my mind and I'm not going to change.") Some people think that all Irish people are alcoholics. These stereotypes are hard to change and they are prejudices. An Oxford University student said, "I despise all Americans, but I've never met one I didn't like." This anecdote suggests that pre-judgments may stand when even overwhelming evidence is against them. Some prejudiced whites may think blacks are criminals, drug addicts or desire welfare. Prejudice, if kept to oneself, causes no great harm except to the mind that possesses it, but if expressed, it may lead to discrimination and/or hostility.

5) Mixed Racial Scripts: Dissonance/Ambivalence

An individual with a mixed racial script displays a mixed valence (both positive and negative) potential and may be both "attracted to," as well as "repelled by" African-Americans. This individual will show racial ambivalence and/ or dissonance that may lead to confusion, anxiety or fear of African-Americans.

This point of ambivalence is illustrated in the next vignette where the child received mixed racial scripts:

- As a child my parents gave me conflicting views about black people. My Dad was the one usually saying something derisive or degrading or just plain mean remarks about blacks and other races. For instance, occasionally I would go to work with him and every time we'd drive into the city, he'd lock the doors because he didn't want any black people stealing our car. My Dad inflicted a negative script in me by doing this along with a hundred other things.

   My mother, however, always tried to raise me to be open minded and understanding. She was always saying things like everybody is different and if you were a good person, it didn't matter what your color was. I would go places and see black people she knew from work and she would talk and laugh with them like she talked and laughter with everyone else.

   The opposite behavior from my Mom and Dad was quite confusing to me. Down the street from where I lived there was a black family and I wanted to go play with the children, but found myself avoiding them out of fear of what my Dad would say or do. Eventually, my sister and I began to slip/ sneak and go to the black family's house but we were always fearful of being caught.

A common coping strategy for children with mixed racial scripts is to seek a one-on-one relationship with individuals of a different race. For one who has been racially isolated, interaction with a black person might have some positive effects as a solution to racial alienation. As one individual wrote:

- Experiencing the individual is much better than judging an individual without any contact with the person. Getting closer to a race provides a stable and accurate perception. It worked for me. Now I live in a suite with four black girls. I have been to steps shows, Spike Lee movies, and Baptist churches to hear gospel music and slowly blacks are becoming less and less foreign and fearful to me.

6) Mis-Match Between Scripts and Discovery: Dissonance/Ambivalence

On the one hand, if the pre-exposure racial script is positive but the discovery experiences are negative, this combination may lead to a vacillation between attraction and avoidance of blacks. It may also influence the development of hostility and Afrophobia or a strong fear of black people as illustrated in the following example:

- I lived in an all-white, middle class environment. Unfortunately, my parents instilled in me a negative approach to black people as well as an avoidance approach. My first discoveries of blacks proved to be negative.

  Nadine was the only black student in my first grade class and one of the few blacks in the school. She asked to see my prized possession, a tiny, copper penny coin ring. She asked if she could wear it during recess. I never saw the ring again. She became very hostile and angry when I asked her for my ring. As a result of this incident, I never spoke to her again.

  Nadine had been my first memorable black encounter resulting in a generalized hostile attitude I carried over to all blacks. The ring incident clouded my young mind by forming a bully image of blacks. After trying to recover the ring, I was scared away. I simply adopted an avoidance attitude of all blacks, which was easily maintained in my white environment.

On the other hand, strong inner conflict may arise when there is a mis-match between the pre-exposure script and the discovery experiences. For example, if there is a ``negative pre-exposure script and a positive discovery experience, cognitive dissonance and conflict may set in. An individual with a positive pre-exposure racial script and negative discovery experiences may develop avoidance tendencies and tend to move away from or avoid associating with African-Americans as shown in the next vignette:

- Although I had positive racial scripts, I do acknowledge a distinct behavioral shift into a form of avoidance upon entering high school. Up until this point racial difference in social groupings in school seemed irrelevant. However, this quickly changed in high school. There was a very high ratio of blacks in my high school and strong racial polarization occurred. There was occasional crossing of racial boundaries, but as a general rule one went with ones' own group or paid severe consequences. Social punishment often came in the form of ostracizing, pejorative labeling and mocking

  My social situation and stance placed me in the avoidance mode. For it was very difficult for me to cross barriers or even show interest without being offensive to others or getting offended myself. Therefore, I was not purposely avoiding contact with blacks due to a negative script. I had become immersed in and internalized my peers' social norms.

On the other hand, an individual with a mis-match of a negative racial script and a positive discovery will experience confusion, anger and hurt. The next vignette will illustrate this individual's feelings.

- Jamie was not like what my parents taught me. I had a very negative pre-exposure racial script, but very positive discovery experiences. I don't remember how old I was when I first heard the cryptic phrases drifting through our house, but they were always spoken in the same somber tone in voices barely above a whisper. "Give THEM an inch and THEY will take a mile. THEY will ruin the school. THEY are dangerous, criminal and inferior."

  I was young and scared of THEM, yet I still wanted to know who THEY were. "THEY are "Niggers," Ann, and THEY are dangerous," my father told me.

I first met one of THEM when I entered school. I was eager to meet new people, forge new friendships and find new adventures. I sat down next to a black child. I had never seen anyone so dark before. She smiled with uncertainty and introduced herself. I was fascinated with her. We did lots of things at school together. I went home and told my parents about my new friend and watched, as my father's face grew red.

"You mean they put you next to a 'NIGGER'" he half-screamed. I was confused. "Daddy, how do you know that she is a 'NIGGER'? I thought NIGGERS are bad and dangerous. She's nice just like the rest of my friends. Only she's Black." My Daddy said, "Ann, she's a 'NIGGER,' because she is black. All black people are 'NIGGERS'." I was hurt and angry. I knew my father was wrong. My discovery of black people taught me that his values were racist."

7) Afrophobic Mode of Interracial Interaction: Fear

Afrophobia involves an extreme, unrealistic fear of African-Americans. People with afrophobia will go to great lengths to avoid black people whom they fear. This is a pathological anxiety experience. This fear or anxiety in the presence of blacks goes deep as the following examples illustrate:

- My experience with black people has been very limited. I grew up in a small rural town. There were no black families living within a forty-five minute radius of my home. The only time I would come in contact with them was when my family went shopping in bigger cities. I used to stare at a black person because I was afraid of them. They had a different color of skin. My parents would tell me to stop staring, but I couldn't stop.

- I began to see blacks through my mother's words and actions. I was about 5- or 6-years-old when we went shopping. My mother would not let me go to the food court by myself because she said there are too many black kids down there and you might be shot. That comment had a distinct impression on me. I developed a fear of blacks. I can remember thinking why would my mother assume that the black kids would shoot me. She told me later that this city was dangerous because of all the blacks. She even bought a gun because she was afraid of being robbed by blacks. She was really afraid for her safety because she did not trust people of another race, particularly blacks. I became extremely afraid of black people, mainly because of her behavior.

- I lived in one of the more prosperous suburbs of New York. I did not meet very many blacks. It is a predominately white neighborhood where being a WASP meant being in the majority. The "bad blacks " lived in Harlem. Harlem is a place known for its poverty, drugs, burned-out buildings, crime and large black population. It was from Harlem that I learned to fear blacks. I was told by my parents never to drive through Harlem for fear of being attacked. On the rare occasions when we drove through Harlem, we would always lock our doors. I was warned never to stop in Harlem. I was told a scary story that my teacher and his wife, upon returning from a dinner party, had had their car stall in Harlem and about a frightening experience they had. All of these stories indicated to me that Harlem was bad and since blacks were the largest population in Harlem, they must be the cause of all the trouble. They were bad and I should avoid them.

- There were just a few blacks in the public and private schools that I attended. I was always hearing my parents comment on the injustice of racism and that blacks are human beings. I was also hearing that the color of a person's skin does not matter. Through all my parents' comments, I still had an internal conflict. For a long time I had an intense curiosity in touching the skin of black people. When I came in contact with a black person I would always think about touching their skin. I knew that it was normal skin, but I could not help think about it. I also had a desire to have a relationship with a black person, but I was never given the chance.

I always thought "afros" were cool. There was this black boy in my second grade class. He was a new kid in my class. I was amazed at his one or one and a half inch afro. I was so fascinated by it that one day I simply reached over and felt his head for about five seconds. The teacher screamed at me "Get your hands out of that boy's hair." I was frightened. I became nervous around black folks from that day on.

In the next situation, this student experienced a very traumatic event that led to her becoming afrophobic.

- I was washing clothes and studying in the laundry room when a black man came into the room and exposed himself to me. I was shocked and scared to death. He blocked my way out of the room, but I pushed past him and ran upstairs. I had trouble trusting any black man for a long time. I was very suspicious and nervous around every black man that I did not know. I tried not to let my anxiety show and avoided contact with black men for a long time. I realize that this incident could have easily happened with a white man, but it didn't. I associated only black men with my fear. I'm somewhat more comfortable now, but I'm still extremely cautious around black men with whom I'm unfamiliar.

8) "Nigger Lover:" Hostile rejection of Interracial Dating

Many whites avoid associating with blacks out of the fear they will be called a "Nigger Lover." To be called a "Nigger Lover" is very demeaning to a white person. This labeling is a form of group thinking: it's the American way. It is not politically correct to associate with or date blacks in this country. Consequently many whites avoid genuine associations with blacks because of this "group thinking." The following vignettes illustrate how this negative label and name-calling cause whites to avoid associating with and/or dating African- Americans.

- Perhaps the most chilling encounter I had with racism occurred during my senior year in high school. I began talking to this guy over the phone. We got along well and had so much in common that he asked me out, sight unseen. When he came to my house both my parents and I were in for a shock. In all our phone conversations I had not realized that he was black. We ended up going out for a couple of months.

  My parents were very cool about the whole situations but the same could not be said for the rest of the community. We began to receive phone calls calling me a "Nigger lover." One time my friend was driving me home and we were pulled over by the police. I was asked if I was there of my own free will and I said "yes."

  The sad thing is that my friend and I would still be together if it were not for the negative reaction of the community. I found it really frustrating that people would not get past the stereotypic barriers. Soon my relationship with this person ended. I began to become fearful about starting any sort of friendship with a black person simply because of the bad experiences I experienced in the past. It is not the black people; in fact, I get along with black people better than with white people. I am just frightened to death of the backlash from "my white friends."

- In the eleventh grade, I began dating a black guy. He was good looking, well mannered, intelligent and athletic—a good catch. However to many members of my peer group, this was wrong. White individuals refused to see his good points and chose to focus on the fact he was dating one of their kind. As we continued dating, many people assumed that we were seeing each other for sexual reasons and would say things like "you know, once you go black, you never go back." They immediately stereotyped him as a "sexual animal" and me as some kind of tramp and "Nigger Lover." We both parted as friends because the stereotyping and degrading comments grew to be too much for us to handle.

- My junior year in high school I started dating Bob, who is black. I went to black weddings, black family reunions predominately black clubs and concerts. I was the only white person at Bob's sister's cotillion. I was always welcome at his family's home and they accepted me with open arms.

Bob and I grew apart mainly because we encountered a lot of racism while we were dating. At school I was called a "Nigger Lover" and most places we went together, everybody stared at us. One night we were leaving a club and Bob and I were play fighting like many couples do. A cop came up and asked me if I was okay, while he frisked Bob. I didn't see him affront any same race couples that were acting similarly.

9) Interracial Dating and Marriage

Sexual myths about the physical superiority and virility of black men have been a part of America's racial ideology since slavery. According to Calvin Hernton (1965) in his book **Sex and Racism in America**:

> The white man, especially the southerner, is overtly obsessed by the idea of the Negro desiring sexual relations with whites.... The race problem is inextricably connected with sex...The sexualization of the race problem is a reality, and we are going to have to deal with it even though most of us are, if not unwilling, definitely unprepared." (Pp. 3-4)

This morbid fear of black-white dating and marriage has been banned in literature even when the relationship involves animals! A few years ago a children's book entitled "The Rabbits' Wedding" was banned from a public library in a Southern city because it contained a marriage of a black rabbit and a white rabbit! Can you believe that?

Sexual issues (miscegenation or the marriage and sexual intercourse between blacks and whites) are often assumed to be at the root of racist attitudes and practices. In particular, whites' fear of interracial marriage was provided as a justification for America's racist ideology. One of the deepest fears of white Americans is that black men will marry white women and produce black babies that will eventually result in the disappearance of the white race (Welsing, 1991). From the Internet, this post was taken:

- Today Blacks, Jews and other people of color threaten the White race. The white race should fight back. We should stick by our white family and teach our kids to hate the colored man. Yes, these groups threaten the white race.... We should have interpersonal relationships with our own; however, regarding teaching our kids to hate the "colored" man. I don't necessarily agree it would be a positive approach. I believe a more positive approach would be to teach our white kids to have pride and nobleness in themselves. Our kids need to be nourished with the realization that they would be proud to be white and not ashamed. One of the biggest problems today is interracial marriage. "Niggers "should stick with "Niggers" and whites with whites." (From Freya Cat 11-5-98)

Blacks and whites are diametrically opposed in their racial attitudes about sexuality. Over sixty years ago the Swedish Social Scientist Gunnar Myrdal (1944) warned us in a monumental work titled **An American Dilemma the Negro problem and American democracy.** In one section Myrdal asked white Southerners to list in rank order of importance things they thought blacks wanted most. Here are their listings:

1) Intermarriage and sexual intercourse with whites
2) Social equality
3) Desegregation of public facilities buses churches, etc.
4) Political enfranchisement
5) Fair treatment in the law courts
6) Economic opportunities (pp.60-61)

Then Myrdal asked blacks to rank order these same items. The blacks listed the items in direct reverse order than the whites.

1) Economic opportunities
2) Fair treatment in the law courts
3) Political enfranchisement
4) Desegregation of public facilities, buses, churches, etc.
5) Social equality
6) Intermarriage and sexual intercourse with whites

We find the same thing today. Black-Americans want improved economic opportunities and fair treatment. Intermarriage is not a high priority.

For many years, television avoided this thorny problem of interracial dating. However, the successful "Ally McBeal" comedy /drama tackled one of TV's biggest taboos, the interracial relationship between a black man and a white woman. ('Ally McBeal ' Tackles TV' biggest. 1999) However, Ally McBeal is not the first time an interracial romance has been on TV. In NBC's "Emergency Room" a black man and a white woman have an on-again, off-again interracial affair. Racial myths about the superior black sexual stud, AIDs, and other diseases have been created to prevent interracial relationships from developing.

In spite of the racial myths about blacks, a significant number of white females indicated they dated black males. On the contrary, a small and insignificant number of white males indicated that they dated black females.

- In high school there was a black guy that I always had a crush on. We suffered through trigonometry together. I ran into him at a party the week before my graduation and we talked a long time. We became very close. I still remember being really surprised that he liked me and being with him immediately changed the way I looked at other couples, especially inter-racial couples.

- During the course of my senior year in high school, I dated many black guys and I had a serious relationship with one black guy.

My parents did not accept this relationship. All of a sudden their daughter was a little too liberal for this small town. They threatened to kick me out of the house if I did not end the relationship immediately.

I was being forced to make a decision that would leave someone out of my life that I cared about very much no matter what I ultimately decided. I had never been so close to someone of another race before.

- I spent summer in the State of Georgia hitting it off with two local girls that I befriended. One day I showed them the prom photo I carried in my wallet of my black date and myself. There was great shock by both girls. I was surprised to discover that they (of my generation) were caught up in old taboos about interracial relationships.

  The following year I went to a prom with another black guy. At this point, a couple of classmates pointed out that it seemed as if I was trying to make some kind of statement with my choice of having a black date both times I went to the prom. Half amused, my black prom date decided to play up on this idea. For the prom, I wore all black and he wore all white.

- My freshman year in college would have been much harder if it had not been for this one black guy. He took care of me when I was down, trying his hardest to cheer me up. He also would go out walking with me at two or three in the morning when I needed to clear my mind. He was always there for me. Then, in the spring, he asked me to his formal and I responded with a quick "yes." Some of my friends approved and simply said to have a great time while others were shocked and pretty much speechless. However, besides a few funny looks, I had a great time that night. This experience changed my beliefs about racism and prejudice.

An additional perspective needs to be stated about interracial relations. Historically, black women have been raped by white men and have experienced all sorts of sexual abuses from white men. Black women have served as white men's concubines, mistresses and secret paramours since slavery. DNA tests performed on the descendants of Thomas Jefferson (the third US President) and Jefferson's young slave, Sally Hemming, offer compelling evidence that he fathered at least one (and probably more) of her children. The report is based on blood samples collected by Dr. Eugene A. Foster, a retired pathologist who lives in Charlottesville, Virginia. This finding undercuts the position of many white historians who have long asserted that Jefferson did not have a sexual liaison with his slave mistress who was about 28 years his junior. It also confirms the oral tradition that has been handed down among Sally Hemming's descendants that Jefferson fathered her children. Sally Hemming's bedroom was right back of Jefferson's bedroom. A door separated the two bedrooms. Further, visit Washington D.C. or any city and observe the white men who hang out in the "red light" district soliciting black prostitutes. White men, unsuccessfully, attempt to disguise their interest in black women. This last vignette tells about the problems that arise between the parents and child when the child decides to date interracially:

- As far as my parents were concerned there was no need to form scripts because it was assumed that my close friends would not be black and that I would never think of dating a black guy. I never thought my parents had such strong feelings about blacks, but I learned differently when they discovered that I had a Black boyfriend.

I came home one day from school to find my mother extremely distressed. In her hand was my yearbook. She said to me. "Sandy I heard you raving about this boy you like and how much he likes you so I decided to look in your yearbook and see who he was. You can imagine how I felt when I discovered he's black.

Jamal was a good friend of mine and my mother didn't like him because he was black. It was one of the most difficult things for me to understand. I tried to appease her by telling her that he and I were just friends. But as the months wore on, our friendship grew into a two-year committed relationship.

During those two years I had to deal with my parents opposition. My parents turned into my enemies. The people who supposedly loved me so much were making me miserable by forbidding my relationship with Jamal.

I tried to help them understand my point of view, but it was impossible for them, as it was impossible for me to understand their point of view. So my parents and I drifted slightly during this important time in my life. It was very hurtful to me they could want to destroy something in my life which I cared about and loved.

It wasn't long until I was convinced that eventually one day Jamal and I would get married. Although the marriage would take place, as my parents would say, "over their dead bodies," I didn't care and was prepared to alienate myself from my parents and my family. I hated them for their prejudices and for their inability to look past Jamal's color.

Jamal's family, unlike mine, completely accepted me. His family adored me. They welcomed me with open arms and made me feel like a part of their family. I felt completely comfortable with them as they did with me. I was treated with as much love and respect as they would have treated his girlfriend if she were black.

I rejected the scripts my parents gave me. I rejected them with every bone in my body and they, to their regret, were never able to make me understand why I was wrong and why they were right. This is because to me, I was right and they were wrong.

CHAPTER VIII:
ACHIEVING RACIAL MATURITY

As a child, I spake as a child,
I understood as a child,
I thought as a child:
But when I became a man,
I put away childish things.

Corinthians 13:11

1) Racial Maturity Defined

Racial maturity means having adequate knowledge and respect for members of other races plus the ability to interact comfortably and effectively with members of different races. It is similar to social maturity or the ability to relate effectively with persons of the opposite sex. As in social maturity, racial maturity develops through appropriate exposure, interaction and socialization with persons of different races. Color blindness is not racial maturity; color awareness and respect is racial maturity. Children who are exposed to early interracial interactions tend to be more racially mature than those who do not.

Racial immaturity results from the exact opposite (i.e., lack of exposure, isolation and or negative and hostile encounters with other races). If, for example, a white child grows up in an all-white neighborhood, attends all-white schools, all-white churches and has no exposure to different races, that child, most likely, will have difficulties as an adolescent or adult when confronted with situations requiring him/her to deal with different races. He/she will not know what to expect, what to say, what to do and will feel extremely awkward and confused.

By contrast, if a white child grows up in a racially mixed community, given positive racial scripts and interacts comfortably with members of other races at school, church and on the streets, the white child is likely to gain the requisite skills needed to effectively interact with people of another race, simply because of his/her experiences earlier in life. This person, along with proper instructions and modeling by parents, becomes racially mature through experiences in his/her experiential world.

The amount of previous quality experience one has with a person of another race is a good predictor of the kind of interaction one will have with persons of the same race at a later time in life. According to psychoanalytic theory, social interest receives its characteristic stamp in the early years of life. Consequently, the next reports will illustrate the importance of strong positive parental racial scripts, living in an interracial environment, going to integrated schools, having interracial friends and having positive early interracial experiences. These individuals will reflect a healthy racial maturity as well as what Helms (1984) describes as a "healthy white identity." Let us examine a few case histories to look at the early experiences these individuals had and the later impact in life.

- From the time that I can remember, I have always had contact with members of other races, most notably blacks. My earliest recollections of primary contact with a black person are Mrs. Stewart or "Stu" as we affectionately called her. Stu was in charge of the four of us when my parents were at work and basically raised us. We referred to her as our black mom. My mother used to say, "You have one white mom and one black mom." When Stu's family had family reunions, we were the only white people there.

When her sister was looking for a house, we found one right next door to my grandparents. On thanksgiving, we used to go to my grandparent's house and still spend part of the time with Stu and her family. We respected Stu's culture and we respected ours.

- I attended a racially mixed elementary school. I had no problem relating to friends of many different races. Because of the diverse racial composition of my school, I learned some things about black history. For example, I learned from a very early age that Benjamin Banneker, a black man designed the layout for our nation's capital. I can remember doing a report with a black girl on Billie Holiday.

- My parents and grandparents were unbiased as far as racial issues were concerned. My grandfather had a heart of gold. I have many memories of him helping people of other races and nationalities.

Every Thanksgiving my family went to a family reunion. Momma Sarah was an African-American who was my great Aunt's maid and housekeeper. I was never taught to treat her any differently than I would treat my own Momma. All I knew was she made the best banana pudding in the whole world. She used to tell me stories from when she was a little girl. I never saw her as a black maid.

My family spent many Sundays attending an all-black church. My Mom liked their worship better as I got older I chose to attend the black church.

I developed a wide range of friendships with both black men and black women. When I started dating black men, I was hit with full-faced racism from both the black community and the white community. It was a huge slap in the face for someone who had been taught the total opposite. Many people disapproved of my decision to date black men. I felt that I had made the right decision. I have two beautiful biracial children and I would not change it for the world.

People may say what they want, but I feel confident and comfortable with the way I treat people of all races

2) Transactional Analysis

Maturity is the function of the "Adult Ego State" (Berne, (1964); Babcock and Keepers, (1976). The adult ego can be used to reason, to evaluate stimuli, to gather and to store technical information. We all have an adult ego state, that is, everyone is capable, to some extent, of testing reality, seeking alternative solutions and estimating the consequences of each alternative, to make a choice or decision. Such information is retained for future reference. What is called immature is the "Child Ego State." What is called mature is the "Adult Ego State."

Thus, a child who was brought up with negative scripts can move into the adult ego state and begin to re-evaluate the old scripts and estimate the consequences of various courses of action. The mature adult is able to minimize the possible racist remarks and/or behavior.

3) Examples of Racial Maturity

Children whose parents teach them positive racial scripts, such as "don't judge a book by its cover," tend to have a greater level of racial maturity than those who are taught negative racial scripts. The following is a description of a person, who had positive racial scripting, but had negative exposure to blacks. His friends were very negative, but he did not "yield" or "acquiesce" to their pressure for him to conform to their racist beliefs. In addition, this student took my Black Psychology class and became not only one of my best students, but an able teaching assistant. In addition, he went on to medical school to earn his M.D. His racial script shows how he moved from racial immaturity to racial maturity.

- As a young child I did not know many black people. I had a black teacher one year and there were three or four black children that attended my elementary school--that was about it. I saw a lot of black people but they didn't live in my neighborhood. When I was in the fifth and sixth grade, one of my friends was black. I never considered his color.

I remember people saying, "Those blacks, they do things differently." This was the beginning of my negative racial belief formation. In junior high school I had very little exposure to black people. There were no blacks in my honors classes, my church and groups that I belonged. Most of what I heard about blacks came from whites--and most of it was negative. I heard several teachers speak poorly of blacks. Many of my friends learned racist behavior at home and they badmouthed blacks as well. I did not follow my friend's beliefs. I had been taught at home that racism was wrong. I experienced many conflicts with my model. I wanted to believe all people are created equal, but I was aware of many differences between the behavior of blacks and whites. Friends and the media told me blacks are lazy, stupid and cause trouble. Blacks I saw congregating in the halls and bathrooms at school seemed to confirm that description.

Coming to the university caused a positive change in my racial identity. My white friends would not tolerate racial jokes or slurs. In addition, I made many new black friends who have helped expose me to black culture. Recently, while at home, I was shocked by the racist comments made by my friends. Realizing I was once in that mindset, I could see how important my exposure to blacks at school had been and what effect it had on me. I am pleased to say I no longer judge people on the basis of their skin color.

During the process of moving from immaturity to racial maturity, some individuals experience guilt and shame over the way whites have dealt with blacks in this country.

- Recently, I viewed the film "From Montgomery to Memphis: Dr. Martin Luther King," I was embarrassed for my race. I felt shame when thinking about the way that the white people in America treated the Black people. Now that my attitudes and feelings regarding black people have changed, my old racist feelings enter my mind less and less. Now, I am immediately aware of them and I try to examine why I think the way I do. My new ideas and lessened racist attitudes have caused me both discomfort and a few conflicts. For instance, many members of my family get together for Christmas. Some of my relatives are really racist. They spend much of their time drinking beer and telling racist jokes. I do not find these jokes funny. They really get to me. They are so stupid and crude and I do not fake polite laughter like I used to in the past.

Another source of conflict is with my ex-boyfriend's racist attitudes. When I began to tell him how I felt about black people, hoping to change some of his racist attitudes, I was bothered and angered by the comments he would make and the things he believed about black people. When I told him what I believed, he became furious and insulted me with some of the racist comments that he made. Well, I decided I could not deal with his closed mind and racist attitudes and I left him.

- It seemed very probable that I was directly connected to the history of white supremacy and the exploitation of blacks. Finding out about my Southern (and racist?) heritage intensified my guilt, resentment and racial self-consciousness that I began to experience because of my whiteness. I had begun to consider myself implicated in the injustice in spite of my own views and behavior. I had begun to wonder anxiously what blacks I encountered in public were thinking about me. I still feel this odd guilty uneasiness when I am around blacks that I do not know.

Another individual who felt guilt and shame explained his situation this way:

- My parents told me how white men in America took Africans and forced them to be slaves in this country. I could not understand how something so wrong could have gone on. I felt very upset and even ashamed. I felt guilt because I am white and it was my race that had treated these people so cruelly. I am a very compassionate and sensitive child and I cried when my parents told me what was done to these people. My parents assured me that I was in no way to blame.

Others have expressed a level of racial maturity in terms of avoiding guilt and shame by evaluating both sides of the racial equation:

- In dealing with my own feelings, I had to consider my attitude toward the black race. I forced myself to define how I really felt. I am white. I offer no apology for being so and I expect no apology from you. But I do expect, as do you, to be accepted for who I am as an individual and not to be stereotyped into the category of "white" and to therein take on all of the negative qualities that may be ascribed to me by the black man.

  I do not want to be a walking apologia for what has happened to your race, but I do want to provide a source of encouragement and wholesome living.

  I choose not to be overwhelmed by guilt, but allow my heart to be touched by the impact of your history. It will take time; but I am thinking ---I am opening my mind--- I empathize with where you have been, who you are and the potential you wish to fulfill. Allow me time.

Some individuals are uncertain of their racial maturity and are still identifying ways to find the medium through which to express their feelings as the following examples will illustrate:

- I am not sure that I have reached the highest level of racial maturity, but there have been three things have helped me become more racially mature. First, my experiences here at college have given me the opportunity to develop relationships with African-Americans and learn about their lives through personal experience. Secondly, my faith in God and belief in Christian truth has provided me with answers about how and why I should act and feel toward African-American community. Lastly, the knowledge that I have obtained from several Black Studies classes in college have allowed me to better understand the African-American experience and the implications that it has on my life as a future educator in America.

With the help of these three influences, I can interact comfortably and effectively with black people and any other race. I have several positive and secure relationships with black men and women. I work on group projects with black peers, at my job where my boss is black and my co-workers who are black. I baby-sit for a black family and I attend black-centered functions to enjoy the culture and traditions of African-Americans. While I do feel comfortable around African-Americans, I do realize there are many differences between their race and mine. I can't claim to understand what it means to be black, but I accept I probably never will.... I was born white, but my identity and beliefs are determined by Jesus Christ (black or white) and not the color of my skin.

• Throughout my experience with African-Americans I believe I have developed a positive racial script. I have had the chance to work with black children more so than adults because this is where my field of interest lies. I wish to become a school counselor; therefore I hope to be educated about other cultures, especially the black community since I will be working with black children and their parents. I would really like to learn more about the black community first hand. I would like to move into a black neighborhood so I can interact more with African-Americans. However, I do have doubts and anxieties about this situation such as will I be accepted? I don't believe so. I am not nervous about black people specifically; I am nervous about what they will think of me.

I will be truthful and say I am not sure I have reached racial maturity. I feel comfortable with African-Americans that I can relate with or who share a lifestyle that correlated with my own. I feel this is how the general population related to other human beings. I am not sure. I do know I would like to interact with more blacks and take every chance I can get.

Am I racially mature? Considering that I have grown up in a white community and have gone to schools that are predominately white, yes. But looking at other white people my age and the experiences they have had with the black culture, I believe I have done a lot towards becoming racially mature.

This individual is at a crossroads and is experiencing anxiety about how she will be perceived by blacks. She should realize that black people, in general, would accept her because she wants to interact positively with them. Of course there may be a few blacks who will not accept her, but the majority will. She should begin to have more interaction with black adults as well. This will give her knowledge of how she is perceived in the black community. At this point, she is not racially mature but she in on the tract to becoming mature racially.

In my class I begin with a model I call "Freeze-Unfreeze-Refreeze" by suggesting that students usually come to the class with "frozen racial scripts." I also state that one of the things this course does is enable the person to examine his/her frozen scripts and unfreeze them and re-freeze them in a different form. Or they may re-freeze them in the same original form. Here is how one individual discussed his frozen racial script:

- There is no question that when I first came to college, I had some pretty solid racist ideas about people who were different than me. My racial scripts were frozen solid and had been for some time, mainly because I came from a small town which was, among other things, predominately white, Christian and very Midwestern. I had a difficult time accepting some of those differences my first year in college, but gradually I came to realize that maybe some one that was different than I was not so bad after all, and that I might even learn something from him/her. One thing that I found much different was the "type" of black people that attended college. Why were they different? How were they different? I came across answers to these and many other questions regarding black people throughout my first two years in college and after taking Black Psychology many things have begun to tie together.

I really wondered if any of my thoughts and ideas about blacks would change after taking this class. I have been pleasantly surprised, for I have learned more than I ever thought I would, especially with respect to their culture. I feel that the things I have learned or discovered in this class will remain with me forever. I find myself, when at home or out in public around black people, thinking back to the many different topics that we have discussed in class. Have my views changed? I think so. The temperature got high enough to unfreeze my ideas so that more ingredients could be added to the mixture. These ingredients include both enrichment materials and preservatives, both of which will undoubtedly remain when the temperature drops, and I have my re-frozen mixture of scripts. I have come to understand, in some respect, the way that blacks think about themselves and about whites and why they think this way. I am beginning to see a person for a person, and not a person of a race, which I consider to be the most important thing I have learned. Finally, I have learned where society has been, where it is, and possibly where it is going in this area or racial harmony. I thus, consider myself in the late stages of immersion, taking the things I have learned, and looking toward the future and my continued growth and security with respect to racial maturity.

One individual wrote a very mature description of where he is with racial discrimination. The paper was titled, "A World Without Discrimination."

- It is easy to recognize a problem exists in our society today concerning racial discrimination and prejudice of one group towards another. Specifically a barrier can be seen to exist between black and white people.

Individual racism is the most dangerous type of racism in existence today. People demonstrating this type of racism actively limit those people in the minority from living up to their full potential. It's this type of racist with whom we, a nation wanting to put an end to the problem, must deal with. We must convince these people that racism is morally wrong; that all people no matter the color of the skin, the ethnic origin, or sexual gender have strong points, which they can offer to society. Most individuals demonstrating racial prejudices usually suffer from a lack of self-confidence themselves and feel threatened by black individuals.

Several of the questions that I asked were: Are you willing to give up your negative racial script? Are you ready to give up your negative thinking about blacks? Are you willing to give up your association with your racist friends? Are you willing to be free and an independent thinker? Are you willing to walk away from racist people who will be very upset? When will you stand up and speak up for what is right? Are you attempting to develop racial maturity?" Some folks are not willing to give up their racist script in order to move on toward racial maturity as expressed in the following examples:

- I don't think I could ever become completely racially mature, for I feel I still have certain biases against blacks. For example, I simply am not attracted to black men, nor could

I ever see dating one. Also, if I know that a neighborhood is completely populated by blacks, I could never see myself living there, for I would feel uncomfortable. These remaining fears prevent me from becoming completely racially mature. I hope I have developed a sensitivity and awareness so I can be objective and understanding about differences in black and white relationships.

- My family is racist, pure and simple. There's not a nice way to say that. I've grown up with their racist views and the views of our racist community. I will always be aware of the separateness of blacks and whites. I have lived twenty years with constant reinforcement of that separateness. My racial scripts are: blacks have bad blood; blacks steal and are lazy; blacks can't be trusted. It's what I was told from day one.

This person has to ask, "Am I living the life of my mother's or father's life"? It really seems that similar persons are living the life their parents told them they should live. If they are to become racially mature they must change these racist scripts.

Let us examine a few accounts of how one's level of racial maturity is tested:

- For all of my life I have lived in a white middle-class neighborhood in a small town. My high school had over 1600 students. Fewer than 20 were African-Americans. This was a very segregated town, which offered very little acceptance to blacks. This created a natural breeding ground of prejudice. However, despite all of this I was lucky enough to escape the ignorance solely because of my mother. Throughout my childhood, my mother exposed me to sensitivity, open-mindedness, awareness, and acceptance. I was taught this world is made up of many different types of people--rich, poor, Black, White, Protestant, Jewish, etc. and we were to respect people's differences rather than ridicule them. She used to explain that people who were prejudiced were ignorant and insecure. I remember my uncle being asked to leave our house because he couldn't keep his racial slurs to himself.

When I was eight, my best friend moved to another city because his parents were getting a divorce. I would spend a month with my friend and he would come back and spend a month with me. I was unaware of the fact that his mother was dating a black man. My mother never mentioned the fact that the man was black before I left to stay with my friend. I believe this was her way of testing whether or not she had succeeded in developing my sensitivity towards other races. I can remember being surprised if for no reason other this was my first extended encounter with a black person. This man turned out to be a great guy who helped to confirm everything my mother had preached. I often wonder what would have happened if she had taught me differently. I am indebted to my mother for what she achieved because I have a strong sense of racial equality, which has allowed me to be very secure in my interracial relationships

The next student is caught between being a close friend to a black male and dating him; her racial script is tested when he asked to take her to the prom:

- I remember the emphasis my parents placed on treating everyone equally, which was the typical golden rule standard: Do unto others as they do unto you. They explained that a black person's skin color did not make him any less or any more of a decent human being. I became a close friend with a black boy. We spent a lot of time together. Since we went to different schools, the time we spent together was usually alone. Just as we were getting along great, something dampened our friendship. He asked me to his prom. At first, I thought "Great, it would be so much fun." We used to go dancing a lot and knew that we would have a great time. But then, I realized that he wanted to start dating. All of a sudden, I felt very uncomfortable. I didn't know if it was because I just wanted to be friends or was it because he was black. I was very uneasy. I was attracted to him, but I knew it would be difficult to date. Then came anger. I became angry at society for establishing these labels. Why did it put these restrictions on us? Both of us were very confused and angry that race had to come into our relationship.

This last vignette poignantly relates how some individuals are struggling with their racial identity and the ugly racial history.

- I am not secure with my skin color. I feel like when black people look at me, they see only my skin color--an unfair judgment for me to make on them. The problem is my inability to deal with my color and the unfavorable white history that preceded me rather than any negative action by a black person.

  I still associate a certain amount of guilt with being white. I am secure in the notion of equality, but I am not all secure of my own race. I don't especially have any pride about being white because I don't associate cultural heritage with it.

SECTION IV

Racism: Its Various Forms
and Expressions

CHAPTER IX
WHITE SUPREMACY
AND WHITE RACISM

1) Definition Of White Supremacy

Slavery is virtually dead but its legacies, white supremacy and white racism, are alive and well. Throughout my discussion, I will use the terms white supremacy and white racism interchangeably. However, white supremacy is a more definitive and descriptive term than white racism. White supremacy will be defined first and, secondly, white racism and its various forms will be discussed. In the next two chapters the purveyors and transmitters of white supremacy and white racism (stereotypes and racial myths) will be discussed.

The Encarta World English Dictionary defines white supremacy as: "The view that Caucasian people are genetically and culturally superior to all other people or races and should therefore rule over them" (p. 2028). White supremacy is a generic term; white racism and bigotry are subsumed under its classification. Inherent in the idea of white supremacy is the notion of a superior/inferior relationship. White supremacy, however, is more than a superior/inferior relationship or domination by one group over another. White supremacy is an ideology or a worldview. It is the ultimate measure of the white's supremacist belief system.

Dr. Francis Cress Welsing (1991) in **The Isis Papers: the keys to color** reports that Neely Fuller in his book, **The United Independent Compensatory Code/System/Concept: A textbook/workbook**

for thought, speech and/or action for victims of racism (white supremacy), states there is only one functioning racism in the world-- white supremacy. She further relates that Fuller concluded that the only valid operational definition of racism is white supremacy. P. 2

An Internet Post (Twaecap, 1998) called attention to some of the thinking about white supremacy. It is entitled "White Supremacy" by Twaecap who gave us permission to quote from this post. He writes:

> ...White Supremacy is probably the most pejorative, emotion-laden racial term that can be used against a white person...Taken literally, the term "White Supremacy" is presumably the belief that the white race is supreme, that it should dominate, rule or exploit other races.

2) Definition of White Racism

There are many definitions of White racism. Feagin, Hernan and Batur (2001) define White racism as the socially organized set of practices, attitudes and ideas that deny African-Americans and other people of color the privileges, dignity, opportunities, freedoms and rewards that this nation offers to white Americans. P. 17

Let me be clear about how I define white racism

> White racism is defined as the organized and systemized abuse of power that leads to physical harm or oppression of an individual or group in the form of discrimination, control, exclusion and/or subordination solely on the basis of skin color. The common denominator of white racism is power or the ability to define social, economic and political reality along with the necessary instruments of domination to uphold that reality. Further, white racism is the activation, operation and/or institutionalization of prejudices, stereotypes, bigotry and abuse of power. It occurs when one takes racial prejudices and forces them on others either individually or institutionally. Finally, white racism involves action and much more than a set of beliefs and ideology.

a)   Effects of Racism on Individual Racists

Little or no attention has been given to the effects of racism on the racist. The focus has been mainly on the effects of racism on the victims (blacks) and not the victimizers [see Kardiner and Ovesey (1951) **The Mark of Oppression**; Karon (1976) **Black Scars**; Gutterman (1971) **Black Psyche**)]. It is my contention that racism affects the victims and the victimizers alike. Thus, the perpetrators of racism, rather than the victims of racism must be closely examined. Just as slavery affected both the slave masters (the captors) and the slaves (captives), racism affects the racists, as well as their victims. It is well known the slave masters lived in dread fear of slave insurrections, uprisings and rebellions by a population that hated them and frequently sought revenge and their freedom. Similarly, the racist lives in grave fear of blacks. The racists see blacks categorically as dangerous, having a criminal mentality and as rapists. These perceptions merely suggest the racist is ignorant to black Americans and their culture. This ignorance results in (1) FEAR (False Experiences Appearing Real) and (2) HATRED. Dr. Cornell West, formerly Professor of Afro-American Studies and Philosophy of Religion at Harvard University, in a speech given at the Sorbonne in Paris, France, stated: "A discussion about racism is a discussion about white fear." (Reep, p. 1)

Racism has the unique characteristic of providing the racist with a set of lenses and blinders (stereotypes, myths and racial scripts) for viewing African-Americans. On the one hand, the lens increases the sensitivity to the most striking aspects of the black person: his/her dark skin color. This what I have called "hypersensitivity" of the perceiver and "hyper visibility of blackness."

As Boguslaw (1971) explained:

> The truism is perception is functionally selective...the hungry man examining the menu "sees" the food items; the thirsty man "sees" the drink items; some men see only the pretty girls on the cover (p, 240)

On the other hand, the racist blinders decrease sensitivity to those aspects of the environment that do not fit into the racist belief system. This is what Ellison called "invisibility" of blackness. That is, the racist lens, which prevents the racist from seeing aspects of the black person that contradict his/her beliefs. Thus, racism itself is a form of distortion and "blindness" based on certain preconceived assumptions, which support or reinforce false belief systems about black people. This description is not too different from the way a delusion is defined: a persistent and false belief held in the face of strong contradictory evidence. (Encarta World English Dictionary, 2000, p. 479)

b) White Denial of Racism

Racists mainly use denial as a primary defense mechanism to avoid facing the reality of a racial situation. For example, not too long ago, (1999 to be exact) the St. Louis Police Department recommended two police officers (one black and one white) to receive its highest and most prestigious award: The Medal of Valor. Both officers rescued three young children and their mother from a burning building. Their supervisor recommended both men for this prestigious award. But, when the award ceremony was held during a luncheon, strangely enough, the black officer's name was omitted. Only the white officer received The Medal of Valor (Bryan, 1999).

The Police Department alleged racism and asked for an external investigation by the Missouri State Highway Patrol. In an eight-page report the Highway Patrol stated that Race was not a factor in the black officer not getting the award (denial). How did the State Highway Patrol arrive at that conclusion? Their report concluded that one of the white judges made "an innocent mistake" that consisted of "accidentally" dropping the black officer's recommendation on the floor and mistakenly putting it in the wrong pile. Further, the report stated that it was a simple error and race was not a factor in the black officer's disqualification. After this incident was widely publicized, the black officer was belatedly given the Medal of Valor. The Executive

Director resigned after this embarrassing "oversight" in which a blunder had deprived a black officer of getting his department's highest award. (Lhotka, 1999).

The above incident reflects one of many situations where denial is a basis for excluding a person of African-American descent. Another example is found in a letter from a white man to a black St. Louis columnist, the late Greg Freeman. This example further shows how whites clearly deny racism by projecting their racist attitudes and attacking blacks.

The man writes:

> *Dear Mr. Freeman:*
>
> *I'm with you except when you write about that black stuff. We get bombarded with black people in our culture today, and I'm bothered when you write from a black point of view.*
>
> *Let me make it clear. I'm not a racist. I'm a white guy…I don't care for your 'angry black man' columns. I've done nothing for anyone, black or white, to be angry with me. But it seems like blacks are always blaming white people, me, for all their troubles, and that puts me on the defensive…* (Freeman 2000, P. B1)

Greg Freeman, the black journalist, responded as follows:

> *We all look at the world through prisms of our lives. My prism is that of a black man. For me to try to look at the world through the eyes of other than those would be inauthentic at best. Being black is part of me. Just as it would be unreasonable to ask David Limbaugh to write columns leaving out "that conservative stuff"…* (Freeman 2000, p B1)

Another blatant example of racist denial is the case of Kevin Miner, a white man, who stood in court before the family of a black teenager he murdered and apologized for his actions. He added that race had nothing to do with the killing. He was sentenced to life without parole. This was a hate crime.

c) White Men-Black Women

The following excerpt is an example of how racist attitudes lead many whites into denial behavior and to misperceive and distort African-Americans' interpersonal relationships. This white male has the arrogance to attempt to explain black male-female relationships. He tries to explain why black men date white women or what he calls "interracial dating disparity."

He writes:

> Ninety-four percent of black-white couples involve a black man and a white woman. I'm not opposed to interracial dating [denial], however there are some issues. The problem lies within black women. This is not a racist comment [denial]. Black women, on the whole, are not perceived as being feminine and attractive (by Western world standards) by a majority of males.

> Many perceive them as being manly with characteristics such as a deeper voice, shorter hair, baggy clothes and a lack of sexiness and flirtatiousness. It is the nature of a man to consider overall attractiveness when choosing a date and looks are a great part of this. This has compelled many black men to look for a white woman to date. Consequently, many black males, which comprise a significant segment of the population, date white women.

> Black women have to shed their "macho," "masculine" and unattractive character and appearance. This will compel black men to actually enjoy dating black women, which will mean more white women for white men.

> Sorry, I know I will offend some, but in my heart I know I am not a racist [denial] and it is for the better and I am not afraid to take any irrational heat. (AOL Internet, 2000)

Two black women responded to this white male's statement on the Internet as follows:

- The level of arrogance of European males is astounding at times.... A white male, who doesn't date a sista (rooting to get the chair next to one is probably as close an interaction as he has ever had with black people) has the unmitigated gall to claim that he single-handedly has figured out the "problem with sistas."

- I appreciate your honesty and your opinion. I am a black woman and I am not the least offended. I attribute your perspective to a lack of exposure. I realize that only age, maturity and an introduction to what you have been missing out on will change that.... I live in Washington DC and I have never had a problem finding a man. What short stick are you talking about? Don't fool yourself into thinking that white men aren't attracted to us just because you aren't. Black men love us; Asian men are fascinated by our mystery; African men admire our strength, intellect and confidence; Latin men adore our curves, sensuality and rhythm; Italian men savor our style and the variety of our shades; "Brits" enjoy our quick wit and zest for life; Australians love our good conversation and love for good beer ...and I could go on!

It is only white American men that admire us secretly. You watch us at work, at school, in the street and you want to get to know us, but your shame wont allow it. You too are fascinated by the mystic. You like the way our brown skin glistens on your pale white skin when we shake your hand, that is!

Short hair is sexy and deep voices are sensual. Just ask your granddad! Black women, my dear, are known nurturers. While your mothers, grandmothers and great-granddads sat and drank tea, we were feeding you, teaching you. We raised you! But there is no need to get philosophical on you. Let's keep it to the here and now!

My advice to you dear is to stop watching Jenny Jones, Cops and Ricky Lake. The sistahs that you see on those shows are not representative of the masses. The sistahs in my circle wouldn't know a pair of baggy jeans if they slapped them in the face. Charm and flirt are our middle names. Validate your research with some exposure. Take your blinders off and feed your ignorance. There's an entire world that YOU are missing out on! (AOL Internet, 2000)

d) Is Racism Unconscious?

I do not believe that racism is unconscious as black psychologist Dr. Halford Fairchild proposes. According to Fairchild (2000):

> Interestingly, contemporary research in social psychology demonstrates that the aversive racist is unaware of his or her racism; much of contemporary racism is an unconscious process, p. b. 7

It is my opinion that racists are fully aware of their behavior. They continue to engage in racist activity because they see it as part of the norm, the right thing to do and the way things are supposed to be. It is the politically correct thing to do. Racial scripts are automatically activated at sight or visual perception of African-Americans. Because of this automatic activation, racist behavior may appear unconscious, because it is activated quickly in a reflexive manner.

e) Racist Distortions

Another major consideration is racist individuals are subject to make quick over-generalizations about black people without doing reality checks on their misperceptions. Their negative evaluations of black people are based on subjective, even second-hand information, rather than on objective data gained from personal experiences. In addition, they are likely to integrate into their beliefs any negative information that confirms or reinforces their hypotheses about the inferiority of black people.

Lastly, the racist mind distorts reality to fit his/her belief system. William Styron's **Confessions of Nat Turner** (1966) is a classical example of how racist distortions may occur. According to Styron's perception, Nat Turner was a cringing, whining, emasculated slave who had an incessant lust for white women. Styron used the full range of popular Eurocentric psychoanalytic jargonese to portray Nat Turner as having self-hatred, being anti-black and having a desire to be white.

Black writers, however, saw Nat Turner differently. The late Dr. Nancy Grant (1968) a black historian at Washington University in St. Louis differed from Styron in her opinion of Turner. She described Nat Turner in this way:

> The party had remained together from twelve to three o'clock when several men joined them-a short, stout powerfully built person, of dark mulatto complexion and strongly marked African features, but with a face full of expression and resolution. This was Nat Turner. (Pp. 53-54)

Styron (1966) admits at the beginning of his book that in areas where little information existed concerning Turner's early life and motivation for the insurrection, he permitted himself considerable "freedom of imagination in reconstructing events." (P 11) It is obvious that his "imaginations" about Turner are distorted products of his racist mind. He selected the kind of pathological stereotypes that perpetuate racist myths of black people.

Dr. Alvin Poussaint (1968) points out the following about Styron's portrayal of Turner:

> Styron is a southern white man who has been raised in a racist society and is not free from the impact of its teachings. How will we ever know how well the author has filled himself of his own white supremacist attitudes as he attempts to project himself into the mind of a black slave?" (p. 17)

Lerone Bennett (1968) Senior Editor of Ebony Magazine, in commenting on Styron's perception of Nat Turner concludes:

> The voice in this confession is the voice of William Styron. The images are images of William Styron. The confession is the confession of William Styron. (P.4)

It is difficult, if not impossible, for a white person to project himself/herself into the psyche of the Black American. Even today so as to prevent whites from understanding them, many black people dissemble themselves in the presence of whites.

Gellert (1933) and Ames (1950) report how this false appearance was expressed in black songs:

> Got one mind for white folks to see.
> 'Nother for what I know is me.
> He don't know, he don't know my mind
> When he see me laughing,
> Laughing just to keep from crying.

f)   Closet Racists

Many whites will not express their racist attitudes verbally or non-verbally, that is, until a situation arises that conflicts with their belief system. Usually this situation is in the area of interracial dating and marriage.

The following excerpt will illustrate:

- My parents were not prejudice people. They always taught me that black people are no different from white people. With this racial script my friendships with black people flourished, especially one in particular with a black guy. He confirmed for me all of the positive beliefs I have acquired about black people. He was genuinely one of the most thoughtful and caring individuals that I have ever met. We dated for a while, but when it was time to go back to college, we decided to go back to the friendship we had built earlier. When I told my parents that we had decided to be just friends, I was surprised to learn they were relieved. They told me it didn't matter how wonderful a person this guy was, a relationship with a black person was too difficult. This upset me greatly because it was the first time my parents had expressed to me their true feelings on interracial dating. I was willing to experience the difficulties of interracial dating, but my parents didn't think it was worth it. It was here that I discovered my parents' racist attitudes.

CHAPTER X:
RACIAL MYTHS AND STEREOTYPES: CARRIERS OF RACIST SCRIPTS

A myth is worth a thousand words
An African Proverb

1) Introduction

The purpose of this chapter is to describe the carriers of racial scripts: myths and stereotypes. First of all, racial myths and stereotypes serve as the primary conveyors of racist scripts. Thus, they are the taproots of racist thoughts and the foundation of racist beliefs. Secondly, society has created an almost limitless number of destructive racial myths as well as racial stereotypes to justify racist beliefs and practices. For example, blacks are portrayed erroneously as welfare mothers, thugs, uneducated, happy-go-lucky, no ambition, dancing fools, criminals, drug addicts, prostitutes, pimps and so on.

Racial myths and stereotypes form the foundation of what I call "racial scripts." Negative themes depicting the Black-American as a psychological cripple, criminal, welfare recipient, drug addict, lazy, dangerous, sexual stud, etc. abound in the scientific and popular literature as well as the media. Whereas Black-Americans are principally described as abnormal beings (i.e., low IQ, low self-esteem, buffoons, over-aggressiveness, etc.), their athletic profiles in major sports such as football, basketball, baseball and track are described as "super heroes." This combination of positive and negative themes presents a contradictory and confusing picture of Black-Americans. The themes point out that Black- Americans have been woefully misunderstood and their images have been extremely distorted.

Not only were the philosophies and beliefs of white researchers one-sided, but their reports were also slanted to emphasize the negative aspects of black life. Instead of searching and looking for strengths of black people and the extent to which blacks have managed to survive in an oppressive society, white researchers focused almost exclusively on pathology. Numerous "victim analyses" were made. To be sure white researchers tuned in specifically to look for and find pathology in the African-American; they found some pathology, but overlooked or ignored the resources, strengths, creativity, spirituality and the harmony in the lives of black people.

Why? The reason for this oversight or slant can be found in Alexander Pope's metaphor:

> All looks jaundiced to the jaundiced eye,
> As all looks infected to the infected spy.

Translated, pathology may be in the eye of the beholder rather than in the beheld. Not only were white scholars' explanations of African-Americans erroneous and faulty, but also for the most part, were highly distorted by racist ideology.

The major source of racial stereotypes and myths is found in one's personal philosophy and belief system. That is, one's inner states, beliefs and fantasies determine to a great extent what one perceives in certain situations, and not what the picture portrays. Gregory Freeman, a former writer for the St. Louis Post Dispatch newspaper, suggested that we deal in myths of each other's racial group instead of actual knowledge.

2) Ten Destructive Racial Myths

Racial myths abound in this American society regarding the Black-American. In the main, white scholars studied and created the myths. Racial myths are similar to what Boorstin (1961) labels man-made or pseudo-events. The term "pseudo" means "false" or to mislead or deceive, and this is what white scholars have done: distorted the image of Black-Americans. Throughout history we have been flooded with pseudo-images.

Pseudo-images are not spontaneous or unintentional; they are planned and their purpose is to perpetuate false images of African-Americans. A further purpose of a pseudo-image (a racial stereotype or myth) is to create a condition known as "Mentacide" a term coined by the late Dr. Bobby Wright (1975). Mentacide is the systematic destruction of a racial group's mind through distorting and/or erasing its history. Mentacide occurs through a process of distorting and falsifying the history of the Black-American.

Carter G. Woodson (1933) in his book **The Mis-Education of the Negro**, clearly warned what happens to a race's mind when it is led to believe certain fallacies:

> ...The Negro's mind has been brought under control of his oppressor...When you control a man's thinking you do not have to worry about his actions. You do not have to tell him to stand here or go yonder. He will find his "proper place." And will stay in it. You do not need to send him to the back door. He will go without being told. In fact, if there is no back door, he will cut one for his special benefit. (p. XIII)

One individual reported how myths influenced her:

- As a child I grew up in a suburban town where there were no blacks. I was exposed to the racial myths concerning blacks. Most of what I learned about them came from racial jokes, which I heard from my friends and some of my family. My friends concerned themselves with the sexual myths and my family made jokes about the slower intellect but superior athletic abilities of blacks. Accepting these myths was not difficult because the only black boy I knew was in the remedial classes and was by far the best athlete in school.

Ten of the most destructive racial myths were selected for examination to show their origins and relationship to the making of pathological images of blacks.

1) Black genetic deficiency
2) Deteriorating black families
3) Cultural deprivation
4) Black language deficiency
5) Black self-hatred
6) Damaged black psyche
7) War between black men and black women
8) Superior sexual stud
9) Superior black athletes
10) The lazy Negro

a)   Black Genetic Deficiency: The Original Myth

The first myth asserts that blacks are genetically inferior to whites. This myth was generated from the King James Version of the Bible. I have labeled it as the "original myth" because it is the basic myth that serves as the foundation for all other myths.

According to religious theory (Genesis 9:19-27), after the forty-day and forty-night flood, God blessed Noah and his three sons (Shem, Japheth and Ham). However, one day, Noah drank too much alcohol, became intoxicated and lay naked in his bed. Ham, the youngest son, went in to view his father's nakedness, but the other two brothers refused to look at their father in his naked state. When Noah awoke, he discovered that Ham had witnessed his nakedness. He became enraged and cursed Ham and all of his descendants to become "servants of servants". Noah blessed Shem and Japheth for their modesty. It is assumed that Ham was black because he was condemned to become a servant. Guthrie (1976) points out:

> The verses said nothing of skin color, but various interpretations held that since the descendants were to be enslaved, it was logical they had to have been black (pp.4-5).

Other versions of this passage exist. The central point, however, is racist theory has it that the doomed tribe of Ham (the Canaanites) provide scriptural authority for the inferior status of the black race and superior status of the white race. Felder (1993) cautions that any reference to the curse of Ham, as a black man is a myth. He says:

> The 'curse of ham' is a post-biblical myth. In fact, the sons of Noah-Shem, Ham and Japheth—do not represent three different races. (It is an absurdity of no small order to claim that Noah and his wife could produce offsprings that would constitute three distinct racial types!) In Gen. 9:18-29, Ham is not the recipient of a curse. The text explicitly says, "Let Canaan be cursed." Further, Ham does not mean "black" in Hebrew; it translates literally as "hot" or "heated." Pix.

The racial myths, however, did not stop there. The biblical interpretation was a mere beginning. Pseudo-scientific foundations were later provided and elaborated by racist theorists to validate the inferiority thesis. In 1840 during a lecture to his class in anatomy, Dr. Samuel G. Morton produced such "scientific evidence" of racial inferiority. Donned as having the world's largest collection of crania, Morton performed numerous comparative racial experiments by measuring the capacity of skulls by filling them first with white pepper seeds and later with lead shots (Stanton, 1960). From these experiments Morton concluded that the brains of five races of man (Caucasian, Mongolian, Malaysian, American-Indian and African-American) became successively smaller as one "descended" from Caucasians to Ethiopians. The Caucasian race was reported to have the largest brain and the black race to have the smallest brain. By equating brain size with intelligence, Morton led his readers to believe that persons with small brains necessarily have inferior intelligence and capacity. The results reported by Morton quickly caught the attention of anthropologists throughout the world, and they accepted the small-brain, black inferiority interpretation as a scientific fact.

As Stanton (1960) points out, the validity of Morton's data is highly questionable. Because of a liver condition, Morton never went into the fields himself to collect crania. He relied completely upon the reports from correspondents as to the central features in research, i.e., and the ethnicity of a particular skull, its location and geological conformation. The main point here focuses on the unreliability of Morton's research on at least three fronts: 1) the ethnicity of the crania, 2) the accuracy of his comparisons and 3) the fallacy of the small-brain theory. Certainly, no modern day anthropologist would accept such laxity in scientific research. But such was the case in the mid-nineteenth century, especially when racial myths were being created.

Another line of scientific reasoning used to support the racist thesis of black inferiority was the 1840 census, which "proved" that enslaved blacks were less likely to be insane than free blacks. The census, based on a series of statistical fallacies, showed that the insanity rate among free blacks living in the North was eleven times higher than that of enslaved blacks living in the South. In Maine, for example, where very few free blacks lived, one out of every 14 blacks (about 7 percent) was found to be insane; in Louisiana where there was a heavy population of blacks, only 1 out of every 4,310 blacks (far less than 1 percent) was found to be insane. According to the proponents of this argument this census provided "unassailable" support for the myth of racial inferiority. John C. Calhoun, then Secretary of State, used the census data as positive proof of the necessity of slavery. He claimed that the African is incapable of self-care and becomes a lunatic under freedom (Litwack,

1961). Secretary of State John C. Calhoun argued for the extension of slavery. According to Calhoun:

> Here (scientific confirmation) is proof of the necessity of slavery. The African is incapable of self-care and sinks into lunacy under the burden of freedom. It is a mercy to give him the guardianship and protection from mental death."

It didn't take long for the critical and logical mind, however, to discover the statistical fallacy of Calhoun's argument. When research samples are of unequal sizes (e.g., 1 out of 14 versus 1 out of 4,000), the differences in proportions are meaningless. Obviously, with small samples it takes a much smaller number to inflate the proportion than with large sample sizes. This same statistical fallacy, as we shall see later, sprang up in 1965 in the famous Moynihan Report on the black family.

In 1853, several works on racial inferiority appeared. Count Arthur de Gobineau of France (Biddiss, 1970) published an oft- referred to multi-volume series entitled **Essay on the Equality of the Human Races.** In his publication, de Gobineau argued in favor of the innate superiority of the white race over the darker ones. The Negroid variety, he claimed, is the lowest, standing at the foot of the ladder (Thomas and Sillen 1972).

b) The Myth of the Deteriorating Black Family

No one would question the all-persuasive influence of the family on personality development. It is here that socialization occurs; but, what if the child is a product of a broken home, a weak or absent father, a dominant mother?

White scholars have ascribed these characteristics to the black family. In 1965, the Moynihan Report, **The Negro Family: The Case for National Action** presented the black family as a "tangle of pathology" and as approaching complete breakdown.

The Moynihan report became another one of the most controversial pseudo-events in the mythmaking process. He hypothesized that the social problems of blacks result from a breakdown in the black family. As soon as the report was released, a storm ensued. Critics argued that he should have emphasized racial oppression, but the myth had been created.

By contrast, black scholars and scientists have studied the black family and community. They report unusual strengths and resiliency rather than weaknesses. Fanon (1963) saw blacks struggling and fighting exploitation, misery and hunger. Carmichael and Hamilton (1967) graphically described black power, not pathology in the black community.

Billingsley's (1968) refutation of the Moynihan Report shows how black families have survived under the most oppressive conditions and suggests strengths rather than weaknesses. Similarly, White (1970) described the black community as providing the unique life-styles necessary for coping with the various forms of racist games. Ladner (1971) found the black mother to be strong, but not necessarily dominant.

Staples (1971) criticized the allegation that the black male is impotent. Also, Staples gives a balanced view of the black family and black male personality. Hill (1971) found five major strengths in the black family as follows: 1) Strong kinship bonds 2) Strong achievement orientation 3) Strong work orientation 4) Strong religious orientation and 5) Flexibility and adaptability of family roles. Thus, whereas the white researcher found a "deviant community" by either misinterpretation or distortion from his observation of the black community, the black behavioral scientist, having a different perspective, found many positive features and strengths among blacks and their families.

c) The Myth of Cultural Deprivation

Frank Riessman (1962) introduced the cultural "deprivation" myth in his book, **The Culturally Deprived Child**. This cultural deprivation myth, which provided an alternative interpretation to the genetic deficiency hypothesis, asserted that the deficiencies of black children are not genetic in nature but environmentally produced. He recommends that compensatory educational programs are needed to correct these deficits. Take the little children to the zoo, the museum, the airport and other places of "cultural interests," because many of them have not been to those places. Since they do not have the proper cultural exposure, they are culturally deprived.

d) The Myth of Black Language Deficiency;

The chief proponents of the language deficiency myth were Bernstein (1960), Bereiter and Englemann (1966), and Hunt (1961). According to Englemann (1967):

> The child of poverty has language problems. These are problems far more crippling than mere dialect problems. Too frequently a four-year old child of poverty does not understand the meaning of such words as long, full, animal, red, under, first, or before. A goal of the Bereiter-Englemann project at the University of Illinois has been to teach young disadvantaged children the meaning of basic language. (p. 1)

In a report by HEW (1977) titled **Preschool Handicapped Children,** from a sample of thirty thousand children, 15, 670 (47 percent) were diagnosed as having speech impairment. Six thousand seven hundred and eight (45 Percent) were further diagnosed as having severe articulation difficulties and 5,680 (38.86 percent) showed expressive language difficulties. My point here is that because of the language deficiency myth of blacks and the bias in testing, these findings are readily accepted and go unquestioned, because they fit the preconceived mold. Many of the children in the head start sample were black and probably did not have "real" speech problems.

In the early 70's Drs. Robert Williams and Wendell Rivers challenged the language deficiency myth and showed quite clearly that test instructions in Standard English penalized the black child (Williams and Rivers, 1972). After changing the language of the test from unfamiliar to familiar terms, without training or coaching, the child's performance on the test increased significantly.

We divided 890 kindergartners, first and second grade black children into two groups of 445 each. Balancing the groups controlled variables of race, IQ, age, sex and grade. We used the standard version of the Boehm Test of Basic Concepts, and a culturally specific version of the same test. The Boehm Test consists of 50 pictorial multiple-choice items involving concepts of space, quantity and time. Black teachers and graduate students translated the concepts and objects into language familiar to the black children. Examples of the basic concepts in standard and the culturally specific versions are as follows:

Standard Version
1) Mark the toy that **is behind** the sofa.
2) Mark the boy who **is beginning to** climb the tree.

Culturally Specific Version
1) Mark the toy that is **in back of** the couch.
2) Mark the boy who **is fixing to** climb the tree.

The results of this study showed striking differences. The children's performances on the culturally specific version were significantly higher than those on the standard version. The findings also suggest that the standard version of the test did not activate the child's linguistic systems to the extent that the culturally specific version did. Grace Holt (1975) puts the situation this way:

> The participants in this rapidly developing drama were scholars who defined themselves as agents of social change. These agents defined black dialect in the good old Anglo-Saxon tradition labeled 'American,' excluding blacks from the decision-making process.... With few exceptions (e.g. Stewart vs. Williamson), the debate over black dialect was for whites only (p. 4).

At a 1973 St. Louis, Missouri Conference on Cognitive and Language Development of the Black Child, a group of black scholars rejected the so-called black language deficiency hypothesis. It was at that conference that Dr. Robert Williams coined a new term called **EBONICS**, derived from ebony (black) and phonics (speech sounds). Ebonics is defined 1) as the African-American's linguistic memory of African languages and 2) as a creative set of expressions generated by blacks exclusively for intra-group communication. The concept of Ebonics has gained wide currency among black scholars. (Asante, 1980; Johnson et al., 1980b; Smith, (1979)

e) The Myth of Black Self-Hatred

First of all, blacks do not hate themselves as the myth asserts. This myth gained support with the works of Kenneth and Mamie Clark (1939, 1940, 1947, 1950 and 1980). Numerous studies have explained in one manner or another the existence of this so-called self-hatred in Black-Americans. Until recently, nobody seriously questioned this allegation.

Black self-hatred conditions are defined as low self-concept and self-esteem. It was simply taken for granted by most researchers. The research questions included: How much of it exists in blacks? Do we have more of it (i.e., low self-esteem) than whites? Do black females have higher self-esteem than black males?

Clement Vontress (1964) author of "The Negro Against Himself" was one of the earliest promoters of the black self-hatred hypothesis. Using such terms to describe blacks as "les enfants terribles" and "deracines" (the uprooted), Vontress reports:

> The dominant characteristic of the Negro personality is that of feeling, feeling that he is inferior, worthless: and since this feeling has been engendered in him by the superior group a paternal figure against whom he cannot vent his spleen, he must hate himself, must punish himself and/or others like himself. (p. 238)

Vontress claims that the Negro personality is bent toward self-destruction, masochism and black-on-black crime. In a later article, Vontress (1971) discusses essentially four (4) components of the black male-all are negative: 1) self-hatred; 2) erratic behavior 3) black compulsiveness and 4) masculine protest.

1) Self-hatred: Defined as not liking being black because blacks are not accepted into white society i.e., since blacks are members of a racist society. Blacks reflect that hatred as self-rejection through the black psyche.

2) Erratic behavior: Erratic behavior is essentially any escapist behavior by blacks. Due to the prolonged effects of frustration, blacks engage in erratic (deviant) behavior, e.g., "passing for white," leaving the country, passivity, identification with the dominant group by assuming their life styles, aggression toward the oppressor, habitual use of alcohol, drugs, etc.

3) Black Compulsiveness: This behavior refers to acting in a non-black manner; it means placing restrictions on natural expressions of black life styles. According to Vontress, these blacks are in a "culture limbo." They are damned if they do (i.e., behave in a black manner) and damned if they don't (i.e., behave as middle class whites do).

4) Masculine Protest: Employing the psychoanalytic mechanisms of reaction formation (i.e., behaving just the opposite of what one feels), Vontress explains why many black men exaggerate the most obvious, external signs of masculinity. According to his thesis, the secondary aspects of black masculinity are the important ones: a big shiny car, flashy clothes, and money in the pocket, a fine lady and not having to work at all. Vontress claims that these goals become the model expectations for young black males in the black community.

Vontress's conclusions sound a note of doom. Since racism "creates" self-hatred and the other three components, and since racism is thoroughly ingrained in this society, Vontress's prognosis for blacks ridding themselves of self-hatred is "not good."

Continuing in this same vein, Pouissant (1968) reports that Black-Americans are suffering from a marred self-image that affects blacks entire psychological being. This negative self-image is equated with self-hatred. Pouissant indicates that integration is partly responsible for the development of the negative black self-concept.

Addressing the topic on the effects of racism on the black psyche, Pouissant states:

> ...the Negro has come to form his self-image and self-concept on the basis of what white racists have prescribed. Therefore, black men and women learn quickly to hate themselves and each other because they are Negroes.... There is abundant evidence that racism has left almost irreparable scars on the psyche of Afro-Americans that burden them with an unrelenting, painful anxiety that drives the psyche to reach out for a sense of identity and self-esteem. (p. 420)

f) The Myth of the Damaged Black Psyche

Abraham Kardiner and Lionel Ovesey (1951), two white psychiatrists, advanced in their book **The Mark of Oppression,** one of the earliest racist theories of the black psyche. Based on psychoanalytic investigative theories of merely 25 black clients the authors formulated the concept of the "damaged black psyche." From these clients the authors gleaned 25 black personality characteristics--all negative. Their central thesis asserted:

> The Negro still bears the psychological scars created by caste and its effects. It is these scars that we have chosen to call "The Mark of Oppression." (P.15)

The authors further claimed that: "The basic Negro personality is a caricature of the corresponding white personality, because the Negro must adapt to the same culture, must accept the same goals, but without the ability to achieve them." (p. 317)

Many black writers including Collins (1952) in *The Journal of National Medical Association* immediately criticized the Kardiner-Ovesey theory. Collins remarked the methodology is shaky, the sample is too small and the investigations were biased.

William Grier (1966), a black psychiatrist argues strongly against the use of white designed psychoanalytic methods with blacks. According to Grier, the problems blacks face in this society cannot be talked away even if we could afford to pay.

From their research, Kardiner & Ovesey, 1951 presented twenty-five (25) personality characteristics of Black-Americans

(1) Superficiality (2) Apathy and resignation (3) Repressed hostility (4) The wish to be white (5) Identification with feces (6) Inter-group aggression (7) White ego ideal (8) Inclined to gamble (9) Magical thinking (10) Inclined to alcoholism (11) Unconsciously resentful and anti-social (12) Weak super ego development (13) Disorderly, unsystematic (14) Sexual freedom (15) Reject education (16) Poor discipline in childhood (17) Maternal neglect and rejection (18) Little respect for parents (19) Psychologically crippled (20) Distrustful (21) Live for the moment (22) Hedonistic (23) Unlovability (24) The diminution of affectivity and (25) Uncontrolled hostility

As if the above descriptions were not enough, Bertram Karon (1958) wrote a negative discourse on the so-called Negro personality, which essentially was based on his doctoral dissertation. Contrary to the impressions one might gain from the title, the book provides neither a unique description of Black-Americans nor does it provide a theory of the Black American personality. Karon conducted a comparative research study, whose primary aim was to discover the differences in black and white personality structures resulting from differences in caste sanctions. His basic postulate was that Northern racism is less damaging to the black psyche than Southern racism. Therefore, one should see fewer "scars on the psyche" of Northern than Southern blacks. Comparative research, as we shall see later, not only is racist in nature; it does not provide a good basis for understanding black personalities.

Seventeen years after his first book, Karon revised the Preface and gave it a more pejorative title: **Black Scars**. Karon pointed out that the original title did, perhaps, mislead readers into believing that there is a distinctive basic personality common to all black people. He claims that because his research dispelled the notion of a black personality, he changed the title to **Black Scars** to reflect the effects of caste on personality formation and development.

As in the Kardiner and Ovesey (1951) study, Karon (1958) made similar methodological errors in the research on Black-Americans. His research was comparative in nature. A group of people cannot be fully understood when they are compared with another group. The only conclusion that can be drawn is that one group is "similar to" or "different from" the comparison group. Not much is learned about the unique characteristics of the group under study. But such is the nature of racist research.

In essence, from the comparative research format, it is virtually impossible for a clear description of the black personality to be gleaned. This point is extremely important from a methodological point of view, because comparative research does not and cannot provide one with unique descriptions of the black personality. From a review of the above questions, it is not surprising that Karon concluded the following regarding the black personality, all of which are based on difference theory.

Another mythmaker is Thomas Pettigrew's **A Profile of the Negro American** (1964). Here he presents a summary or collection of research reports on blacks through the late 1950s and 1960s (the eye of the black revolution). He provides a lopsided and often distorted view of black people--their personality, genetic composition, mental and psychological health, intelligence, crime rate and reactions to racism. Pettigrew offers neither a personality theory nor a critical review of the black personality; he merely reports the mythical conclusions as others present them.

Pettigrew reports several recurring negative descriptions of the black personality: the wish to be white, weak super-ego development, repressive hostility, rejection of education, psychologically crippled, distrustful, etc. Obviously, Pettigrew's account of the Black-American is not only pathological but is fraught with negative distortions as well.

Using Clark and Clark (1939) studies as a focus, Pettigrew interprets the preferences of black children for white dolls as evidence of self-hatred. He argues that these feelings are intensified during the period that black youth are in more contact with the white world. Pettigrew further buttresses his argument of black self-hatred theory by using studies based on questionable projective psychological tests. According to Pettigrew (1964), "These Negro youth typically told stories in which the hero, presumably themselves, is hated reprimanded, restricted or injured." (p. 12) White youth of the same age gave more positive responses to the projective. Another perspective on these findings in light of Weaver's study (1978) is that black youth may have been rejecting the "white hero" in the stories because of the differences in race and, presumably, the hatred, hostility and injury were representative of real feelings (anti-whiteness) the youth had toward white people rather than anything that has to do with self-concept.

In addition, Pettigrew believes that the residual effects of slavery cause many present "shortcomings" of the black family. The main shortcoming he asserts is the matrifocal or, mother-centered black family that unquestionably creates personality disorders in black children. The chief personality problems that develop are delay of gratification (Freud's pleasure principle) and confused sexual identity. Black males, in particular, attempt to correct their problems with masculinity through over-compensation, i.e., substituting toughness for masculinity or by joining a gang.

Pettigrew bases his assumptions concerning the lack of masculine identity in males on results of the MMPI. He claims that this test, more so than any other, shows that black males often make "feminine choices."

g) The Myth of the War Between Black Men and Black Women

The newest destructive racial myth concerns a "war" between black men and black women. Although its origins are difficult to establish, what is quite evident is that this myth is evolving into fact and many blacks are now validating it. We need not go into detail describing the principle of the self-fulfilling prophecy, but let us paraphrase the words of Woodson presented in one of the previous chapters: "Lead a man or woman to believe certain fallacies and you can control his thinking."

Ebony magazine (July 1979) presented the issue as "The War Between the Sexes: Is It Manufactured or Real?" Is it merely food for the media because it will sell? Have black people swallowed it "hook, line and sinker" without stopping to analyze its accuracy?

Two opposing camps have emerged. On one side are the opponents who assert that the issue is a "red herring." On the other side are the proponents who assert that the war is real. The participants on both sides incidentally are black men and black women arguing about the existence or non-existence of a war between the sexes. Let us first examine these arguments, and then provide a critique of their principal points.

Dr. Frances Welsing (1979), a noted black psychiatrist, is an opponent of the war myth. Unquestionably, there are problems between the sexes, but not a war. Welsing states that the so-called war is manufactured in the same manner that other myths and pseudo-events have been created. She adds that the man-woman conflict is only symptomatic of a deeper problem: "We have fighting that goes on between black males and black females that is caused by racism..."(p. 34)

Another opponent of the war myth is Dr. Nathan Hare, a black psychologist who believes that there is a conflict that has been escalated into a war. The real problem, according to Hare, is an economic problem with black males being the loser. Dr. Alvin Pouissant (1979) shares the same position as Hare but adds that the media contributes to the false images of the black male.

Michelle Wallace (1978) fanned the flames of the war myth in her highly controversial book, **Black Macho and the Myth of the Super Wo**man. Wallace analyzes the myth from a feminist perspective:

> I am saying, among other things, that for perhaps the last fifty years, there has been a growing distrust, even hatred, between black men and black women. (p. 13)

She further criticizes black men, charging that their male macho image made them insensitive to the needs of black women and children.

Another proponent of the black male-female war myth is Ntozake Shange, who wrote the hit play "For Colored Girls Who Have Considered Suicide When the Rainbow Is Enuf." This play is a direct attack on black males. The most shocking and disturbing part comes when Willie Beau misuses Crystal, his girlfriend. He gets her pregnant twice, beats her and then, to top it all, drops their two children to their deaths from the 5th floor apartment to the pavement below. The book is loaded with negative behavior of black men. Ms. Shange could have presented more balance to her book. Black men are not all Willie Beau's!

Dr. Robert Tucker of Yale University and his wife Dr. Leota Tucker developed a "Black Love" workshop aimed at closing the gap between the sexes. The Tuckers feel that black women must deal with a double jeopardy: rejection from white and black men. In addition, the Tuckers feel that black men are deserting black women for white women. Resentment between the sexes increases because black men are not taking care of black women who are not soft and seductive the way white women allegedly are.

The origins of the war-between-the-sexes-myth began, perhaps, with the charge by whites that black women are castrating black men. Without completely analyzing the source and validity of the myth, some black men may have reacted with a strong, defensively bitter response directed toward the black woman. Obviously, the next step was for black women to retaliate. Thus, the alleged war between the sexes was underway. The fact that a conflict led to this situation points out why racist charges are made in the first place. In transactional analysis, an interesting version of this game is called "Let's You and Her Fight." Many black men could see through this ploy and recognized it as such.

My concern is with an analysis of this particular myth because it could erupt to destroy the natural love between black people. First of all, I believe that the war myth is another one of those pseudo-events created to divide and conquer. Frantz Fanon put it aptly: "When the oppressed become too weak to fight the oppressor, they begin to fight among themselves." Such appears to be the case where black men and black women, caught in the stranglehold of racism and oppression, began to fight each other. What we do not understand is how oppression affects the mind.

h) The Myth of the Superior Sexual Stud

One of the best-known stereotypes of black men in our society is the prowess of the black male phallus. This stereotype has been converted to a myth about the size of the white man's penis in comparison to the size of the black male's penis. The black male is perceived as the super sexual Stud with a very large penis, or a walking phallic symbol,

Psychologist Phillip Rushton measured not only head and brain size of whites and blacks, but also, breasts, buttocks and genitals. He reported that blacks have larger penises than whites but smaller brains. Rushton believes that whites have larger crania than blacks and therefore are more intelligent. Conversely, blacks have smaller brains but larger penises and are therefore sexually superior to whites. Rushton's school, The University of Western Ontario, reprimanded him for soliciting people in a local shopping mall by asking them how large were their penises and how far could they ejaculate.

On the contrary, Dr. Francis Cress Welsing (1991) believes that the real issue is not black's large genitals, but instead the real issue is fear of black male passing of his dominant gene and the subsequent annihilation of the white race. The phallus is not only a source of generative power, but in a deeper sense, a source of genetic power. Is this the real reason that the white race feels threatened of the black male? Blacks possess the dominant gene and whites the recessive gene. Therefore, whites fear the genetic power of black genes. Black males possess the greater potential to annihilate the white race. Acts of the fear and curiosity were vividly displayed when the genitals of black males were attacked and taken away by whites during the age of lynching.

According to Calvin Hernton (1965) in his book **Sex and Racism:**

> The white man, especially the southerner, is overtly obsessed by the idea of the Negro desiring sexual relations with whites.... The race problem is inextricably connected with sex...The sexualization of the race problem is a reality, and we are going to have to deal with it even though most of are, if not unwilling, definitely unprepared." (Pp. 3-4)

i)   The Myth of the Superior Black Athlete

Blacks domination in certain sports leads many people to assume or to speculate that blacks are genetically superior to whites in certain athletics. Amongst the sports in which blacks dominate are basketball, baseball, boxing, sprinting, jumping and long distance events. Many coaches, scientists, as well as black athletes themselves believe that blacks have a natural ability to excel in sports over whites. There is simply no scientific proof that has been found to support this claim.

Certain differences between the muscular structures of blacks and whites do indeed exist. In general blacks are found to have a more dense, compact skeletal frame with less fat on the extremities. Blacks are also found to have more fast-twitch muscle fibers than whites, suggesting that blacks will excel at sports in which explosive bursts of energy are used such as in power sports, sprinting and boxing. Whites are found to have more slow-twitch muscle fibers than blacks, suggesting whites will succeed in the long distance or endurance events such as marathon races. However, recent marathon victories by Kenyan men and women show different results. Kenyan men have won 14 of the last 16 Boston Marathons. Kenyan women have won three in a row and six of seven Boston Marathons. These findings raise questions regarding the fast-twitch and slow-twitch muscle theories.

Jimmy "The Greek" Snyder perpetuated the myth of black athlete superiority by stating that blacks were bred for superior physical qualities. These are not only ludicrous but racist statements as well. One serious consequence of the black superiority myth is that many coaches as well as the general population assume that since blacks are genetically superior, they lacked the intellect to think strategically and manage a team. Al Campanis, a former General Manager of the LA Dodgers, claimed that blacks are not fit or capable of fulfilling a managing position because of their weak intellectual capacities. The truth of the matter is that any athlete who has become successful has used both hard work and intelligence to get as far as he/she has.

j) The Myth of the Lazy Negro

The lazy Negro is perhaps the most insulting, dehumanizing and degrading of all anti-black caricatures. In this myth, blacks are portrayed as a lazy, easily frightened, chronically idle, inarticulate buffoon. These portraits characterize the lazy Negro as the "coon" and Stepin' Fetchit. The coon acted childish, but was an adult. The coon who often worked as a servant was not happy with his status. He was simply too lazy or too cynical to attempt to change his lowly status. The coon character was created during American slavery. Slave masters and overseers often described slaves as "slow, lazy and trifling." As we know many slaves worked from sun up to sun down. Clearly, that amount of labor is not the sign of a lazy person. However, the myths were created as a method of controlling blacks.

Stepin' Fetchit allegedly was the greatest coon of all time. Born Theodore Monroe Perry in Key West, Florida, he ran away from home at age 14 and toured the South with minstrel shows, carnivals and later vaudeville as a singer, dancer and comic. Fechit's character appearance was always a head scratching, tall and lanky buffoon with a shaven head. He spoke with a whiny, slow talking broken speech. He always appeared wearing clothes too large for him. When he grinned it was very wide teeth, very white eyes bulging and very large feet. Fetchit had become a living symbol of what millions of white Americans thought or hoped black people were really like: slow witted, slow moving, lazy, shiftless and avoidance of hard work. For African Americans Fetchit was/is an embarrassment to the race.

These myths have been reviewed in detail, first to demonstrate the origin, and secondly to show how they influence belief systems and consequently, the image of black people. .

Myths are, also, powerful image-makers. They create certain images which influence and shape perceptions of self and others. Interestingly, the term "image" is derived from the Latin "imago" and is related to the Latin term "imatari" which means to imitate. Webster's New Collegiate Dictionary defines image as an artificial imitation of representation of the form of a person or thing. Racial myths (images) in particular, possess the following characteristics:

1) They are planned and created by man for a specific purpose or to give a specific purpose. The genetic deficiency myth was no accident. Its purpose was to bolster a belief system: white supremacy.

2) They are designed to shape, fit into or reinforce a particular belief system. Myths serve no purpose if no one believes them.

3) They must create a controversy or "positions" so as to remain visible and alive. Such is the case of the IQ myth of black intellectual deficiency.

Fact or fantasy, the image becomes the "real thing." For the very purpose of myths and images is to overshadow reality. Racial myths have been quite effective in not only overshadowing reality but distorting it as well.

Lerone Bennett, in **Challenge of Blackness**, discusses the dangers of negative images:

> ...men act out their image. They respond not to the situation, but to the situation transformed by the images they carry in their minds. In short, they respond to the image-situation, to the ideas they have of themselves in the situation...the image sees... the image feels...the image acts...and if you want to change a situation, you have to change the image men have of themselves and the situation.

3) Racial Stereotypes

a) What is a Stereotype?

Walter Lippman (1922) in his book **Public Opinion** introduced and defined a stereotype as an oversimplified picture of the world, one that satisfies a need to see the world as more understandable and manageable. Stereotypes provide the function of being able to have ready-made words and terms to easily classify people and place them in compartments quickly. Stereotypes create thinking in terms of "allness" rather than "uniqueness." They are "broad brush" judgments that lead to false perceptions and conclusions. A stereotype functions to preserve one's belief system.

Racists rely on stereotypes to make easy and quick overgeneralizations about racial groups without adequately checking their perceptions with reality. For example, blacks described as lazy, dangerous and welfare seekers may be true of a limited few blacks, but certainly not all or the majority of blacks. It is also true that some whites are racists, but not all whites are racists. It is a terrible mistake to generalize any form of behavior or characteristics to all members of any racial group. Further, it is inappropriate to judge the majority of group members by the actions of a few members of a group.

b)   How Stereotypes Work

Stereotypes serve as overgeneralizations about a group of people. Stereotypical views are used to justify one's behavior towards members of that group, especially when one's behavior may have negative impacts. When a stereotype influences a person's perception there is a tendency to exaggerate the differences between "them" and "us." As a consequence, stereotypes lead to alienation or polarization of racial groups.

Through the mechanism of generalization, stereotypes interfere with the proper perception of individual cases. That is, the perceiver does not see the characteristics of the individual member, but instead the pre-conceived stereotypical nature of the group of which the individual is a member.

The following is an example of how a generalization develops:

Carol was the only black student in my first grade class and one of the few blacks in the school. She asked to see my prized possession, a tiny, copper penny coin ring. She asked if she could wear it during recess. I never saw the ring again. We had never been close friends. As a result of this incident, we grew even farther apart. Carol had been my first memorable black encounter resulting in a generalized hostile attitude I carried over to all blacks (generalization). The ring incident clouded my young mind by forming a bully image of blacks. After trying to recover the ring, I was scared away. I simply adopted an avoidance attitude of all blacks, which was easily maintained in my white environment.

Stereotypes block out relevant information. They serve as a filter that allows only a limited view of the qualities of a people within a stereotyped category. The following list contains a summary of over-generalizations (stereotypes) given by whites on The Williams Racial Survey Questionnaire:

1) Black fathers don't seem to care about their children.
2) Black men have children out of wedlock.
3) Black schools are bad.
4) Blacks have no desire to succeed.
5) Black families tend to be large and unstable.
6) Blacks have little or no culture.
7) Blacks are harder to educate than whites.
8) Blacks are inferior to whites (i.e. ignorant).
9) Blacks are lazy.
10) Blacks are dangerous.
11) Blacks steal.
12) Blacks are happy-go –lucky.
13) Blacks are athletically superior to whites.
14) Blacks are sexually superior to whites.
15) Blacks are pleasure loving.
16) Blacks are religious.
17) Blacks are musical.
18) Blacks are criminals.

It should be noted that the statements listed above are false. They are over-generalizations. An over-generalization usually implies that a statement may be partially true and partially false. A statement, however, cannot be partially true and partially false. It is either true or it is false. As such, an over-generalization is false. It is a loose cannon that may have many hits, but in the wrong places.

The racists' negative conception and evaluation of black people are based on subjective rather than objective data. In addition, they are likely to integrate in their beliefs negative information that confirms or reinforces their hypothesis about the inferiority of black people. Racists do not, therefore, subject their belief system to critical tests at appropriate times. The energy for the racists' élan vital (life force) is derived from their being anti-black and pro-white.

Below is a summary of the characteristics of stereotypes:

1) Stereotyping is a common part of racist thinking.

2) Stereotyping represents a shorthand method by which information about individuals is processed.

3) When racists meet African-Americans they tend to focus primarily on certain "salient attributes" (e.g., skin color) and ignore other characteristics. Generalizations are then made about African-Americans on the basis of the salient attributes.

4) Stereotyping leads the racists to make false generalizations about individuals because they believe that the group to which they generalize is a homogeneous rather than a heterogeneous group.

5) Stereotypes are resistant to change. Even if racists meet people who do not fit the stereotype they do not change their opinion. They ignore, misperceive or forget counter-examples.

6) Racial, ethnic and religious groups are made salient in American society.

Thus, our challenge is to change the myths of a negative black image and replace them with truths. Patrica Raybon (1989 put the true situation succinctly when she stated:

> I want America to know us—all of us—for who we really are. To see us in all of our complexity, our subtleness, our artfulness, our enterprise, our specialness, our loveliness, our American-ness. That is the real portrait of Black-America—that we're strong people, surviving people and capable people. That may be the best-kept secret in America. (Newsweek, October 2, 1989, p. 11.)

CHAPTER XI
INDIVIDUAL RACISM

1) Introduction

Carmichael and Hamilton (1967) in their book ***Black Power: The Politics of Black Liberation*** defined two forms of racism: individual and institutional as follows:

> Racism is both overt and covert. It takes two closely related forms: Individual whites acting against individual blacks, and acts by the total white community against the black community. We call this individual racism. The first consists of overt acts by individuals, which cause death, injury or the violent destruction of property. Television cameras can record this type and it can frequently be observed in the process of commission. The second type is less overt, far subtler and less identifiable in terms of specific individuals committing the acts; but it is not less destructive of human life. The second type originates in the operation of established and respected forces in the society and thus receives far less public condemnation than the first type.
>
> When white terrorists bomb a black church and kill five black children, the act is of individual racism...But when in that same city-Birmingham, Alabama-five hundred black babies die each year because of the lack of proper food, shelter and medical facilities, and thousands more are destroyed because of conditions

of poverty and discrimination in the black community, the act is a function of institutional racism. (p.4)

2) White Racism Defined

This chapter focuses on significant cases of individual racism to illustrate the irrationality of white racism. Regardless of whether it is called traditional or modern racism, the generic name is white racism or white supremacy. "A rose is still a rose by any other name." Feagin, Vera & Batur's (2001) book **White Racism: basic issues** give the following definition of white racism.

According to these writers:

> White racism can be viewed as the socially organized set of attitudes, ideas and practices that deny African-Americans and other people of color the privileges, dignity, opportunities, freedoms and rewards that this nation offers White-Americans. (p. 17)

3) Traditional forms of Individual Racism

a) Verbal Hostility

Individual racism consists of overt hostile acts (verbal and physical) that may cause psychological and/or physical damage to individuals of a different race. Several examples will illustrate:

Michael Richards, the actor, was performing at a Hollywood Comedy House when he lashed out at hecklers with a string of racist obscenities and racial epithets. Richards ranted: "Throw his a—out. He's a Nigger. He's a Nigger. He's a Nigger." Richards says he does not consider himself a racist. (CNN NEWS, November 18, 2006)

Four New York police officers fired 50 shots at Sean Bell, a 23-year old Black man on November 23, 2006. Bell was exiting a club the night before what should have been the happiest day of his life, his wedding day. One of the officers "thought" one of the men had a weapon. Bell was unarmed. He had no arrest record. The police chief said the 50 shots were not excessive force.

In Tempe, Arizona (December 2, 2006) a white police office required two black men to perform a rap in order to avoid getting a littering ticket.. Sergeant Chuck Schoville told the two men, "You know why you say I'm right? Because I got a gun and badge. I'm always right. That's the way it works, right?

In the late 90s, Fuzzy Zoeller's made remarks about Tiger Woods. Mr. Woods' dramatic 1997 Masters victory was still fresh when Zoeller called the new champ a "little boy" (Tiger Woods was 21 years old). Mr. Zoeller wondered aloud if Tiger would want "collard greens and fried chicken" at the 1998 Master's dinner. The media quickly criticized Mr. Zoeller's remarks. One Editorial (Fuzzy Thinking, 1997) stated: "Mr. Zoeller's remarks were definitely not funny and the swift reaction against him should make him tone down the jokes, if not his own prejudices." (P B6)

Cesar (1997) reports Zoeller later apologized for his racially insensitive remarks:

> Following the Masters, I said something I realize I should not have said and that I deeply regret saying. I've apologized publicly for those comments. My comments were not intended to be racially derogatory...and I apologize for the fact they were misconstrued in that fashion. Everyone who knows me knows I'm a jokester, but that is no excuse for what I said. Jokes aren't funny when they hurt people. I realize that what I said hurt many people and I apologize to anyone who was offended. (p. 2)

As a consequence, two things happened to Zoeller: 1) K-Mart ended its long sponsorship of Zoeller because of his remarks and 2) Zoeller pulled out of the Greensboro Open Golf Tournament where he had played for 21 consecutive years.

Cesar (1997) further reports that Davis Love, a pro golfer stated in a somewhat condescending fashion, "I wouldn't expect Tiger to know how to handle this situation, but I would expect some people that are working with him to know how to handle it." (p.2c) How many times have we heard similar remarks about African-Americans?

Let us examine Tiger's level of maturity and see how he handled these racist comments. Mr. Woods calmly stated:

> At first, I was shocked to hear that Fuzzy Zoeller made these unfortunate remarks.... His attempt at humor was out-of - bounds and I was disappointed by it. But having played golf with Fuzzy, I know he is a jokester; and I have concluded that no personal animosity toward me was intended. ...I respect Fuzzy as a golfer and as a person and for the many good things he has done for others throughout his career.... I know he feels badly about the remarks. We all make mistakes and it is time to move on. I accept Fuzzy's apology and hope everyone will now put this behind us. (Woods to Zoeller, 1997, p. 3 d.)

In my opinion, Mr. Wood's statement was mature and very professional. He couldn't have said it better. I don't think his "handlers" prepared that statement for him. I listened to Tiger on the Oprah Winery Show soon after his 1997 Master's victory where he showed the same level of spontaneous maturity and professionalism the above statement reflects. What is reflected in Davis Love's statements are the same kind of stereotypical racist remarks by whites, i.e. implying "That blacks do not have the intelligence to handle certain situations." Tiger Woods and Fuzzy Zoeller met face-to- face in a scheduled luncheon and both agreed to get on with the business of playing golf. Tiger later said, "Fuzzy and I had a nice lunch and a nice conversation." ("Nice Lunch," 1997, P. 8) To further demonstrate that Tiger had settled with Zoeller, the next year they were paired in a tournament together. Both felt that it was no big deal—just two professional golfers playing together.

Tiger stated that he receives many death threats. According to Woods (Tiger Woods…1997):

Unfortunately, I've had my share of threats since I was 16…That's just the way of life when you're playing a sport that traditionally hasn't been a minority sport. (P. 54)

Woods has special security guards at every golf event.

However, Tiger Woods is not alone in experiencing racial epithets hurled against him. The super tennis stars, Venus and Serena Williams were victims of racial slurs during a tennis match in Indian Wells, California. Richard Williams, father of the two sisters, reported that people kept calling him the "N-word" when he and Venus were walking down the stairs to their seats. ("Williams Sisters Victims,", 2001). The predominately white crowd booed during Serena's final match because they expected to see a match between Serena and her sister, Venus, but Venus had to pull out because of knee tendonitis.

A former athlete, Paul Hornung, a 1956 Heisman trophy winner and an alumnus of Notre Dame suggested, in a radio interview, Notre Dame should lower academic standards in order to get black athletes. Hornung said,

"We can't stay as strict as we are, as far as the academic structure is concerned, because we've got to get the black athletes…We must get the black athlete if we're going to compete." (Notre Dame Alum Hornung regrets, 2004, pp. 50-51)

Later Hornung regretted he made such insensitive and insulting remarks.

b) Physical Injury- Lynching

Violent manifestations of physical injury to blacks are not new. Franklin (1974) reports:

In the last sixteen years of the nineteenth century there had been more than 2500 lynchings, the great majority of which were of Negroes, with Mississippi, Alabama, Georgia, and Louisiana leading the nation…In the very first year of the new century [twentieth century] there had been more than 100 Negroes lynched, and before the outbreak of World War 1 the number had soared to more than 1, 100. Pp. 322-323

c)   Racial Hate Crimes 1986-2004

Racial hate crimes have reached "epidemic proportions" in this country according to a study released by the National Council of Churches. (Study Reveals Hate Crime Epidemic, 1988) Numerous forms of racism are seen in the hate crimes perpetrated on blacks. FBI crime statistics show that hate crimes have increased in the past few years. More than one-half of the 7, 755 hate crimes committed in 1998 were motivated by racial prejudice. Of those crimes committed, 3, 573 (53 percent) were committed against blacks. Whites committed 2, 084 or 58 percent of the hate crimes against blacks. ("FBI Study" 2001,)

The following is a chronology of racial hate crimes during the periods 1986-2004:

a)   Howard Beach, New York December 1986

Howard Beach, New York is a white middle-class community in an isolated corner of Queens, N.Y. Michael Griffith, a twenty-six-year-old African-American, was stranded at a New York Pizzeria in Howard Beach with two black friends. Apparently their car had broken down and they pushed it to the nearest lot in order to remove it from the busy intersection where it became inoperable. It was dark and they were in Howard Beach, a neighborhood that is ninety-eight percent white. On this particular night a group of white youths returning from a party in the neighborhood spotted the three black youths and returned to the party to grab some friends and a few baseball bats. This group turned out to be a racially motivated violent mob headed down to the closed pizzeria. They proceeded to attack the three blacks.

The blacks, outnumbered four to one, were beaten and chased by the mob of 12. The whites relentlessly chased Michael Griffith until he met his death by running onto the Freeway. A car driven by a man believed not to be related to the mob hit Griffith. On that fatally tragic night, Howard Beach was destined to be the focal point of a nation, one that was enraged at the resurgence of racism in America. When the charge of murder brought against the twelve white youths resulted in only three counts of manslaughter, hundreds of blacks held demonstrations. The Howard Beach incident and many other similar racial incidents that followed indicate that racism is on the increase. (Johnson, et al. 1987)

b)   Miami, Florida 1989:

The fatal shooting of an unarmed black motorcycle motorist by a white police officer, William E. Lozano, erupted into three days of rioting in Miami, Florida. (Schmalz, 1989) Clement A. Lloyd, a 23-year-old black motorcyclist, was being chased by another police officer when Officer Lozano shot and killed him. A passenger on the back of the cycle, Alan Blanchard age 24, died of injuries sustained when the motorcycle crashed.

c). Brooklyn, New York 1989

The Bensonhurst neighborhood is an Italian area in Brooklyn where a young black man was shot to death. This was a racially motivated crime. Yusef Hawkins planned to meet with a man selling a used car. Some white perpetrators were on the lookout with weapons for a group of blacks who had been invited to a local party. They spotted Yusef Hawkins and killed him.

d)   Denver, Colorado 1990

Denver received immense public attention by hosting the Oklahoma City bombing trial. But after several weeks of racial violence involving racist skinheads, Denver attempted to curb the violence. A skinhead who used an officer's gun to commit suicide shot to death first, in a series of racist acts, a police officer, after a high-speed chase. A week later, an African immigrant, who was saving money to bring his family to this country, was waiting for a downtown bus when he was taunted and then shot and killed by two young white supremacists. When a white mother intervened and tried to help, she was shot and paralyzed from the waist down. In a cold-blooded, heartless interview with local TV stations, the suspect smiled and said: "I'd had my gun in my waist...and I'd seen this black guy at the bus stop and I kind of thought how easy it would be for me to take him out right there."

e)   Chicago, Illinois March 1997

Then, in Bridgeport (Chicago) a racially motivated case involved a 13-year-old African-American boy who was savagely beaten and left for dead by at least three white teenagers. The perpetrators even bragged about taking care of a black boy who had wandered into their neighborhood. They smashed the boy's head against a wall and left him for dead in an alley and he was in a coma for nearly a week. Though he is making progress and is able to walk and talk, he still remains brain damaged and his recovery will take months of rehabilitation. He may never fully recover from the attack. President Bill Clinton asked Americans to pray for the youth. The President said, this was a "Savage and senseless assault driven by nothing but hate."

Two young white men Victor Jasas, 18, and Michael Kwizinski, 21, were given minimum sentences for their actions in beating the black boy. They were given two years probation for aggravated assault and required to serve 300 hours of community service. A third man, Frank Caruso, was convicted earlier of aggravated battery and a hate crime. He was sentenced to eight years in prison.

A *USA Today* poll showed whites fear black neighborhoods, but believe blacks are largely safe in white neighborhoods. However, given the Howard Beach incident and now the Bridgeport (Chicago) beating, are blacks really safe in white communities?

f) Elk Creek, Virginia August 1997

One of the most heinous racial crimes involved two white men, Louis Ceparano and Emmett Cressel, Jr., who invited a black man, Garnett Johnson to a party. Later in the evening the two men dragged Mr. Johnson into the yard, doused him with gasoline, set him on fire and then beheaded him. They later bragged about the horrible murder. Residents of the city insisted that such a crime could not happen among their own and only an outsider could commit such a terrible crime. (Levinson, 1997)

g) Hampton, Virginia, February 23, 1998

A white man in Hampton, Virginia was sentenced to three years in prison after pleading guilty to a felony account of burning a cross outside the home of a black family on the day they moved in to his neighborhood.

h) New Jersey March 1998

Two white men attacked a black woman in the stairwell of her apartment. They rubbed her face in feces, cut her hair and marked an "x" on her forehead. Then they said: "We don't want any 'Niggers' in our town."

i) Jasper, Texas June 1998

Then there is the most ghastly and grisly racial crime within the last thirty or forty years: the dragging and murder of James Byrd a forty-nine year old disabled black man who was a father of three. (Shlachter, 1998) To fully grasp the sickening horror of this tragic event, one would have to drive the full length of the road where Byrd was dragged until he died. It happened one night when Byrd was hitchhiking. He was picked up (four blocks from his home at 2:30 a.m.) by three white men in a Ford Pickup truck. Apparently he was drunk and was on his way home from his niece's bridal shower. Three white men: Shawn Berry, 23, Lawrence Brewer, 31, and John King, 23, offered Byrd a lift. (Pressley, 1998) Byrd accepted the ride, which was his fatal mistake. Police say that Byrd was savagely beaten before he was dragged. Strung out over three miles were pink, spray-painted circles where parts of Byrd's body were strewn along the road: head, arms, legs, dentures, torsos, etc.

According to the sheriff's report one of the men looked out the truck's back window and remarked: "That f----r's bouncing all over the place." Byrd's headless torso was cut loose and left in front of a black cemetery. Police say that each of the suspects was covered with tattoos indicating white supremacists beliefs and affiliations.

Two white supremacists, Lawrence Brewer and John William King, have been sentenced to die by lethal injection for the dragging and death of James Byrd. A third white supremacist, Shawn Allen Berry, received a life-in- prison term.

j)   York, Nebraska September, 1998

In York, Nebraska the Associated Press reported a white mob attacked the home of a white woman who was dating a black man. While carrying a confederate flag, the mob shouted racial slurs, broke car windows and attacked the home of the woman.

k)   St. Louis Missouri May 2000

A black Army Captain, Garick Benson, was charged with raping a white woman. (Lhotka, 2000) He spent two days in jail and two weeks as a suspect before prosecutors dismissed charges of rape, sodomy and burglary. Thanks to modern DNA test that cleared Benson of any wrongdoing. Captain Benson felt he was arrested because he was black. Benson has an exemplary background. He joined the Army as a lieutenant in 1989 after graduating from the Citadel Military College in South Carolina. He served in Germany and served combat in the Desert Storm.

l)   May, 2000-St. Louis Missouri

Three black youth ages 15, 16 and 19 were injured in what authorities believe was a racially motivated fight. The teens were assaulted outside a home where a party was ongoing. They were trying to pick up a friend when a white man confronted them, yelled racial slurs and punched one of them in the face. As they ran down the street, others from the party chased them, punched and kicked them and yelled racial slurs. A white guest at the party, Andrew Amelung, intervened and drove the three black youth safely from the scene. Scott Edward Schroeder, age 21, with a history of arrests for assaults and other offenses, pleaded guilty in the attack on the three black teenagers. The prosecutor, however concluded that this was not a hate crime. ("Police Search, 2000;" "Beating of three teens", 2000; Rowden, 2000a; Rowden 2000b)

m) June 2000   Kokomo. Mississippi

The hanging death of Raynard Johnson, a black honor student, in Kokomo, Mississippi raised suspicions of a racial lynching (Hanging in Mississippi, 2000). His father found Johnson's body hanging by a belt in front of their home. Johnson was friendly with two white girls. Medical examiners ruled the death suicide but there are many unanswered questions. The boy had just purchased his first computer the day before his death. He was also looking forward to a family picnic the day before his death.

n) July 2000 Grant Town, West Virginia

Two seventeen-year-old white boys, David Parker and Jared Wilson, savagely beat and kicked a 26-year-old black man J.R. Warren to death in a vacant house. (Reeves, 2000) They then dumped his battered body into the road and drove over it several times to make the crime look like a hit-and-run. Residents of the community are convinced that Mr. Warren was murdered because he was black, or gay or both.

o) September, 2000 Troy, Illinois

A white man from Troy, Illinois was charged with a hate crime after he allegedly tried to run down two back women with his pickup truck. (Franklin, 2000) The two women were walking home around midnight when Jason T. Oliver drove up on the curb and almost struck one of the women.

p) Springfield, Missouri 2004

Five white men of Springfield, Missouri were charged with attacking two black men in a Denny's restaurant. Two white women accompanied the two black men. The white men, wearing T-shirts touting white supremacy, stabbed one of the black men with a knife and threatened the other black man. ("Five White Men Face Charges" Jet, 2004)

Further incidents of racial hate crimes are reported frequently in local daily newspapers. A 25-year-old black man is in serious condition after he was assaulted by a group of white men and dragged for a mile behind a car in Mississippi. Authorities say the assailants shoved an object into the man's rectum and then dragged him behind a car on a rural road (Man dragged, 2002). As reported earlier, three white men in Jasper, Texas dragged James Byrd to his death on June 6, 1998. One year later forty-two-year-old Ray foster, a black man, on June 6, 1999 was kidnapped, assaulted and dragged by a vehicle near

Hernando, Mississippi.   Foster suffered irreversible brain damage, partial paralysis and was rendered permanently disabled. A white man, George Hunsucker, was tried and convicted, but later fled Alabama.

In Belleville, Illinois three white teenagers allegedly dragged a black teenager (Goodrich, 1998). The three white men hurled racial epithets at the black teenager. The attorney for the white males said that one thing was clear; this was not a hate crime. Then if it was not a hate crime, what was it? Strangely, all four of these draggings occurred during the month of June.

Hate crimes are the most violent kinds of individual racism. Are we in a period where whites feel that it is OK to physically harm African-Americans? These crimes bring back memories of horrific crimes of earlier periods: fourteen- year-old Emmett Till who was lynched and thrown into a Mississippi river in 1955 with a cotton-gin fan tied around his neck; One Sunday morning in September, 1963 in a Birmingham Baptist church, four little black girls entered the basement where a bomb had been planted. The lives of Cynthia Webster, age 14, Annie Mae Collins, age 14, Carol Robinson, age 14 and Denise McNair age 11 were snuffed out. These were acts of racial hatred and individual racism. Over thirty years later, two former klansmen were arrested and charged with the 1963 Birmingham, Alabama church bombing that killed the four girls. A third man was convicted in 1977 and died in prison. A fourth suspect, never charged, is also dead.

4) Police Brutality Against Blacks

McCall (1994) asserts that individual racism is so prevalent in this country that it makes him want to holler! Pick up a newspaper from any section of the country on any given day and one will most likely find that an African-American was killed or brutally beaten by a white police officer. Blacks have been, and continue to be, the victims of excessive police force. Frequently, the police officer is white and the victim is black. But even if the police are caught on tape beating black suspects, often they are not prosecuted. A review of 19 recent cases involving such tapes shows that the police officers captured on film often face no criminal charges. (Lewin 2000) Prosecutors, defense lawyers and other legal experts say bystanders' videotapes rarely capture a complete picture of an incident. They say the video often misses the behavior that provoked the attack, or it captures only the last few seconds of a violent chase or confrontation.

The following examples over the past few years will illustrate only the tip of an iceberg of police brutality. Many incidents of police brutality go unreported and undetected. The Congressional Black Caucus (CBC) launched an investigation into police brutality, racial profiling and racism in five U.S. cities: New York, Chicago, Atlanta, Los Angeles and Houston:

a) Los Angeles, California March 1991

George Holliday, a white store manager, video taped the savage beating of Rodney King by Los Angeles policemen. The videotape shows fifty-six blows delivered in eighty-one seconds while King was lying on the ground. Doctors reported King suffered extensive body damage, multiple lacerations, nine skull fractures, a shattered eye socket, a broken leg, a concussion, injuries to both knees and facial damage. (Mydans, S. 1991) Eleven policemen stood by and watched while the brutal beating took place. Racial tension increased during and following the Rodney King's beating by LA cops. An all-white jury in Simi Valley, California acquitted the four officers charged with beating Rodney King. In Los Angeles, the verdict set off riots that took more than 50 lives and resulted in one billion dollars in property damage. Two years later, two of the officers were convicted in a federal court of violated King's civil rights. King was eventually awarded $3.8 million in damages for his injuries.

b) Detroit, Michigan 1992

Malice green was killed by two white police officers that kicked and punched him after he refused to obey their orders. Green was struck on the head about 14 times with a heavy flashlight, a case of excessive force. Green suffered a seizure and died on the way to the hospital. A white policeman was sentenced 7 to 15 years in prison for the death of Malice Green. ("White Ex-Cop" 2000)

c) Prince Georges County, Maryland 1993

A twenty-four-year-old black man, Archie Elliott, was shot and killed by two police officers. He was shot fourteen times while his hands were handcuffed behind his back as he sat in the front seat of a police cruiser.

d) Pittsburgh, Pennsylvania. 1995

Following a traffic stop, white Pittsburgh police, killed Johnny Gammage, a cousin of Pittsburgh Steelers defensive lineman Ray Seal. Gammage was beaten and stomped to death by five policemen. Police officers claimed Gammage, who was unarmed and had no police record, was driving suspiciously. None of the police officers was indicted, but all were later fired.

e) St. Petersburg, Florida 1996

A white policeman shot and killed a black teen. The shooting of Tyron Lewis by Officer James Knight set off a night of rioting in St. Petersburg's black neighborhood, which resulted in at least two-dozen fires and several injuries. Knight said he shot Lewis after Lewis tried to run him down with a car after a traffic stop. Knight was cleared of any criminal wrongdoing, but the police department suspended Knight for two months without pay after the shooting. Knight appealed his suspension to an arbitration panel, which ruled the sanctions were unjustified. It ordered that Knight be paid his back wages and recover the seniority he lost while suspended.

f) Brooklyn, New York 1996

As he sat in a car, Aswan "Keshawn" Watson, a 23-year-old black man was shot twenty-three times by two undercover policemen. The officers claimed he was in a stolen car and he reached for something. However, Watson was unarmed and eyewitnesses reported that Watson had his hands raised when the policemen approached him. (Village Voice, 1996)

g) New York City 1997

Kevin Cedeno, a sixteen year-old black youth, was shot and killed by a police officer who claimed that Cedeno lunged at him with a machete. The medical report indicated the Cedeno was shot in the back.

h) New York City 1997

Albert Louima, a Haitian immigrant, was brutalized by three white New York police officers. One officer held him down while another officer shoved a broken-off broom handle into his rectum and mouth in a Brooklyn police station house bathroom. Louima, whose hands were handcuffed behind his back, suffered severe internal injuries. One of the officers was sentenced to 30 years in prison. The judge said the 30-year-sentence was adequate to punish the cop for barbarous misuse of power. ("Ex-Cop Sentenced" 2000) Louima received a 9 million settlement from the New York Police Department. City residents criticized the amount of the settlement by saying it was not enough. (The Challenger, 2004)

I) Trenton New Jersey 1998

White New Jersey troopers shot three of four young black men after a traffic stop. They were handcuffed, forced to lie in a ditch and strip-searched. The troopers wounded three of the young men. One of the men was raising his hands in the air when one of the troopers opened fire on him. In addition, the remaining indictment alleges the troopers falsified records to hide the race of motorists they stopped, obviously to prevent charges of racial profiling.

A Trenton, NJ Judge threw out all the criminal charges against the two state troopers. The judge ruled that the overzealous prosecutors had set up a "minitrial" before the grand jury and they violated the troopers' constitutional rights. Official misconduct charges against the troopers still stand as well as pending civil suits. (Jet, May 17, 1999, 95, 24, p, 37)

The State of New Jersey later agreed to pay 12.9 million to the four men for the racial profiling incident.

j) Gainesville, Florida, February 2, 1998

University of Florida President, Dr. John Lombardi, referred to Dr. Adam Herbert, Jr., the new black Chancellor of the State of Florida University System, as an "Oreo" meaning black on the outside and white on the inside. Dr. Lombardi agreed to step down after causing a furor by using a racial slur. Dr. Herbert, Jr. is the first black Chancellor of Florida's 10 public universities.

k) Broward County, Florida 1998

A grand jury would not indict a Fort Lauderdale police officer of any wrongdoing in the beating of a schizophrenic man, John Clements, videotaped by two Polish tourists. The grand jury was unconvinced that it had enough information about what happened off cameras. Clements settled his civil suit for about $208, 000.

l) New York City   1999

Amadou Diallo was shot and killed by four New York policemen outside his Bronx, New York home. (Jet, Feb 22, 1999) Police fired 41 bullets at the unarmed Diallo, hitting him 19 times. The medical examiner reported several of the bullets hit Diallo as he was falling, or while he was on the ground. At least one of the bullets hit the bottom of his shoe. The doctor who performed the autopsy reported Diallo could not have been upright to sustain (the toe wound) unless someone was underneath the floor shooting upward. Critics say the trial of the four officers who killed Diallo was similar to the Rodney King trial of 1992 that was moved to Simi Valley. (Getlin, 1991) The family of Amadou Diallo agreed to a 3 million dollar settlement against the City of New York. (Family of Amadou Diallo, 2004)

m) Riverside, California 1998

In Riverside, California a black woman, Tyisha Shenee Miller was shot and killed by two white officers. Ms. Miller was lying unconscious in her car at a gas station with a handgun in her lap. Her car doors and windows were locked and after failing to rouse her, two white officers broke her windows and tried to remove the gun from her lap. They fired twenty-four rounds at Ms. Miller, hitting her twelve times when she awoke and reached for her gun. The officers made racist comments and rejoiced at the killing by "high fiving" each other in joy and glee.

The City of Riverside, California reached a settlement with Miller's family, said to be between three to five million dollars. Attorneys for the family said "racial animus" led the officers to fire the 24 shots that killed Tyisha Miller. (Pringle, 2003)

n) St. Louis 2000

The cold-blooded killing of two black men, Earl Murray and Ronald Beasley sparked an outrage among the black citizens of St. Louis. On a pretext of a "drug investigation," several police agencies surrounded the car of Murray and Beasley in broad daylight in a parking lot of a Jack-in-the Box fast food restaurant. When Murray and Beasley tried to pull away, the car spun and two police pumped 20 shots into the car killing the two unarmed men. Beasley was not even a suspect. (Kennedy, 2000)

o) Philadelphia, Pennsylvania 2000

Millions of television watchers witnessed disturbing images of Philadelphia police officers kicking and punching a black carjacking suspect over and over. A random survey showed a divided Philadelphia over the beating. White Philadelphia's appeared more sympathetic to police. In the Black community, the public sentiment ran against the police. (In Philadelphia, reactions, 2000)

p) Detroit, Michigan 2000

A white Detroit police officer shot and killed a black man who was deaf. (Detroit Police Officer, 2000) The man could neither hear nor speak. He was carrying a wooden-handled rake when he was shot in cold blood. The victim's mother stated she pleaded with the police not to shoot her son because he could not hear them. The police officer has been charged with manslaughter, but records show that police officers usually are not convicted for these homicides. Even police caught on videotapes are often not prosecuted. (Lewin, 2002) Prosecutors say often force is justified because the suspects resisted arrest. Even when the cases have made it to court, juries have acquitted police in controversial cases.

q) Cincinnati, Ohio 2001

In Cincinnati, April 2001, a white police officer shot and killed unarmed black 19-year-old Timothy Thomas. Thomas had 14 outstanding warrants, most of which were misdemeanors. Officer Stephen Roach was charged with negligent homicide but was acquitted of all charges. Three nights of rioting causing dozens of injuries and more than 800 arrests occurred following the shooting. Thomas was the fifth black man killed by Cincinnati since November 2000. In all, Cincinnati police officers have killed 15 black men since 1995. (White Cincinnati Officer acquitted. Jet, 10, 15, 2001 P. 46)

r) New Jersey 2002

A white officer who mistook her identity arrested Kindra Wright, a black woman. The trooper handcuffed the woman, lifted her by the hair and pushed her face into the ground. She received an $800. 000 settlement with the New Jersey Turnpike Authority. (Black female motorist, 2002)

s) Inglewood, California 2002

Has it happened again? It has been over10 years since the Rodney King beating. A white police officer of Inglewood, California was caught on videotape July 6, 2002 pummeling a handcuffed black teenager. A bystander taped Officer Jeremy Morse on slamming 16-year-old Donovan Jackson on the trunk of a squad car and punching him in the face. The officer has been indicted on assault charges. (Officer indicted, 2002. The defense attorneys argued the slam culminated a fierce and long struggle during which Donovan Jackson grabbed, kicked and punched the officers. This beating has drawn comparison to the Rodney King case. His attorney says Officer Jeremy Morse will plead innocence. Another officer Bjorn Darvish, Morse's partner was indicted for filing a false police report. Although the officer was charged with assaulting and slamming Jackson onto a car trunk and hitting him, a mistrial was declared in the case. (Marosi & Wride, 2003) Hutchinson (2003) states it takes more than nailing a cop with a videotape to get a conviction.

t) Columbus, Georgia 2004

In Columbus, Georgia, a local sheriff's special unit targeted four black men riding in an expensive SUV as possible drug suspects. These four men were dragged from their vehicle at gunpoint and forced to lie on the side of a major interstate like animals. One of the sheriffs made a decision to shoot Kenny Walker in front of the head twice with an assault rifle. The policeman said he made a "judgment call" because he couldn't see Kenny's right hand. Kenny Walker was a loving husband, devoted father and had never been in trouble with the law. When his records were searched, not even a speeding ticket was found. All four men were college graduates, as well as responsible citizens. (Lemon, 2004)

u) Alton, Illinois 2004

An African-American woman reported that the Alton, Illinois police kicked down her door and entered her house without a warrant and choked her 14-year-old son. The Alton police acknowledged they did enter without a warrant but said they were "legally justified" because they suspected that a boy was in the house who had stolen a car. The police said they had a right to enter the house without a warrant under the "Terry Stop case," a reference to a 1968 U.S, Supreme Court ruling (Hampel, 2004)

v) New York City 2004

A white New York Police Department housing cop shot and killed 19-year-old Timothy Stansbury on a rooftop. Timothy was going to his apartment to get a CD to be played with his friends and he had no police record. The police chief quickly responded to the tragedy by announcing the shooting was unjustified. The officer had encountered Stansbury when both arrived at the exit door at the same time. The cop had his gun drawn and when he opened the door, the gun fired and hit Stansbury who fell down four flights of stairs where he died. (Boyd, H. 2004)

w) Seattle, Washington 2004

Two 16-year -old boys turned them selves in to police for burning a cross in a black minister's yard. The minister said he wants to forgive the boys and offer them guidance. The cross burning occurred in Arlington, Washington, a town whose population is 90 percent white and about 2 percent black. (Pastor wants to help, 2004, p. A4)

x) St. Louis, Missouri 2004

A pair of St. Louis police officers fired 28 shots at a fleeing car following a traffic stop. A man, his wife and three children were in the car. The officers said they did not know children were in the car. Strangely, one of the officers had argued with the driver and ordered him out of the car. How could he not have known that children were not in the car? Only one of the shots hit anyone, the driver, in the car. The Chief of Police, Joe Mowka said the two police officers might have violated department procedures. The Chief immediately fired one officer who was on probation. (Bryan, B, 2004a, April 8). He said the shots were not justified and the second police officer was suspended and there is a pending investigation.

y) May 2005 California

California sheriffs shot at Winston Hayes, A black motorist, one hundred and twenty times (120). Was this shooting justified or was it racism? Reverend Al Sharpton said it was a reckless display of human life.

z) October 2005 New Orleans, Louisiana

Two officers of the New Orleans Police Department, long plagued by allegations of brutality and corruptions, were suspended for repeatedly beating a 64-year old black retired schoolteacher.

A videotape showed an officer hitting the man at least four times on the head and another officer kneeing the man and punching him twice.

5) New Expressions of Individual Racism

a) Modern Forms of Racism

The modern forms of racism exist where whites are seen as more conservative and critical of governmental policies that seem to favor blacks, e.g., affirmative action, President Clinton's Initiative on Race, cries of reverse discrimination, etc. Modern racism holds the belief that discrimination no longer exists and blacks are making unwarranted demands. They argue modern racism is without hostility or hate. It contains a little discomfort, uneasiness, disgust, fear rather than the previously destructive behavior.

Although traditional racism may be declining, new forms have sprung up. For example, if we ask the question: Are whites against affirmative action? The answer is yes. Every major research study of white attitudes shows white opposition to affirmative action. Frank Riggs (R.Calif.) introduced a bill in Congress aimed at banning affirmative action at most universities and colleges. Fortunately, the proposed bill was defeated. The measure would have ended a generation of admissions practices intended to increase minority enrollment. Riggs's intent was to spread the provisions of California Proposition 209 to the rest of the country. That measure, enacted in 1996, banned race- and gender-based affirmative action in college admissions, government hiring and contracting programs in the State of California. (St. Louis Post Dispatch May 11, 1998, p4)

b) Reverse or Black Racism: Does It Exist?

Former Congressman, Gus Savage, explained unequivocally blacks couldn't be racists, because

"Racism is white.... There are no black racists." Savage defines racism as "the unfair power of one race over another." Saturday, June 30, 2001 9:53:21

Feagin and Vera (1995) state black racism does not exist:

> Racism is more than a matter of individual prejudice and scattered episodes of discrimination designed by African-Americans to exclude White-Americans from full participation in the rights, privileges, and benefits of this society. Black (or other minority) racism would require not only a widely accepted racist ideology directed at whites but also the power to systematically exclude whites from opportunities and rewards in major economic, cultural and political institutions. While there are Black-Americans with anti-white prejudices, and there are instances of blacks discriminating against whites, these examples are not central to the core operations of U.S. society and are not part of an entrenched structure of institutionalized racism...p. I

Bruce Jacobs (1999) in his book **New Race Manners: Navigating the Minefield Between Black and White Americans,** argues that one of the ten worst ideas held by blacks is that only whites can be racists. He states that the attitude that black hatred cannot be racism is fallacious. He asks further what do you call it when embittered black teenagers kick white passersby because they can no longer stand the sight of white people? Or what is it when a black youth gestures at a white person? Use any term as ethnic hatred, revenge and reciprocal prejudice; but it all boils down to racism, says Jacobs.

My position is a minority of blacks may be prejudiced and/or anti-white, but very few are racists. Black racial prejudices are frequently referred or interpreted as black racism; these prejudices are not the same as white racism.

c) New Expressions of Racism

There really is not a "new racism," only re-engineered and re-designed forms of racism that have been reformulated into new expressions. For example 1). Racial Profiling or "Driving While Black (DWB)," 2). "Shopping While Black (SWB)," 3). Working While Black (WWB),

4). "Red Lining,"5). Mortgage rejection, 6). Predatory lending and 7). Environmental Racism---all represent some of the newest manifestations and expressions of racism in this country.

1) Racial Profiling: Driving White Black (DWB)

DWB refers to the process by which police stop drivers based on their skin color rather than the way they are driving or for a violation. According to the American Civil Liberties Union, in the State of Florida 80 percent of those persons stopped and searched by police were African-American and Hispanic although they constituted only five percent of the drivers. These humiliating and illegal searches are violations of the Constitution. Although stories of DWB have received wide media attention recently, racial profiling has its origins in slavery when blacks had to carry identification papers proving their identity or risk being seized by slave catchers.

Another name for DWB is "racial profiling" which refers to a similar practice of police officers using race as the sole criterion in deciding to stop or question an African-American or Hispanic person when investigating a crime or enforcing traffic laws. Many law enforcement agencies deny they engage in racial profiling. The U.S. Civil Rights Commission reports the New York Police use improper racial profiling against African-Americans and Hispanics. New York Mayor, Ralph Guiliani, denied the charge and called the conclusion a "political report that bears no relation to reality." Nonetheless 51 percent of the people stopped and searched in Staten Island in 1998 were black while the borough's population is only nine percent black. (St. Louis Post Dispatch, June 17, 2000, p. 20) Now, as we enter the 21st century we face a growing crisis of police brutality that is based on racist actions.

Two of President Clinton's highest-ranked African-American aides were recent victims of racial profiling. Bob Nash and his wife, Janis F. Kearney,

Recently we were the victims of racial profiling by Montgomery County Police. Until that moment, we had an intellectual understanding of the bogus crime of Driving While Black. But, in a few terrifying moments, we felt it more deeply and more personally than any words could ever convey. .... We want to take this opportunity to tell you in our own words.

First of all we were returning from a dinner at a relative's home and had not violated any traffic laws whatsoever. Suddenly, approximately eight police officers surrounded our vehicle and pointed spotlights, pistols and shotguns at our vehicle. At gunpoint, we were directed to walk backwards with our hands on our heads for approximately 40 feet. At this point neither one of us had said one word to the police and we followed each and every order very carefully and slowly because we feared for our lives given the large number of pistols and shotguns pointed at us.

We were both handcuffed by the police officers. The pistols and shotguns were aimed at us until we were handcuffed. At this point I asked a police officer why we were stopped and treated in the manner described above. He responded by asking if I owned the vehicle I was driving. I said yes ... At that point, they took the handcuff off of us...I then told an officer that my wife and I worked at the White House and had not broken any laws; an officer then apologized to us and let us go. (The Challenger Newspaper, October 12-October 18, 2000, p. 2)

Racial profiling has gotten so bad that black parents now warn their children--especially black males--of the dangers in being stopped by police when they're driving, bicycling or just standing around on the street corners.

Instructions given to black children go something like this:

If the police stop you, do exactly what they tell you. Answer their questions politely with 'yes sir' or 'no sir.' Don't get loud. Don't give them any attitude. Don't run away even if you're scared. If they tell you to get on the ground, do it." Minneapolis Star-Tribune, July 23, 2000.

2) *Shopping While Black (SWB)*

For black youth shopping is hardly a free and relaxed situation. Shopping While Black (SWB) or retail racism is common for black youth who are routinely the objects of suspicion. They do not usually know they are being watched the entire time they are in the store. Typically, black youth will be approached by security guards and questioned about some apparel. Then the youth are asked to accompany the security guards to the security office where they are searched. This is a demeaning and humiliating experience for the shopper. Former employees of retail stores report their supervisors inform them to watch black customers carefully.

One individual gave this account of SWB:

- My aunt owned a shop in Chicago and it had been robbed several times. When a few black teenagers would enter their store, she would say to her husband "Keep an eye on those black kids. They're exhibiting certain non-verbal actions that I'm sure they are going to steal something.

A black college student recalls a shopping trip to a local mall while in Oklahoma. She says:

I was carrying a bag from J.C. Pennys into the Sears store and my friends and I were followed…. They saw a bag and asked to search it. But that's not what they look at; they look at your color. (Howlett, USA Today, 1989) p.6a

3) *Redlining*

"Redlining" refers to the process by which mortgage companies and banks simply refuse to lend money on properties that are considered to be at risk of losing value because blacks are moving into the area. Do these procedures exist? Of course they do, not perhaps as a written policy but as de facto ones. Approximately 25 percent of African-Americans were turned down in St. Louis, Missouri for a loan compared to 17.5 percent white Americans. Nationally, 49 percent of African-Americans were rejected for conventional mortgages whereas whites were rejected at 25 percent. The size of this gap, plus the history of redlining, point to institutional racist practices. Bankers, however, are quick to deny racism by saying the racial gap point to economic factors. They claim that blacks have worse credit histories than whites.

However there is mounting evidence that low-income blacks are being victimized by unscrupulous home mortgage lenders by a process of "predatory lending."

Predatory Lending is another manifestation of institutional racism. These procedures represent loans at exorbitant interest rates, pre-payment penalties, balloon notes and thousand of dollars in extra charges. These loans are made to persons (i.e. Blacks) who ordinarily could not get mortgages because of poor creditor shaky employment.

4) *Predatory Lending*

A study by The Association of Community Organizations for Reform Now (ACORN) showed that the majority of blacks pay significantly higher interest rates than whites. The ACRON study cited a case of a black couple who was paying an interest rate of 12.5 percent whereas the usual rate charged is 2 percent above the prime rate of 8 percent. In addition the couple paid $5,700 for credit life insurance and $5,200 for an origination fee.

HUD and the Treasury Department released a joint report detailing recommendations on legislative, regulatory and other steps to curtail increasing occurrences of predatory mortgage lending. Secretary Cuomo said "Predatory lenders are greatly destroying families' life's savings and destroying good neighborhoods all across the country."

5) *Environmental Racism*

Another recently identified expression of racism is environmental racism that threatens black communities. Bullard (2000) defines Environmental Racism as follows:

> Environmental Racism refers to any environmental policy, practice or directive that differentially affects or disadvantages (whether intended or unintended) individuals, groups or communities based on race or color. Environmental racism combines with public policies and industry practices to provide benefits for whites while shifting costs to people of color. Environmental racism raises it ugly heads through unequal enforcement of environment al, civil rights, public health and transportation laws. It allows people of color to be adversely and disproportionately exposed to harmful chemicals, pesticides, and other toxins in the home, school, and neighborhood and workplace. p.1.

Black communities become dumping grounds for landfills, municipal waste combustors, or hazardous wastes. African-Americans are 50 percent more likely than whites to live in communities with hazardous waste facilities. This exposure increases the risks for ethnic minorities of getting asthma, prostate cancer and other deadly diseases. Blacks in West Oakland, California are concerned by the high levels of vinyl chloride, a gas that has been linked to rare forms of liver cancer.

Alabama is a major "dumping ground" for garbage and toxic landfills because, for one thing, they are a source of revenue. Several examples of Alabama's Environmental Racism will be reported here:

- Sumter County, Alabama is 71.8 percent black. This rural county is the home of one of the nation's largest hazardous waste landfill. Chemical Waste Management, Inc. in 1978 opened a giant waste treatment, storage and disposal facility. It was coined "The Cadillac of the Dumps." Black residents thought they were getting a brick plant.

- Macon County, Alabama the home of Tuskegee University has a population of 86.4 percent black. An 800-acre landfill was proposed for this area. Were it not for grassroots opposition, this landfill would have been built that would have accepted 5, 000 tons of garbage and toxins daily.

- Lowndes County, Alabama has a black population of 75.7 percent. The Alabama Department of Environmental Management approved a 200-acre landfill permit on the "Selma to Montgomery Historic Trail."

CHAPTER XII
INSTITUTIONAL RACISM

1) Institutional Racism Defined

Most discussions centered on individual racism until Carmichael & Hamilton (1967) identified and defined institutional racism. Institutional racism refers to those customs and practices that systematically support doctrines of racial superiority and inferiority in American society. It develops from the beliefs of people to meet their needs, reinforces their beliefs and through repetition, it becomes a standardized method of operation. Institutional racism ranges from the subtlest to the most blatant forms. Easily identified forms of institutional racism are found in the employment sector where the ratio of blacks to whites is low; in professional schools where the percentage of blacks is under-represented; in housing where blacks live in slums and run-down neighborhoods. Frequently, however, it is the more hidden forms of institutional racism that produce the most blatant and frustrating consequences.

Many race-based discrimination charges have been filed with the Equal Employment Opportunity Commission (EEOC). People may not be using the "N-word" but other forms of discrimination exist. Armour (2000) reports that more than 5000 claims have been filed with the EEOC during the first nine months of year 2000 which is an increase of approximately 2000 from the previous year.

Feldstein (2004) reports that minorities are still facing workplace discrimination. In the twenty first century African-American workers are finding it tougher to get a job or a promotion (Armour, 2002).

African-Americans tend to be the last to be hired when the economy is booming and the first to lose their jobs when a downturn hits. Michelle Johnson (2004) suggests Working While Black (WWB) is a recently recognized form of racial discrimination witch is still in existence.

2) Institutional Racism in Stores

The following example of institutional racism occurred on February 2, 1998 in a Home Depot Store. It is, however, a situation that happens to many African-Americans but is not reported. Most often the African-American simply departs from the scene. In this case the individuals contested the racist's actions.

> Mr. Sarah Thompson, director of Love Thy Neighbor (LTN), a non- profit primarily African-American community-based organization serving low-income families in Washington DC, went to a HOME DEPOT store in Oxon Hill, Maryland. She had a $1000.00 gift certificate which was purchased and donated to LTN by a corporation and the certificate was to be used for renovation of the LTN building.
>
> After spending 45 minutes picking out floor tile and other merchandise, Ms. Thompson and the three volunteer youth directors presented the certificate to the cashier. The cashier treated them with suspicion, as if they had stolen the certificate. The cashier refused to accept the certificate even though Home Depot had issued it. The gift certificate had been paid for several weeks prior to this time. The cashier refused the purchase and told them to come back in two weeks.
>
> Ms. Thompson asked for the manager. After making them wait another 45 minutes, the manager spent an additional hour trying to clear the certificate through the computer system five times and each time it cleared. The manager was still suspicious. Ms. Thompson gave them the telephone number of the organization

that bought the gift certificate so they could verify its validity, but the manager refused to call.

Ms. Thompson spent over four hours in the store to no avail. They left dejected and without the merchandise. Ms. Thompson said she felt discriminated against. She said there is no question in her mind that she was treated with suspicion of theft and the certificate was rejected because she and the volunteers were African-Americans.

3) Racial Covenants

Racism expressed in a written policy by a company, organization or by law in government is defined as de jure; racism expressed in unwritten discriminatory practices is referred to as de facto, that is, existing in fact whether legally recognized or not. Racial covenants are examples of institutional racism by policy. Recently, an article appeared showing a racial covenant in Silver Lake, a section of Los Angeles, Calif. The covenant stated:

> "No part of said premise shall be sold to, conveyed to, leased to or rented to, nor shall the same ever be used or occupied by any person of either the Negro, African or Asiatic race, or any person not of the Caucasian race, whether the owner, tenant or any other person, except, however that these covenants and conditions shall not prevent the employment upon said premises of Negro, African or Asiatic servants."

The deed also required that buyers obey the conditions, otherwise their ownership would be revoked. In Shelly vs. Kramer (1948, 334 U.S. 1) the U.S. Supreme Court ruled racial land deed covenants were unconstitutional.

4) Death Penalty Disparities

A study by the Justice Department showed wide racial disparities in U.S. death penalty cases. A disproportionately greater number of blacks are recommended for the death penalty. From 1995 to 2000, U. S. attorneys forwarded 682 cases of defendants who faced capital charges for review. Twenty percent (136) were white and 80 percent (546) were minority members. U.S. attorneys recommended the death penalty for 183 of them, 26 percent (48) white and 74 percent (135) minority members. The attorney general approved the death penalty for 159, of which 28 percent (45) were white and 72 percent (114) were minority.

5) Racism in the Workplace is Costly

Racism is costing corporate America millions to fend off complaints of racial discrimination. Feagin, Vera and Batur (2001) state

> "…racism is extremely expensive and wasteful for all Americans, as individuals and collectively. The eradication of racism is vital not only to the interests of African-Americans and other Americans of color but also the long-term in terms of all white Americans." (P 221)

For example, lawsuits cost GMAC $100 million, Coca Cola $192 million, Adams Mark Hotels $8 million, Denny's Restaurants $2.5 million, Avis Car Rental $2.1 million, Enterprise Leasing 2.3 million, Unitrin Inc. Insurance Company $27 million, Winn Dixie $33 million, Shoney's $132.5 million and Texaco $176.1 million. Class action lawsuits are now being levied against other major corporations as Boeing Aircraft, Reliable Life Insurance Company, and Ford Motor Company.

a) GMAC

GMAC has a class action against it for $100 million. The pending charge alleges that GMAC charges blacks more money for financing than whites. A study by Debby Lindsey, a Howard University Law Professor, showed black consumers pay 48.9 percent higher finance charge markups than whites. James E. Farmer, a GMAC Vice President, denies these charges and vows to fight the case. He states, "This Company strictly adheres to a zero tolerance policy on racial discrimination. We're going to fiercely and vigorously challenge these allegations." (The Challenger Newspaper, December 21- December 27, 2000, p1 and p 5)

b) Coca-Cola

Coca-Cola announced on November 16, 2000, it would pay a record $192.5 million to settle a racial discrimination suit by black employees. (Curry, 2000). The suit charged Coca-Cola of discriminating against black employees in pay, promotions and evaluations. Although Coca-Cola never admitted to practicing racial discrimination, nevertheless the company agreed as part of the settlement to pay $113 million to African-American employees, $43.5 million to boost salaries of blacks to be comparable with whites, $36 million for program to monitor the company's employment practices and $20 million for the plaintiff's legal fees.

c) Adams Mark Hotels

President and Chief Executive Officer of the Adam's Mark Hotel, Fred S. Kummer III, issued a public apology (in writing) to African-Americans. The apology was sent as a result of the controversy that includes a suit by the U.S. Justice Department which charged that black guests were treated differently than other guests. Black guests were required to wear orange wristbands and pay higher room rates than white guests. The Hotel agreed to an $8 million settlement.

The apology stated:

We apologize to you and to any member of the African-American community who has felt any pain or discomfort due to any of our actions, because such feelings are inconsistent with the Adam Mark's philosophy. We will continue to do everything within our power to avoid problems, and to correct any mistakes that have been made. (St. Louis PD. Nov 17, 2000, p A2)

James Buford, CEO of the Metro Urban League of St. Louis, asked groups to avoid holding meetings at the Adam's Mark Hotels until the Justice Department settled the lawsuit. Buford did not use the word 'boycott," but it was strongly implied when he said some form of punitive action is needed against those who discriminate against people of color. (Urban League Chief, 2000, p. A1.)

An additional class-action suit, alleging that the company discriminates against minorities, was filed against the Adam's Mark hotels after the $8 million settlement. Black workers contend that the company fostered and conducted a racially hostile environment. Employees were humiliated, intimidated, demeaned and subjected to frequent inappropriate racial comments [and] the company refused to take action against co-workers or supervisors who engaged in racial harassment and retaliated against employees who complained. (O'Connor 2001, p.7.)

d) Beverly Enterprises

Beverly Enterprises, one of the nation's largest nursing home operators, agreed to pay 1.2 million to nine former employees following allegation that a white administrator targeted blacks for racial discrimination and for firing. (Jonsson, 2001 P. B1) C. Felix Miller, an attorney for the EEOC said, " She [the administrator] apparently decided she wanted to get rid of black employees and replace them with white employees" (P. b1) The EEOC also said applications for employment were coded differently for black and white applicants. A sticker with a "smiling face" was placed on white applications whereas a sticker with a "frowning face" was placed on black applications.

e) Denny's Restaurant

A major food restaurant chain, Denny's restaurant was lambasted for institutional racism. As a result Dennys increased top-level minority management from zero to 119. Their action improved services and sales. Denny's owners settled two class-action discrimination suits for 45 African-Americans. Denny's paid one million dollars and pledged another one-and-a-half million dollars to several civil rights groups and the United Negro College Fund.

f) AVIS Car Rental

In Wilmington, North Carolina, an AVIS car rental company was charged for discriminating against would-be-auto-renters solely on the basis of their race. AVIS agreed to pay 2.1 million dollars to black patrons to settle the lawsuit. That North Carolina franchise has been terminated. (Jet, May 25, 1998, 93,26, p. 24)

g) New York Brokerage House

A New York Brokerage House, portrayed as a cesspool for vulgar sexual and racial abuse of its employees, will pay $1.75 million to 17 former employees and promise to prevent sexual and racial abuse in the future (New York Brokerage House settles, 1998)

h) Enterprise Leasing

Enterprise leasing will pay $2.3 million to settle a racial discrimination lawsuit. The agency was charged with denying black employees promotions and transfers in favor of less-qualified or less experienced white employees. Black employees trained some of the white employees who were promoted and transferred. (Jet, May 27, 2002, p.8)

i) Unitrin Inc. Insurance Company

Unitrin Inc. Insurance Company was ordered to pay $27 million to black policyholders who were overcharged for life insurance. The monies will go to approximately a half million of the policyholders who held policies from the 30s to the 1970s. Black customers were charged more than whites on the assumption that blacks have shorter life spans. ("Unitrin Inc. Insurance Company," 2002, p.39)

j) Boeing Aircraft

Forty-one minority workers sued The Boeing Co. in Seattle, Washington seeking millions of dollars for racial discrimination. The lawsuit accuses the aerospace giant of a hostile work environment, biased hiring practices and failing to promote minorities.

k) Ford Motor Credit Company

Black employees at Ford Motor Credit Company sued for 600 million dollars, claiming racial discrimination in hiring, evaluation and promotion of workers. Black employees said they were asked to train new employees, only to have white hires soon surpass them in pay and position. They also said they were punished more harshly than their non-black employees.

l) Reliable Insurance Company

Reliable Life Insurance Company's agents were told not to sell standard life insurance policies to African-Americans, instead to sell them overpriced "burial" policies, according to a class-action lawsuit filed against the company. Reliable specializes in selling life insurance policies for small amounts usually to low-income (black) people. Reliable told its agents not to offer better insurance policies to black clients. Reliable charged higher premiums to black than whites the suit charges. (Gallagher, 2000a; Gallagher 2000c)

m) New York Police Department

Twenty-four New York minority policemen were awarded $1.2 million by a jury that determined their constitutional rights were violated when they were transferred to a troubled area. Police officials admitted they deliberately moved 35 officers because of the color of their skin. The transfers were made after Abner Louima had been sodomized by a group of white policemen. (Black Cops awarded $1.2 million, 2000)

n) Norfolk Southern Corporation

Current and former black employees of Norfolk Southern Corporation will be paid 28 million along with new promotion policies in order to settle a race bias lawsuit. Black employees charged they were denied a promotion to management due to race. (New Jersey to pay (2001).

o) City of New York

The City of New York settled a racial bias suit for $26.8 million. The City agreed to pay black and Latino officers who complained of racial harassment, hostile work environments, wrongful termination and unfair disciplinary methods. (New York City Settles, 2004)

o) Boston Transit Authority

The Boston Transit Authority awarded a black woman $7.6 million in a bias suit. In her lawsuit, Roberta Edwards, charged that she was ostracized and harassed by senior officials after she appeared supportive of a woman who brought a discrimination suit against the transit company. Two years before her settlement a black foreman at the transit company was awarded 5.5 million after charging that he had endured years of race baiting. (Black Woman Executive Wins 2001)

p) Supercuts, Inc.

In August 2003, EEOC settled a racial discrimination case against Supercuts, Inc, a nationwide chain of hair salons for $3.5million. An African-American regional vice president was terminated because he refused to endorse a plan to reduce the number of blacks employees.

q) Texaco Oil Company

Texaco, one of the world's largest corporations, agreed to pay $176 million to 1,348 black employees. Tape recorded conversations among senior Texaco executives revealed the executives had called black employees "black jelly beans" who cannot rise up the corporate ladder. The "jelly beans" were stuck to the bottom of the beanbag. (Feagin et al 2001).

r) Sodexho Mariott Services, Inc.

Sodexho Marriott Services, Inc, agreed to pay $80 million to settle a lawsuit brought about by thousands of black employees. The settlement will mean payout to black employees who charged that they were routinely banned from promotions.

s) Shoney's Restaurant

Shoney's restaurant agreed to pay $105 million to settle a lawsuit charging the company had turned away back applicants and relegated the few it hired to menial jobs. One former employee stated she was advised to darken the "o's" in Shoney's logo to indicate that the applicant was black.

t) FedEx

FedEx has agreed to pay $500, 000 to settle charges that a company it bought (American Freightways) had discriminated against African American employees at its terminal. The workers charged that the American Freightways terminal was a racially hostile workplace where employees used racial epithets and sprawled racial graffiti in bathrooms. (Shinkle, 2005)

There are many, many more cases that have been settled and some that are still pending, that I have overlooked. The total of the cases presented here comes to one billion four hundred thirty one million dollars.

6) Proposition 209

With the passage of Proposition 209 in the State of California, people of color admissions have drastically plunged. (Krauthamer, 1997) The number of Blacks, Hispanics, and Native Americans offered admission for the fall of 1998, the first affected by the so-called race-blind policy, plunged by 61 percent. At the University of Texas-Austin the minority admissions were down 85 percent. Ward Connerly, the African-American University of California Regent, ironically led the fight to drop race and gender preferences in admissions. As a consequence of Proposition 209, the number of Native Americans, blacks and Hispanics admitted to the University of California system for Fall 1998 declined significantly from 1997. Black students are in conflict over whether they should attend California Universities because of Proposition 209.

Students are saying they feel unwelcome and unwanted at the California Universities. (Jones, 1998).

The State of Washington voters were faced with a similar ballot (Initiative 200) as California (Proposition 209). Ward Connerly provided financial support through his Sacramento-based America Civil

Rights Institute (a Coors supported organization). The Washington proposition reads as follows:

> The State shall not discriminate against race, sex, color, ethnicity or national origin in the operation of public employment, public education or public contracting." (McMahon, 1998, p. 3). Unlike former California Governor Pete Wilson who supported Proposition 209, Washington State Governor Gary Locke is an outspoken opponent of Initiative 200.

Complaints against race-based scholarships increased in the last few years. Washington University-St. Louis reversed its position of allowing blacks-only scholarships or face federal investigation. (Ervin Scholars, 2004 pp.1& 7) The University's John Ervin Scholarship for African-Americans will now be open to students of any race beginning in the fall of 2005.

James E. McCloud, Vice Chancellor for Student Affairs at Washington University-St. Louis, noted:

> Given the Supreme Court's decision last year involving the University of Michigan undergraduate admissions program and other legal developments, and in light of guidance we have recently received from the Department of Education, we believe it is no longer possible for Washington University to lawfully operate this scholarship program on a race-exclusive basis. (Ervin Scholars, 2004 p. 1.)

The impetus for change is coming from two groups: The Center for Equal Opportunity of Sterling, Virginia and the American Civil Rights Institute of Sacramento, California. (Race and Opportunity, (2004). Both groups oppose racially exclusive programs and scholarships, by seeking to make colorblind equal opportunity. St. Louis University recently replaced its Black-Only Calloway Scholarship with a Martin Luther King Scholarship open to all students. St. Louis University and

Washington University were among the five schools against which the two organizations filed complaints. (Leopoldt, 2004).

At the University of Missouri, -Columbia a white student offered a $200.00 "White Scholarship" presumably in protest of scholarships reserved for minorities. Colin Kerr, a white student established the scholarship from donations. He stated:

> No one realizes the injustice of race-based scholarships until it's offered to a white student...We want people to question the nature of a scholarship being offered based on race." (Gurman, 2004, p1)

The "white only" scholarship drew quick reactions from the college community. (Lamprich and Beauchamp, 2004) University of Missouri students quickly responded by stating that the white-only scholarship misses the point entirely. In an online poll students were asked, "How do you feel about Colin Kerr creating a scholarship solely for white students? The results follow:

1. (52%) There are scholarships for minorities, so it seems fair to me.

2. (20 %) It seems to be more of a mockery than an actual scholarship

3. (13%) Sounds like Kerr is ignoring the basic history of minorities in the United States.

4. (15%) He is trying to set race relations at MU back another 30 years.

Adapted from the MANEATER, April 20, 2004, p. 3
Friday, August 18, 2006

CHAPTER XIII
CULTURAL AND
SCIENTIFIC RACISM

1) Cultural Racism

Cultural racism is a term first used by black psychologist, Dr. James Jones (1972), of Delaware State College. Cultural racism is defined as the individual and institutional expression of the superiority of one race's cultural heritage over that of another. It is an act of cultural racism when the achievements of one race are fully ignored, negated or plagiarized. It is also an act of cultural racism when cultural differences are interpreted as cultural deficiencies. Further, it is cultural racism when the language pattern, folkways, mores and lifestyles of a people are considered to be deviant particularly, when the cultural factors differ from the mainstream culture. Glazer and Moynihan (1963) took the matter to the extreme by asserting black Americans have no culture to protect.

The works of behavioral scientists, particularly those of Berieter and Englemann (1966), gave birth to the racist myth that black children have a paucity of speech and that their speech is illogical and deficient. Unfortunately, such racist statements are abound and have been used as the basis for designing curriculum for early childhood programs. One needs to listen to rappers Little Bow Wow or Master P's boy (Romeo) to understand black children are verbal. Generally, black children do not respond to white interviewers who represent unfriendliness; they respond better to black people with familiar faces and to those with whom they feel comfortable. Labov (1972) reported this finding early in discussions that centered on the verbal skills of black children.

A well-known former president of the American Psychological Association suggested much of social research is less than objective George Albee (1982) stated:

> I have come to believe that I have had the whole "scientific" process reversed. Instead of facts being useful as the objective building of blocks of theories, rather it is more accurate to say that people, and especially social scientists, select theories that are consistent with their personal values, attitudes and prejudices and then go out into the world or into the laboratory, to seek the facts that validate their beliefs about the world and about human nature, neglecting or denying observations that contradict their personal prejudices. (p. 5)

Thus, many of the demonstrations of deficiencies are the result of biased scientific research.

2) Scientific Racism:

The black community has become the white researcher's hunting ground, indeed, an experimental laboratory. In many medical schools, prisons and laboratories numerous menacing scientific experiments are being conducted on black people. So alarming has the situation become that black professional organizations began to monitor so-called "high-risk" research. It already has disclosed one hideous result: scientific racism or the cold, inhuman, sadistic experimentation with poor, powerless and helpless black human beings. "High-risk" research is also another scientific method used to document theories of racial superiority and inferiority.

Scientific racism in the United States has reached such hideous proportions that it threatens the survival of black and poor people. Slater (1973) estimated that approximately 600 psycho-surgical operations are performed each year. The subjects are frequently black and almost invariably poor people. Prisoners, especially black ones, seem to be fair game for the psycho-surgeon's knife.

The late Dr. Charles Thomas (1970), former President of the Association of Black Psychologists, put the grim situation as follows:

> White psychologists have raped black communities over the country. Yes, raped. They have used black people as the human equivalent of rats.... They have been vultures..." (p.52).

a)   The Tuskegee Experiment

The Tuskegee Syphilis experiment is a glaring and shocking disclosure of scientific racism. During a 40 year federally funded study, 600 Alabama black men were used as human guinea pigs by researchers who withheld treatment so that scientists could study the progress of the disease. While this disclosure is shocking, it points to the kind of sadistic research conducted on black people. At the time of the study, it was well known that syphilis was a highly contagious, dangerous and debilitating disease which when left untreated, can cause sterility, blindness, deafness, bone deterioration, nervous system degeneration, heart disease and eventually death. Even after the discovery of penicillin, a cure for syphilis, the men were still denied treatment. Records from the Center for Disease Control in Atlanta, Georgia disclosed that 70 participants died as a direct result of syphilis. Another 154 persons died of heart disease that may have been caused by syphilis. These poor black men were tricked into participating in the experiment. They were offered such tempting bait as free transportation to and from the hospital, hot lunches, medical cure for ailments other than syphilis and, or course, free burial.

Some might argue the study was a scientific experiment where consent was obtained and needed to be done to inform people of the long-term effects of syphilis. According to Jack Slater (Ebony, 1973), scientists already knew the effects of long-term, untreated syphilis from data obtained from a study conducted in Oslo, Norway on a population of 1,976 untreated syphilitics from 1891 to 1910. Says Slater, "Apparently, however, the conclusions of the Oslo study did not suit the needs of the founders of the Tuskegee report." (p. 178) President Bill Clinton went on national television and apologized to the living victims and their families of this racist study.

b)   Sterilization of Black women

But the Tuskegee Experiment is just the tip of the iceberg, the instance of scientific racism that stirred up nationwide indignation occurred on June 14, 1973. It was then that a white Alabama doctor performed tubal ligations on two black sisters, 14-year-old Minnie and 12-year-old Mary Alice Relf. Since both were considered to be mentally defective, under Alabama law they could be forcefully sterilized. Alabama is simply one of 26 states that have laws requiring forced eugenic sterilizations of persons labeled as mentally defective.

Sterilization is still used in several states as a means of reducing the number of welfare recipients by making sterilization a condition for medical care to continue to receive welfare payments and even requirements for parole from prison. Hospital records in Aiken, South Carolina revealed over one-third of the welfare mothers who had babies under Medicaid were required to undergo sterilization. Sterilization was the policy of the county's three obstetricians who told the welfare mothers they would have to agree to sterilization before the doctors would deliver their babies. The records show that 18 welfare mothers had been sterilized during the first six months of the year. Of these, 17 were black mothers.

c)   Columbia University

In addition to the Tuskegee Syphilis Experiment, a recent government funded study revealed that poor black and Hispanic boys and girls were given a now re-called drug to test for violent tendencies. Scientists at an institute affiliated with Columbia University of New

York were testing the brain chemistry of 34 black and Hispanic children using Fenfluramine (Fen), a drug which has been taken off the market because of its suspected links to heart -valve damage. The boys were given a "Fen" pill and were kept in the hospital for five hours with catheters in their arms of blood samples. They were without food for at least 17 hours. The scientists wanted to know whether levels of serotonin in the brain could signal aggression. Fenfluramine induces the brain to release serotonin, a neurotransmitter or chemical that transmits messages across the gaps between adjacent brain cells. Serotonin is produced in the brain and is derived from foods high in protein such as meat and dairy products.

Critics say the experiment offered no medical benefits and put the children at great risk. These racist and morally offensive studies put minority children at risk in order to prove they are generally predisposed to be violent in nature, said Vera Hasssner Sharaav, Director of Citizens for Responsible Care in Psychiatry and Research. The researchers defended their efforts as a legitimate attempt to understand the roots of violence.

d) The University of Texas-Galveston

A medical school at the University of Texas in Galveston conducted a controversial study primarily on black babies from 1956 to 1962. The researchers withheld an essential fatty acid from babies' formula that humans need for the growth of the whole body and nervous system. Those babies were used as laboratory animals and several of the infants died during the study. (reported by Cosby, 1998)

e) The Johns Hopkins University

In still another study, the federal government funded The John Hopkins University to conduct an experimental program of genetic testing of 6,000 juvenile delinquents in a Maryland state school and 7,500 black youth from Baltimore who were attending a free medical clinic there. The purpose of the study was to search for XYY chromosome patterns in delinquents. The XYY chromosomes are supposedly an abnormal pattern of genes that are related to criminal behavior.

f) Sickle Cell Anemia

At a National Conference on the Mental Health Aspects of Sickle Cell Anemia held at Meharry Medical College in Nashville, Tennessee, Dr. Bertram Brown (1972), former Director of the National Institute of Mental Health, eloquently addressed his attention to the questions of exploitation, ethical and moral violations of researchers in leading to the flagrant abuses of rights of black people. He pointed out that whereas only one drop of blood is required to make a slide to examine cells for sickle cell anemia, a disproportionate amount was taken from blacks:

> Yet, in a few recent sickle cell blood studies, 22cc of blood were taken from large black populations. Hidden agendas are always feared and a good many blacks were asking...What else are those blood samples being used for? They have a right to ask. Any agency or scientists dealing in this area have an obligation to deal honestly and sincerely with the subjects.

It is precisely this lack of concern expressed by Dr. Brown that disturbs the black community. In the past years there have not been enough precautions taken to insure protection of subjects generally and black people in particular.

g) Prison Studies

Allen Hornblum's (1998) book, "Acres of Skin," reported widespread medical experiments that went on for 23 years inside Philadelphia's Holmesburg prison. Hornblum, an employee of the prison at the time, said he was shocked to see dozens of inmates with adhesive tape on their faces, their arms and their backs. Most of the inmates involved in the studies were black men and relatively uneducated. Hornblum's work led to a lawsuit, charging the medical experiments exposed the inmates to infectious diseases, radiation, dioxin and psychotropic drugs--all without their informed consent. Johnson & Johnson confirmed that it had tested cosmetic products on inmates at Holmesburg during the late 1960s and early 1970s.

h)   Racist IQ Theories

The IQ Myth: Scientific Racism

Six men, two Englishmen, two Frenchmen and two Americans are preeminent in the creation and perpetuation of scientific racism in psychology. Indeed, these men are the "Fathers of Scientific Racism" which still affects the development of scientific research and psychological thinking.

Charles Darwin (1859) published his classic work "On the Origin of the Species," which theorized that human groups are at different stages of biological evolution. He hypothesized the older races (the Mongolians and the Europeans) were on a higher rung of the evolutionary ladder than the younger races (Negroes). They are, therefore, more intelligent than the younger races.

Social Darwinism involved the struggle for existence or the survival of the fittest. The younger races, (presumably the Africans) are the weakest and have juvenile and poorly developed minds. They are, therefore, less able and less fit for survival than are the older races.

Darwin's theory was, of course, developed long before British anthropologists Dr. L.S.B. Leakey and his wife Mary in 1959. Ironically, 100 years after the publication of Darwin's treatise, the Leakeys made the stunning discovery of the African genesis of man. On July 17, 1959 the Leakeys found a fossil skull near the bottom of a gorge in Tanganyika of a species, which was sufficiently, like modern man to be included in the same genus. This species, Homo Erectus, is estimated to be about 2.5 million years old. This important anthropological discovery confirmed the belief that the first man on earth was black

(African) as opposed to white. This is an extremely important finding because it revolutionizes scientific thinking concerning the origin of man. Certainly, Social Darwinism will have to be re-examined in as much as it has influenced the works of psychologists and sociologists throughout the 19th and 20th centuries.

How IQ Test Development influenced racist thinking

In psychology, the development of the mental testing movement gave the greatest impetus to the search for a scientific basis for racial myths. Sir Frances Galton (1869), the second Englishman and cousin of Charles Darwin, is credited with giving birth to the mental measurement and eugenic movements. Galton's first major piece, "Hereditary Genius: An Inquiry into Its Laws and Consequences" attempted to show that genius and nobility run in families. Based on this theory, Galton founded the Eugenics Society in 1871. Eugenics is the science of heredity, which promotes the idea of racial breeding through selective mating and sterilization of the mentally unfit. The Eugenics Society's purpose was to educate scientists and government officials to the advantages of race betterment. Galton argued that only through "selective breeding" (eugenics) could a master race be achieved.

The Society needed an instrument to verify its views and did not have one until 1905 when two Frenchmen, Alfred Binet and Theodore Simon, constructed one of the first tests at the request of the French government. However, Binet and Simon never intended their instrument to be a measurement of intelligence. Its purpose was to identify "feeble-minded" children so the government could arrange for their special schooling.

Two Americans, Henry H. Goddard and Lewis Terman, popularized the Binet Scales in the United States as IQ Tests. In 1908, Goddard translated the Binet-Simon Scales into English. Terman, a follower of Galton, published his ideas of black inferiority on tests in his book. The Measurement of Intelligence (1916) that contained the Stanford-Binet Scales. Terman reported genetic dullness among various racial groups, (viz., African-Americans, Indians and Mexican Americans). According to Terman (1916)

> *Black and other ethnic minority children are uneducable beyond the nearest rudiments of training. No amount of school instruction will ever make them intelligent voters or capable citizens in the true sense of the word...Their dullness seems to be racial, or at least inherent in the family stock from which they come...Children of this group should be segregated in special classes and be given instruction which is concrete and practical. They cannot master abstractions, but they can be made efficient workers...There is no possibility at present of convincing society that they should not be allowed to reproduce, although from a eugenic point of view they constitute a grave problem because of their unusual prolific breeding." Lewis Terman, The Measurement of Intelligence, (1916) in Nobles, W.W. (1986) African psychology: Toward its reclamation, reascension and revitalization, Oakland: The Institute for the Advanced Study of Black Family Life and Culture.*

Through the years there have been "timed" releases of these racial myths in popular magazines, newspapers and journals. All of which serve the purpose of reinforcing the racial inferiority myth.

McGraw (1931) made public the results of a study that further reinforced the belief of white supremacy. Based on a comparative research design, McGraw tested 128 black and white babies, aged eleven months to two years. McGraw interpreted the findings to mean that black babies were only about 80 percent as mature as white babies. This report was used as scientific proof of black inferiority.

A little more than 10 years later, Audrey Shuey (1942) published her study comparing black and white students on a college entrance examination. Shuey created a pseudo-event by concluding that socioeconomic factors are not the primary cause of the lower scores made by blacks. Rather, Shuey inferred that genetic factors were responsible. Similarly, McGurk (1956) in U.S. News and World Report released still another article "Psychological Tests: A Scientist's Report on Race

Differences," which summarized and reinforced all other pseudo-events.

Many scholars (black and white) have criticized the genetic inferiority hypothesis rather carefully and extensively. The overwhelming conclusion is that not only are the allegations of racial and intellectual inferiority unjustified, but also the scientific data for the thesis may have, in fact, been fraudulent. Kamin's (1976) disclosure of the fact that the eminent English psychologist, the late Sir Cyril Burt doctored, reportedly, invented, his data and created a big credibility problem for the hypothesis that intelligence is largely genetically determined. Of particular note is the fact that Burt's data were quite influential in establishing the notion that IQ is genetically linked.

The genetic theories of black IQ Inferiority advanced by Jensen, Shockley and others present a strong genocidal threat to blacks. Jensen (1969) and Shockley (1972) claim that a so-called "dysgenic trend," considered to be the accumulation of bad or low IQ genes, is present in the black population. According to this claim certain black mothers should not be allowed to bear more children, and their offsprings should also be sterilized. Jensen claims the rate of mental retardation among blacks is seven times higher than among whites and that because of the eugenic trend, black mothers are giving birth to mentally retarded children.

Jensen (1969) used Burt's findings in his highly controversial Harvard Educational Review article. The article proposed there is a large genetic component of intelligence (80 percent) and this might account for the racial differences in IQ scores between blacks and whites.

One of the earliest racist works created a firestorm of controversy about IQ testing was Arthur Jensen's 1969 Harvard Educational Review piece titled "How Much Can We Boost IQ and Scholastic Achievement?" Jensen's second work "Bias in Mental Testing" published in 1980; Jensen made several denigrating conclusions in these two publications about IQ testing:

1) His first false assumption is that IQ tests are valid and reliable measures of intelligence.

2) His second irrational hypothesis is that IQ is highly heritable--80 percent genetic and 2) percent environment. IQ is a set of scores earned on an IQ test. You cannot inherit an IQ. IQ and intelligence are not synonymous.

3) His third and most ridiculous postulate is that since blacks score 15 IQ points (on the average) lower than whites on IQ tests these differences are genetically determined. It may also be fact, but not a truth. All truths are facts but not all facts are truths.

4) His fourth and most racist supposition is that a DYSGENIC trend threatens our society; black genes are dysgenic (bad, dysfunctional or defective).

5) His fifth supposition is compensatory education has been tried and failed.

CHAPTER XIV:
RACIAL SOLUTIONS

I refuse to accept the view that mankind
is so tragically bound to the starless midnight
of racism and war that the bright daylight
of peace and brotherhood can never become a reality.

I've Been to the Mountaintop,
Dr. Martin Luther King, Jr. April 3, 1968

1) Ending Racism: Fixing versus Healing

Ending racism in this country is problematic. Let's face it. America is a racist nation and racism is buried deep in the fabric of the American Society. Further, racism is a national problem that requires healing rather than fixing. Healing and fixing are two different characters. Fixing is doing whatever it takes to cover up, disguise or postpone solutions to the racial problem; that is "the squeaky wheel gets the oil." Healing, however, requires in-depth, long-term solutions. Healing recognizes there is no medicine available to cure racial hatred. In addition, healing recognizes there is neither a "one-size-fit all" solution, nor is there a magic bullet that will end racism.

Over the years this nation tried to "fix" the racial problem by focusing on the African-American—the victim. The race problem is not solely a Black problem. Racism involves both black and white Americans. As former U.S. Senator Bill Bradley stated:

> As long as white America believes the race problem is primarily a black problem of meeting white standards to gain admittance to white society, things will never stabilize and endure…the issue of race can never be a black issue alone.

2) Will Apologies be Sufficient?

The U.S. Government has been asked to offer a formal apology for the years of slavery and discrimination against black people. The question is: Will apologies heal the racial hatred in this country? I don't think so. Much, much more is needed.

Former President Clinton apologized for the horrific Tuskegee Syphilis Study. . which he called one of the most disgraceful sins committed by this nation. The Aetna Insurance Company apologized for its shameful role in slavery in the U.S. Similarly, the Hartford Courant, one of the nation's oldest newspapers, ran an apology for having published advertisements, which supported slavery in the 1700s and 1800s. The paper stated that through its advertisements, it acted somewhat as a slave broker. (St. Louis American, p B1, July 6-12, 2000). Apologies are the first step, but they cannot and do not lead to racial healing; aggressive programs designed to end racism are needed.

In addition, various groups have demanded reparations. Representative John Conyers (Michigan Democrat) proposed a bill in 1989 demanding reparations. The bill called for the government to provide monetary restitution to the descendants of slaves.

Rather than monetary reparation, I suggest the government give descendents of slaves free education, health, housing and legal benefits for the next 100 years. A monetary award would most likely end up within the establishment in less time than a year! Some whites have adopted a "paternalistic script" or one that leads to a protective feeling for blacks.

These whites feel blacks need "helping" and "protecting" in some fashion. Here is one example illustrating the "paternalistic script":

- I truly believed racism was a horrible thing and hardships had been caused for minorities because of it. I also internalized the "myth" that black people needed white people to "save" them; they needed wonderful, charitable people with open-minds (like me of course) to feed, clothe and house them. This mistaken belief manifested itself quite plainly when I turned sixteen.

  As I gained more exposure to black girls in my school, many of whom were extremely high achievers, I began to re-work the myth that whites had to "care for" blacks. I rejected the myth that blacks needed and wanted white people to take care of them. Through various other experiences, I began to change my belief to one that racism was more prevalent, systematic and organized than I had previously thought. I concluded that white people need to become human beings and stop throwing "crumbs" to black people.

In the above example, "experience" enabled this person to re-examine the script and make changes to a more real level. This individual dismissed the paternalistic perception of black people. Many whites, however, still have the perception that Blacks "need" to be given to rather than be respected and treated as equals. There are two questions that must concern us here:

1) How did this paternalistic attitude originate?
2) Why are folks still holding on to this belief?

3) Need for National leadership:

I strongly believe we need a "top down mandate" from the President of the United States and the Congress to initiate a "war against racism." When the country made a decision to go to the moon, it did. When the U.S. decided to send a space ship to mars, it did. When it decided to find or locate Saddam Hussein, it did –in a hole. Thus, I believe this country can end racism if the U.S. decided to do so.

One monumental effort to eliminate racism in this country was initiated by former President Bill Clinton. His bold vision of **One America** proposed to have a racially diverse community in which we all respect, and celebrate our differences which embrace the shared values that would unite us.

On June 17, 1997, President Clinton delivered his anti-racist address at the University of California-San Diego. The President's Initiative on Race kicked off a campaign to improve racial relations. He focused on racial healing. Clinton stated:

> I have launched a national initiative on race to help us recognize our common interests and bridge the opportunity gaps that keep us from becoming one America…We have torn down the [racial] barriers in our laws. Now we must break down the [racial] barriers in our lives, in our minds and in our hearts.… Ten years from now people can look back and see that this year of honest dialogue and concerted action helped to lift the heavy burden of race from our children's future. We will have given a precious gift to America. (Conversations of Race, St. Louis Post Dispatch, 1997)

Clinton wanted a colorblind society, one in which the color of one's skin was transcended. However, Clinton was urged to abandon the idea of a "colorblind" society as a way of ridding the nation of racial stereotypes. The Advisory Board of Clinton's Racial Initiative stated that stereotypes are at the core of American's perceptions of minorities.

John Hope Franklin, Chairman of the Board wrote a letter to Clinton:

> The idea that we should aspire to a 'colorblind society' is an impediment to reducing racial stereotyping… Given that research has demonstrated that the best way to reduce racial stereotypes is

to be conscious about racial differences. It is important to present a thoughtful alternative to the 'colorblind society' concept.

Clinton said his background of growing up with blacks made him more sensitive to the racial issues than many whites. His Initiative, however, was not continued under the Bush administration. In fact, the Bush administration opposed affirmative action and filed a brief opposing the University of Michigan's affirmative action point system.

The 15th Amendment to the Constitution gave blacks the right to vote, but Jim Crow Laws (literacy tests, poll tax etc.) prevented blacks from voting in the South. We must not forget that President Lyndon B. Johnson signed the Voting Rights Act in 1965 and amended by President Ronald Reagan. The rights of black people to vote in America will expire in the year 2007. Blacks are the only group of people in this country who need permission by an act of Congressmen and Congresswomen to vote. We do not have the permanent right to vote under the U.S. Constitution. In 2007, Congress will convene to decide whether or not blacks should retain the right to vote. Thirty-eight out of 50 states must approve the extension. How long will the extension be this time? We need more than an Act to give blacks permission to vote; we need this change in the U.S. Constitution.

4) Opposition to Ending Racism

An ultra conservative group announced on April 29, 1998 the formation of the *Citizen's Initiative on Race and Ethnicity* as an alternative to President's Bill Clinton's *Initiative on Race*. The group, led by Ward Connerly, a black member of the University of California Board of Regents who led the fight to end affirmative action in California, unveiled plans to write and increase the discussions of race that the president's panel opened. Connerly is also chairperson of the American Civil Rights Institute, a national group fighting affirmative action. An AOL Internet post featured an article entitled "Spread the Coors

Boycott" by indicating, Coors funded Ward Connerly and the right wing attack on affirmative action.

A conservative, black talk-show host in Los Angeles claimed that blacks were deceived by the President's Initiative on Race and the measure was an ineffective, worthless venture. (Williams, 1998)

I have no panacea to ending the racial problem, however, I have done extensive research to determine what national, state, local and community organizations have done to ameliorate the racial problem. The following sections will provide examples of programs designed to end racism.

5) Racial Climate in the Home Environment

a) Parental attitudes

First, let's examine the wrong way to instruct children in racial relations: Not too long ago a black businessman went to a white residence and rang the doorbell. A small white child, about six or seven years old, answered the door. Her mother asked the child who was at the door, to which the child replied, "Mom, it's a 'Nigger'." The mother screamed in a frightened voice, "Quick, close the door. Do not let him in." This is only one example of how racist attitudes may be planted and encouraged in the home. This child must have learned the"N-word" from one or both of her parents. However, in a racially sensitive environment, the mother would have taken a different strategy by explaining the proper way to respond to such a situation and giving the proper language. But what did she do? She reinforced the child's use of racist language.

During a forum on race relations, a student reported a situation in which a white child, not attending the conference, remarked to her mother, "Look at all those black people, mother." The mother said "shut up" and quickly rushed the child out of the building. What message did that parent give to the child? What did the child think? Perhaps the child thought, "I have done something wrong, but what was it?" What should the mother have done in this situation? She could have used this opportunity to provide her child with positive racial attitudes by explaining the reason why such a large number of black people were present.

b) Handling parental disagreements about race

Let's suppose two parents disagree over how to raise the child, especially as the racial scripting process is concerned. Perhaps one parent is a racist, lived in a racist environment, and works with blacks and dislikes them. The other parent was brought up in a very liberal environment with the belief that "all men and women are created equal."

Rule #1:

Do not argue racial differences of opinions in front of the child. Seeing mother and dad disagree can cause anxiety and lots of discomfort in the child. It also may put one of the parents in a "one down" position. Instead, the two parents must step aside and discuss how the racist ideas are inappropriate and unreal in today's world. Keep in mind to have differences is one thing but to discuss these differences in front of the child is another. An African proverb states, "When two elephants fight, the grass suffers. Res Ispa Loquitur. (The situation speaks for itself)

Rule #2:

Pick the right moment to discuss your differences.

Rule #3

Watch your non-verbal cues.

Rule #4

Listen to each other carefully and do not engage in a lose-lose game.

Rule # 5

Fight fair—do not use "You always," "you
never" and avoid negative language.

Rule #6
Go for help.

In the following vignettes, several examples are given to show how
parents properly instructed their children:

- I do not recall the first time I was exposed to a black
person, but I do know it was not a major excitement in my
life. I do remember an incident that taught me a lot. In
the fourth grade, I was outside during recess when for no
reason at all, a rather large black girl in my class pushed me
against a fence and kept pushing me until I cried. After
this situation I was afraid of this girl and therefore would
not associate with any black people. I felt all black people
were out to get me. For a ten year old this is not hard to
believe. After discussing this incident with my parents,
they made me realize that my attitude towards blacks was
wrong. They understood how I felt, but they told me to
think about what I was doing by not associating with
blacks. They taught me a valuable lesson about prejudice
and from that day on I have never looked down on a black
person. In fact, it infuriates me to hear a white person
talking badly about a black person.

- My first memory of a racial issue is an incident that took
place when I was about five years old. Somewhere in the
neighborhood I heard someone yell to someone "A fight,
a fight, a "Nigger" and a white." I don't remember exactly
where I heard this said and I'm sure that no such fight was
taking place. Of course I really did not understand the real
meaning behind this rhyme, but it sounded cool, so I ran
inside and yelled it to my brother who was in the kitchen
with my mother. My mother got very angry and sent me to
my room until dinner. She explained to me that "Nigger"

was a bad word that meant mean things about people who were black. She stressed to me that black people were not "Niggers." They were regular people who were black. I never used that term again.

- I was about nine or ten years old and we had just moved into a racially mixed housing complex. My brother and I were outside playing on a swing set with neighborhood kids. We were both shouting out the word "Nigger" as if to say, "look what word we know." Before we could gloat over our recently learned vocabulary, our mother was out of the house and at the playground. She embarrassed us in front of the other kids by dragging us by the ears into the house. I had never seen my mother so mad, she stood in front of us, her blood boiling, her fists clenched as if any moment she might hit us. My mother appeared to have grown to a monstrous size and I suddenly felt incredibly small.

My brother wondered what we had done that had affected our mother so deeply. When she finally did speak, her words were all threats. If we were ever to use that word again, our mouths would be washed out with a bar of soap. My mother had been personally offended, and what offended her offended me. Ever since that day, I have never used that word again. I learned that words could be used as weapons. When people use the "N-word" in front of me, I get very angry and upset. They usually learn not to use it around me again. My mother's lesson had taught me not to make racist remarks and I cannot recall ever having done so.

One individual described how children should be taught:

- My goal is that someday we can live in peace and harmony with one another. This will only happen when we learn to better educate our children. Parents who teach their children to be racist, who teach their children that their race is superior to all others are dong them a great disservice. Parents first need to model good behavior to their impressionable young ones. Following the *golden rule* is key to teaching children about equality. These two main points are imperative to non-racial tension. This education must be consistent with the physical actions of parents, as well. Education that contradicts common practice is usually invalidated. The fate of our future is in the hands of our children. It is our duty to train them well.

Few child-rearing books address teaching methods to aid children in understanding and rejecting racism. However, Reddy (1996), in her book ***Everyday Acts Against Raising Children: a multiracialworld*** presents a number of examples for parents to teach their children anti-racist beliefs.

c) Individuals:

Whitney Young called for a "special effort" by private, public and voluntary organizations to launch a massive attack on the complete range of economic and social ills facing blacks. One individual recommended going a step further by making a "supreme effort" to end racism. On how to improve race relations this individual proposed what she called the "supreme effort" to resolve racism by stating:

- Let white people make a supreme effort in their resolve to contribute their share to the solution of the racial problem. Whites should abandon once and for all their inherent, and at times subconscious sense of superiority, to correct the tendency towards revealing a patronizing attitude towards members of other races. Whites should persuade through their intimate, spontaneous and informal association with them of the genuineness of their friendship and the sincerity of their intentions and to master their impatience of any lack of responsiveness on the part of a people who have received so long a period of such grievous and slow healing wounds.

Let the black people through a corresponding supreme effort on their part show by every means in their power, the warmth of their response, their readiness to forget the past and their ability to wipe out every trace of suspicion that may still linger in their hearts and minds. Let neither black nor whites think the solution of so vast a problem is a matter that exclusively concerns the other. Let neither think such a problem can either easily or immediately be resolved. Let neither think they can wait confidently for the solution of this problem until the president's *Initiative on Race* has taken effect and the favorable circumstances created. (Laurie M 9, AOL Internet, June 28, 1998)

This individual talked about the supreme effort to end racism. That supreme effort happened in Minnesota when a white man, Brad Higar donated one of his kidneys to a black man, Kevin Harris. The two were roommates in college and both were cross-country bicycling enthusiasts. When Higar learned about Harris's illness, he said he didn't think twice about donating the kidney to his long-time friend. "I told him I was there for him…I told him if he needed a kidney, I had one for him." (Jet September 14, 1998 Vol. 94, no.16, pp19-21)

A second example of the "supreme effort" occurred when an African- American woman, Rhonda DeLaremore, also, needed a kidney transplant. A white woman, Margie Goralski Stickles, gave DeLaremore the gift of life--one of her kidneys. DeLaremore stated, "We are more alike underneath than some of us want to believe." (Jet Jan 18, 1999, 95 pp. 26-27)

Jane Smith, a white woman of Fayette, N.C, made another supreme effort. Ms. Smith, a middle-school teacher, donated her kidney to her African-American student, Michael Carter. Ms. Smith received the National Kidney Foundation's *Gift of Life* medal for her donation. *The Gift of Life* medal is the highest award given by the foundation. (Jet, July 17, 2000 p. 5)

6) Schools and colleges

Education can be a powerful weapon in the war against racism. Each school, each community, each home has a vital role to play in helping children be free of racists scripts and behavior. Schools have a major role in ending racism. Classes in racial relations must be held in order to enable students to learn about the races of others. As one student stated about her racial education in middle school:

- The best education I received was in the seventh grade when our school held a seminar on race relations. It was a meeting that ended the avoidance between black and white students. At the seminar, we discussed racism, prejudice and desegregation... words that I had heard before, but had never thought about. I began to understand why people were hateful and why I was not close to my black friends. However, after the seminar and after my school committed itself to teaching diversity, I found myself getting closer to my black friends. We were able to discuss our differences and openly discuss race relations instead of ignoring them. This atmosphere encouraged us to explore the obvious, and not so obvious, meanings of racism.

Antioch College in Yellow Springs, Ohio developed an innovative approach to ending racial conflict. Four college students were expelled from the college for tying a noose around the neck of a black mannequin and hanging it on a tree. The interim President, Bob Devine, stated the following:

Hanging a dark-colored mannequin creates a climate of fear, intimidation and anger... and creates a hostile and unsafe community environment by invoking the horror of centuries of racial oppression and intimating threat of such violence upon community members.

The President also said that he planned to develop "Undoing Racism" workshops on the campus and make it a central theme in student orientation.

I recall a similar incident that happened at Washington University during the early nineties. As the new psychology building was under construction, some of the white workers hung a black mannequin from one of the site's windows and the mannequin had a rope tied around its neck. This was directly in line with my path to my classroom. African-American students were very upset by this incident and I immediately called the Chancellor of the University, Dr. William Danforth, to come and witness this display and suggested the owners of the construction company give a public apology. He viewed the hanging mannequin and demanded the perpetrators remove the mannequin. An apology appeared in the next edition of the students' newspaper,

7) **Future Projection**

In my classes, I employ a "future projection" technique, a procedure which requires one to look into the future to decide certain actions that one plans to undertake later in life. Here are several of the responses:

- I envision myself as a mother. I will have an extremely powerful tool to foster positive attitudes for black people in my children. I will expose them to diverse cultures and help them grow respect and love for other races. Along with my children, I will also continue to grow and educate myself.

- I do intend to teach my children of the beliefs I have gained from both of my parents and those I have obtained on my own. Ever since I can remember, my parents have always taught me that all people are created equal, regardless of ones color or race. I will teach my children the same. From the time I was a little girl, there was no difference, in my eyes, between my black friends and my white friends; everyone was just friends.

- I think the real hope for all of us lies mainly in the future generations. We may not be able to change the racial scripts and attitudes already internalized by our parents, but we can influence the racial beliefs formed in our own children. I hope to raise my children with positive views of other races.

- I plan to contribute to the development of civil rights and abolishing prejudice in two particular ways. Within my family, I will teach my children about equality and about society and the differences and similarities within people. I want my children to be able to detect and understand prejudice and racism so they can understand the weak minds of such people that perpetuate myths and hamper the livelihood of people, and the development of our country. Another important factor, I will live in an area that has people of all different races, religions and social-economic classes because I feel that living with people different from you forces you to learn about them and it is this exposure, which leads to truth and acceptance of others. I believe it is when one lives isolated with only people like themselves causes ignorance, fear and ultimately prejudice.

- I will bring my children up in a home where racism does not exist. The home will express the oneness of mankind. I hope I can teach them to respect people for who they are. I want them to appreciate differences in people. Differences should be appreciated, not ignored. This does not mean painting a pretty picture of a harmonious world where racism does not exist. In my opinion, if children are taught to recognize racist actions and language and are also aware of their negative connotations, then they will not be the ones innocently spreading prejudice through schoolyard talk.

- My goal is to live in peace and harmony with one another. This will only happen when we learn to better educate our children. Parents who teach their children to be racist, who teach their children that their race is superior to all others are doing them a great disservice. Parents first need to model good behavior for their impressionable young ones. Following the *golden rule* is key to teaching children about equality. The fate of our future is in the hands of our children and it is our duty to teach and train them.

8) The Media

A reporter from *Jet* magazine called me and stated she was doing an article on "Laughter and Racism" (Jet, July 27,1998, pp. 14-18) The writer asked if there were instances in which racism could be laughed off with a sprinkle of humor? I found this to be a very interesting question that required a serious response. I answered as follows:

> Racism is not a laughing matter. We don't want to use laughter to cloak over or overlook the reality of racism. I wouldn't agree that we could laugh racism off. It's a very severe issue for African-Americans. To laugh it off is a kind of denial that overlooks and takes away from the reality of racism. There are silly racial acts just as there are racial jokes that we laugh at, but that doesn't mean we should justify or deny racism. We know that there are racial jokes that can be funny, but they all hurt. (Pp14-17)

There is no way we can laugh off the dragging of James Byrd in Jasper, Texas, the killing of Dr. Martin Luther King, Jr. or the incarceration of President Mandela for 27 years.

a)   National Erase the Hate and Eliminate Racism Day

To commemorate the first officially designated "National Erase the Hate and Eliminate Racism Day," the USA television premiered a National Hate Test on April 30, 1998. This program was inspired by the movie, "Not in This Town," that promoted understanding and respect for individual differences. The National Hate Test asked viewers to examine their own prejudices and think about their personal values.

The National Hate Test featured a series of vignettes, scenes from everyday life, that revealed hidden biases viewers may have had about topics related to race, religion, disabilities and sexual orientation. For example, one showed two boys on a basketball court that engaged in a friendly competition of basketball. One is African-American and one is Asian. Viewers were asked to select the winner, African-American or Asian.

A very timely article containing recommendations was written by Gregory Freeman, St. Louis Post Dispatch. (March 30, 1997p 4b) A variety of persons offered solutions to ending racism. None of them laid the blame on blacks or whites. Their suggestions were straightforward and positive. Two of their suggestions appear in the following:

- The plainness of truth is African-Americans and European-Americans are different.... We are all uniquely different, and difference does not mean that one or more ethnic group is superior or better than the other. It simply means we are of diverse cultures that give many different skin colors, hair and skin texture, different eye colors, etc. We must start teaching our young the principle of love, or universal love. Racial harmony should be taught in our schools, churches, temples, synagogues and most importantly, our homes.

- Provide a forum where people can ask questions of each other about races. No judgment, just a way to understand the ins and outs of one's culture and background.

Here is what a 15-year-old Wisconsin girl and a 16-year-old Michigan High School boy had to say about their roles in ending racist comments:

- Finally, I had to stand up for what I believe. I go to a fairly small high school, which is all white except for one black guy. Usually the white guys at school are nice to the black guy, but as soon as he walks away, most of them make fun of him or the way he talks. This breaks my heart. I'm sure he knows what goes on. Everyday at school I hear a racial slur or a racist joke. I used to just sit there through all this. I'd fume, but I'd keep my mouth shut. Because this made me feel horrible, I'd make excuses to myself for why I didn't stand up for my beliefs. Then one day I stopped excusing myself and started speaking up to the people to let them know that I don't believe in racism. I hope these words will reach some people's hearts. Please, at least rethink why you discriminate against someone and put yourself in his or her shoes.

- Many of my friends told a variety of racial jokes. At first, I went along with the jokes and laughed with them. Later, I realized what I was doing was wrong. I decided to confront my friends and tell them what I thought about it. I told them they did not have a very good attitude toward blacks and I no longer wanted to be a part of their jokes. A few of them realized what I meant, but others did not and slowly grew distant from me.

b) Hate Watch

What is Hate Watch?

Hate Watch is a not-for-profit group that monitors the growing and evolving threat of hate groups on the Internet.

1) *How did Hate Watch originate?*

Hate Watch was originally a Harvard University library called, "A Guide to Hate Groups on the Internet." Soon the scope of this guide grew too large for a library WebPages, and the need for a more activist oriented organization was obvious. As a result, in 1996, Hate Watch began and started to actively monitor and confront bigots on the Web. The group offers assistance to academicians; activists and victims of hate crimes.

2) What is Hate Watch's definition of a hate group?

A hate group is defined as, "an organization or individual that advocated violence against or unreasonable hostility toward those persons or organizations identified by race, religion, national origin, sexual orientation, gender or disability. Also including organizations or individuals that disseminate historically inaccurate information with regards to these persons or organizations for the purpose of vilification."

3) Does Hate Watch believe in censoring hate groups or hate speech on the Internet?

Absolutely not. Hate Watch holds that once politically disagreeable, even hateful speech is censored, even for "good reasons," it imperils all speech regardless of content.

4) Does Hate Watch make it easier for racists to find hate groups?

Like cockroaches, hate groups feel powerful in their own obscurity because it allows them to do their racist and sometimes violent work in a covert manner. These groups do not enjoy popular support, but their ideas are pernicious and they need to be shown for what they are, hate and harmful. By letting people of good conscience see what these groups say, feel and believe in an unadulterated form, it provides all of us with good information that we act out of knowledge not ignorance. It will be our ignorance of these groups and their ideologies that will allow the spread of these vile and poisonous ideas to continue Hate Watch can be found on the Internet at www.hatewatch.org.

9) Community Anti Racist Initiatives

a) ERACISM: Dialogue is Prologue to Action:

"ERACISM" is the slogan for the group ERACE formed in New Orleans, Louisiana the summer of 1993. It seeks ways, through person-to-person communication, to show a commitment to treating fellow human beings of all colors with love and respect.

ERACE defines racism as

Any philosophy that is opposed to treating fellow human beings of all colors with love and respect.

ERACE provides a forum for people of all colors to talk to each other and get to know each other in an informal setting. At the Saturday meetings, ERACE wants people to practice the principles of Eracism in their conversation. ERACE believes that everyone in the dialogue groups believes in *Eracism* and is working toward a common goal. ERACE encourages members to think critically about views put forth by others. They, however, attempt to create an atmosphere in which people feel free to explore differences of opinions without fear of ridicule or personal attack. They encourage participants to stay focused on issues rather than on attacking individuals. Bumper stickers and t-shirts carry the group's seven-letter message: ERACISM, against a background of red, white and blue waves.

ERACE gets people to talking across racial lines by establishing dialogue and communication. People are able to develop new and more meaningful relationships with a person of a different race. This helps to promote racial diversity. This leads to more flexibility in one's thinking and behavior. Eracism is not a "magic bullet" or a panacea, but it is a step in the right direction.

b) Students Concerned About Racism Ending Diversity (SCARED).

Code of Conduct

To combat racism in my community I agree to follow the SCARED Code of Conduct. I will follow these rules and educate other people if they break the rules. My aim is to stop racism from ending diversity.

1. I won't use racial slurs.
2. I won't display insulting racial symbols.
3. I won't mimic or stereotype people by race.
4. I won't make racial jokes.
5. I won't judge people's abilities by their race.
6. I won't assume a person's attitude based on where they live.
7. I will educate people about anti-Semitism and racism.

In complete darkness, the only thing that makes us different is wisdom and knowledge."

> SCARED
> West Side Citizens Organization
> 625 Stryker
> St. Paul, MN 55107

c) Shasta County Citizens Against Racism (SCCAR)

Shasta County Citizens Against Racism (SCCAR) was founded on May 19, 1988 in response to a racially motivated shooting in Redding, California. Those forming the group felt it was time for an organization to speak out against racially motivated attacks that had too long gone unanswered in the largely white (90 percent) county. It was felt that the open racism so frequently experienced by non-white residents of Shasta County could only be alleviated by creating a climate whereby the residents of the area would see racism as wrong. This would be done through publicly speaking out and condemning racism, as well as educating and pressuring local law enforcement to vigorously prosecute all racially motivated violence.

Since 1988 SCAAR held annual Civil Rights Award Dinners to honor people who performed outstanding deeds on local civil rights issues. The group intends to demonstrate that fighting racism is a noble cause and help create a climate of racial tolerance by having local elected officials honor these individuals.

SCAAR maintained a working relationship with local police and school administrators over issues of racism and racial violence. Educational seminars on hate crimes are held for local law enforcement.

Racial crises have led to healing racial division in the past. Although I do not recommend this activity, it happened in Toledo, Ohio in the fall of 1963, when a white off-duty officer shot a six-year-old black boy in the leg. The policeman said the boy had been throwing rocks into his backyard swimming pool. Several days later, the policeman's house was destroyed by fire. These two racial incidents brought together the two separate worlds that were divided and did not communicate with one another. In an effort to heal the wounds, the community had discussion groups, parties and picnics. Improved racial relationships followed these activities.

Guidelines for dealing with Racial Crises

1. Don't ignore a racial joke or slur; don't let an incident pass without comments. To do so will indicate that you are in agreement with such behavior or attitudes. The intervention may not always take place at the exact time or place of the incident if it is inappropriate and would jeopardize the safety of children or others; but it must be addressed as soon as appropriate.

2. Explain and engage the person or persons when raising the issue; don't preach or be self-righteous.

3. Don't be afraid of possible tension or conflict. In certain situations it may be unavoidable. These are sensitive and deep-seated issues that won't change without some struggle.

4. Be aware of your own attitudes, stereotypes and expectations and be open to discovering the limitations they place on your perspective. We are all victims of our misconceptions to some degree, and none of us remain untouched by the discriminatory images and behaviors we have been socialized to believe.

5. Project a feeling of understanding, love and forgiveness when events occur; don't guilt trip.

6. Recognize that it is a long-term struggle, so try not to get too frustrated. The "isms" won't be eradicated in a day or from one discussion. It is a constant process of change and growth.

7. Be aware of your own hesitancies to intervene in these situations. Confront your own fears about interrupting discrimination; set your priorities and take action

8. Be a role model. Always reflect and practice the positive values you are trying to teach. Don't compartmentalize your responses.

9. Be non-judgmental, but know the bottom line. Issues of human dignity, equality and safety are non-negotiable

10. Distinguish between categorical thinking and stereotyping. For example "blacks" is a category, but "Blacks are lazy" is a stereotype.

Individuals

- I think once we start to know one another, the respect will come. The thing we need to do before we start to learn about each other is throw out everything we were taught in the past and come with open minds. When I say throw everything out, I don't mean "everything." I mean all the stereotypes we've been fed, so that our preconceived notions will not cloud our judgment. (Ms Sangria, AOL Internet, October 7, 1998)

Education
In addition to focusing on *white privilege*, the One America report outlined ten actions to promote racial harmony. That section is titled:

Ten Things Every American Should Do To Promote Racial Reconciliation

One of the most striking findings from our work is that there are many Americans who are willing to accept that racial prejudice, privilege and disparities are major problems confronting our nation. Many of them told us that they would welcome concrete advice about what they should do. To fill that need, we offer a brief list of actions that individual Americans could take that would increase the momentum that will make us *One America* in the 21st century.

1) Make a commitment to become informed about people from other races and cultures. Read a book, see a movie, watch a play, or attend a cultural event that will inform you and your family about the history and current lives of a group different than your own.

2) If it is not your inclination to think about race, commit at least one day each month to thinking about how issues of racial prejudice and privilege might be affecting each person you come in contact with that day. The more that people think about how issues of race affect each person, the easier it will be for Americans to talk honestly about race and eliminate racial divisions and disparities.

3) In your life, make a conscious effort to get to know people of other races. Also, if your religious community is more racially isolated than your local area, encourage it to form faith partnerships with racially different faith groups.

4) Make a point to raise your concerns about comments or actions that appear prejudicial even if you are not the targets of these actions. When people say or do things that are clearly racially biased, speak out against them, even if you are not the target. When people do things that you think might be influenced by prejudice, raise your concerns that the person or institutions

seriously consider the role that racial bias might play, even unconsciously.

5) Initiate a constructive dialogue on race within your workplace, school, neighborhood or religious community. The One America Dialogue Guide provides some useful ideas about how to construct a dialogue and lists some organizations that conduct dialogues and help with facilitation.

6) Support institutions that promote racial inclusion. Watch television programs and movies that offer racially diverse casts that reflect the real world instead of those perpetuating an inaccurately segregated view of America. Support companies and nonprofit organizations that demonstrate a commitment to racial inclusion in personnel and subcontracting. Write the institutions to let them know of your support for what they are doing.

7) Participate in a community project to reduce disparities in opportunity and well being. These projects can also be good ways of getting to know people from other backgrounds.

8) Insist that agencies that teach about our community accurately reflect the nation's diversity of our nation. Encourage our schools to provide festivals and celebrations that authentically celebrate the history, literature and cultural contributions of the diverse groups that comprise the United States. Insist that our children's schools textbook, curricula and libraries provide a full understanding of the contributions of different racial groups and an accurate description of our historic and ongoing struggle for racial inclusion. Insist that our news sources--whatever print, television or radio--include racially diverse opinions, story ideas, analysis and experts. Support ethnic studies programs in our colleges and universities so that people are educated and that critical dialogue about race is stimulated.

9) Visit other areas of the city, region or country that allow you to experience parts of other cultures, beyond their food. If you have an attitude that all people have histories, cultures and contributions which you could benefit from learning, it is usually not difficult to find someone who enjoys exposing others to their culture.

10) Advocate that groups you can influence (whether you work as a volunteer of employee) examine how they can increase their commitment to reducing racial disparities, lessening discrimination and improving race relations. Whether we are a member of a small community group or an executive of a large corporation, virtually everyone can attempt to influence a group to join the national effort to build One America.

The following suggestions are not "magic bullets" but they have proved to be helpful in developing or improving interracial relationships:

1) Develop a meaningful relationship with a person of a different race.

2) Use a support group consisting of African-Americans. You cannot get rid of racial script alone.

3) You also need a set of positive experiences with black persons.

4) The next step is to admit you are a racist or prejudiced. It is not going to kill you.

5) Express that thought without embarrassment and without denial. Denial is one of the biggest blockages to ridding oneself of racism

6) It is useful to write a letter to a black person, a white person and to yourself to confess to being a racist or prejudiced.

7) It is useful to have a particular black person who works with you on a regular basis. Increase your social contacts with blacks.

10)   National Organization

National Urban League

Hugh B. Price, President of the Urban League, states we should all pledge to improve racial relations as one of our primary responsibilities. In a press conference held by the National Urban League and the Anti-Defamation League, Price suggested eight ways to begin to fight racial bigotry. They are:

1) Intensify community-based efforts to promote racial harmony.

2) Expose the evils of racism and anti-Semitism, and teach tolerance for racial, religious and ethnic differences

3) Encourage the prosecution of perpetrators of hate crimes

4) Eliminate police abuse of citizen's constitutional rights.

5) Encourage colleges and universities to address the problems of the racial divide in this country.

6) Create multi-ethnic coalitions to press for just public policies.

7) Affirm the nation's commitment to inclusion.

8) Call on political and community leaders across the country to speak out against bigotry and violence.

He closed by stating:

> Above all, let us remember.... That the responsibility for promoting racial healing rests with all Americans. With those who could act, but don't. With those of us who should act,

but won't. We must all resolve... that it's our individual and collective responsibility to act." (12-29-95)

I end this book with these two stories:

1) One night around 11:30 p.m. an elderly African-American woman was standing on the side of an Alabama highway trying to endure a lashing windstorm. Her car broke down and she desperately needed a ride.

Soaking wet, she decided to flag down the next car. A young white man stopped to help her, generally unheard of in those conflict-filled 1960s.

The man took her to safety, helped her get assistance and put her into a taxicab. She seemed to be in a big hurry! She wrote down his name and address, thanked him and rode away.

Seven days went by and a knock came on the man's door. To his surprise, a giant console color TV was delivered to his home. A special note was attached. It read:

> *Thank you so much for assisting me on the highway the other night. The rain had drenched not only my clothes, but also my spirits. Then you came along. Because of you, I was able to make it to my dying husband's bedside just before he passed away. God bless you for helping me and unselfishly serving others.*
>
> *Sincerely,*
> *Mrs. Nat King Cole.*

2) The second story is similar, but just as touching. It is titled: *Not All White People are Bad*

You know, Joe, a 6'4" burly white man almost didn't see the old black woman stranded on the side of the road. But even in the dim light of day, he could see she needed help. So he pulled up in front of her Mercedes and got out. His 1965 Pontiac was still sputtering when he approached her. Even with the smile on his face she was scared. No one had stopped to help for the last hour or so.

Was he going to hurt her? He didn't look too safe. In fact, he looked poor and hungry. Joe could see that she was frightened, standing out there in the cold. He knew how she felt. It was that chill that only fear could put in you. The man said, "I'm here to help you ma'am. Why don't you wait in my car where it's warm? By the way my name is Joe."

Well all she had was a flat tire, but for an old lady, that was bad enough. Joe crawled under the car looking for a place to put the jack, skinning his knuckles a time or two. Soon he was able to change the tire. But he had to get dirty and his hands hurt. As he was tightening up the lug nuts, she rolled down the window and began to talk.

She told him she was from St. Louis, and was only just passing through. She couldn't thank him enough for coming to her aid. Joe just smiled as he closed her trunk. She asked him how much she owed him. Any amount would have been all right with her. She had already imagined all the awful things that could have happened had he not stopped. Joe never thought twice about the money. This was not a job to him. This was helping someone in need, and God knows there were plenty of people that gave him a hand in the past. He had lived his whole life that way and it never occurred to him to act any other way.

He told her that if she really wanted to pay him back, the next time she saw someone who needed help, she could give that person the assistance that they needed, and Joe added "...and think of me." He waited until she started her car and drove off. It had been a cold and depressing day, but he felt good as he headed for home disappearing into the twilight.

A few miles down the road this old lady saw a small café. She went in to grab a bite to eat, and take the chill off before she made the last leg of her trip home. It was a dingy looking restaurant.

Outside there were two old gas pumps. The cash register was outdated. The whole scene was unfamiliar to her.

Her waitress came over and brought a clean towel to wipe her wet hair. She had a sweet smile. The old lady noticed that the waitress was about eight months pregnant, but she never let the strain and aches change her attitude. The old lady wondered how someone who had so little could be so giving to a stranger.

Then she remembered Joe. After the old lady finished her meal and the waitress went to get change for her $100 bill, the lady slipped out the door. She was gone by the time the waitress came back with the change. She wondered where could the lady be; then she noticed something written on a napkin under which were four $100 bills. There were tears in her eyes when she read what the lady wrote. The note said:

> *Take this gift. You don't owe me anything. I have been there too. Somebody once helped me out the way I am helping you. If you really want to pay me back, here is what you do: Do not let this chain of love end with you.*

Well there were tables to clear, sugar bowls to fill and people to serve, but the waitress made it through another day. That night when she made it home from work and climbed into bed, she was thinking about the money and what the lady had written. How could the lady have known how much she and her husband needed it? With the baby due next month, it was going to be hard, she knew how worried her husband was, and as he lay sleeping next to her, she gave him a soft kiss and whispered softly and low," Good night Joe. Everything's going to be alright."

REFERENCES

Ahmad, I.L (2001, May 31-June 6). Dodson retired with back-up pay), St. Louis American, P. 1.

Alabama's largest real estate company settles racial discrimination case. (1998, June 1) Jet, 94, 1, P.48.

Alabama Librarian-Activist. (2000, June 19). Jet, 98, 2, P. 23.

Allport, G. W. and Kramer, B. M. (1946), Some roots of prejudices. Journal of Psychology, 22, 9-39.

Allport, G. W. (1954) The Nature of Prejudice, (Reading, Massachusetts: Addison-Wesley Publishing Company.

"Ally McBeal" Tackles TV's biggest taboo: interracial love. Jet, March 1, 1999, vol. No 95, No. 13, pp. 62-63.

Ames, R. (1950). Protest and irony in Negro folksong. Science and Society. 14, 193-213.

Amir, Y. (1969) Contact hypothesis in ethnic relations. Psychological Bulletin, 71, 319-342.

Amir, Y. (1998). Contact Hypothesis in ethnic Relations. In Weiner, E. (ed.) The Textbook of Interethnic Coexistence. New York: Continuum Publishing. Pp. 162-181.

A mother worries about racial profiling. (2000, September 19). St. Louis Post Dispatch, p. F 6.

Annual poll shows that most people believe racial profiling by cops is common. (2000, January 10), St. Louis Post Dispatch, p. 6.

Anti-felon laws bar 1.4 million blacks from voting. (2000, September 22), St. Louis Post Dispatch, p. A 8.

Armour, S. (2000a, October 31). Minorities say job advancement blocked. USA TODAY, P. 1a

Armour, S. (2001b, January 10). Bias suit puts spotlight on work place diversity. USA TODAY, p. 1b.

Armour, S. (2002c, December 9, p. B1). Job hunt gets harder for African-Americans, USA TODAY, P. 1b.

A travesty in Columbus, Georgia: innocent man murdered. (2004, January 5). AOL

Autman, S. For teen-agers, mixing among races is common: Polls show their attitude is more liberal than that of their parents. (1998, March 8) St. Louis Post Dispatch, p. C1 and C9.

Avis Franchise in Wilmington, NC will pay $2.1 million to settle lawsuit filed by black customers who say they were refused rental cars because they were black. (1998, May 25) Jet 93, 26, p. 24.

Babcock, D.E. & Keepers, T.D. (1976). Raising Kids O. K.: Transactional Analysis in human growth and development. New York: Grove Press, Inc.

Bailey, A. (1999). In Whiteness: Feminist Philosophical Reflections. In Cuomo, C.J. & Hall, K. Q. (eds.) Lanham, Maryland: Rowman and Littlefield Publishers, Inc.

Ballard, S. (2002, July 29). How to handle racism Jet, 102, 5, pp. 15-18.

Bell, D. (1992). Faces at the Bottom on the Well: the permanence of racism, New York: Basic Books.

Bennett, L. (1968). Nat's Last White Man. In Clark, J. H. (ed.) William Stryon's Nat Turner: Ten Black Writers Respond. Boston: Beacon Press, pp. 3-16.

Bentley, R. (2000, July 23). Black parents warn kids of dangers of racial profiling. Minneapolis Star Tribune, p.1.

Bereiter, C. & Engleman, S. (1966). Teaching disadvantaged children in pre-school. Englewood Cliffs, New Jersey: Prentice-Hall

Berger, J. (2000, November 17). Founder of Adam's Mark Hotels apologizes. St. Louis Post Dispatch, P. A2.

Berne, E. (1964). Games People Play. New York; Grove Press.

Berne, E. (1972). What do you do After You Say Hello? New York: Grove Press.

Biddiss, M.D. (1970). Father of Racist Ideology: the social and political thought of Count Gobineau, London: Weidenfeld and Nicolson.

Black colleges across US target of hate mail. (2000, January 24). Jet, 97, 7, pp.4-5.

Black cop files race, gender lawsuit against supervisor. (2001, May 31-June 6). St. Louis American, P. A 7.

Black Cops awarded $1.2 million in suit over transfer to Brooklyn precinct where Haitian immigrant was sexually assaulted. (2000, July 3). Jet, 98, 4, pp. 5-6.

Black Farmers Association leaders say Agriculture Department lawyer referred to him with racial slur. (1998, June 22) 94,4 p.9.

Black female motorist reaches $800,000 settlement in N.J. Trooper assault case (2002, Feb. 25). Jet, 101, 10, p.19.

Black FBI agents reach a settlement in 10-year bias suit. (2001, May 21). Jet, 99, 23, p.35.

Black leaders denounce white Senator's racist remarks. (2003, January 6) Jet, 103, 2, p. 5.

Black man sues Taco Bell over spit in nacho chips. (1998, April 27) Jet, 93, 22, p.47.

Black N.J. woman victim of blatant racial attack: rubbed with man's feces (1998, March 14) Jet, 93, 24, P. 6

Black owner of upscale restaurant files $50 million discrimination lawsuit. (2002, June 3). Jet 101, 24, p.10.

Black workers file bias suit against Goodyear. (1998, June 22). Jet, 94, 4, p. 12.

Black Reps press for end to racial profiling during meeting with Attorney General Ashcroft. (2001, March 19), Jet, 99, 14 pp 6-8.

Blacks and whites share some attitudes in some areas of race relations. (1998, May 11). Jet, p. 8.

Blacks file $5 Billion Bias Suit against Microsoft. (2000, Jan 22). 99, 6, pp. 23-24.

Blacks file $100 million racial bias suits against Cracker Barrel restaurant chain (2002, January). Jet, 101, 3 pp.4-5.

Blacks get $80 Million Settlement in Bias Lawsuit. (2005, May 16). Jet, 107,20, p. 39.

Blacks much more likely to face death penalty, study says. ((2003, May 12). Jet, 103, 20 pp. 14-15.

Black South Carolina man learns bone marrow donor befriended two years ago is white. (2001, April 9) Jet, 99, 17, pp. 54-56.

Blacks win $28 million lawsuit against Norfolk Southern in race bias case. (2001, Jan. 29). Jet, 99, 7, p. 21.

Black television characters more likely to appear on sitcoms and comedies, study finds. (2002, June 24). Jet, 102, 1, p. 12-13.

Black woman executive wins $7.6 Mil. (July 2, 2001). Jet, p. 39.

Black workers accuse Amtrak of racial bias. (1998, April 27). Jet, 93, 22, p.16

Black youth treated more harshly by juvenile justice system than whites: report. (2002, May 15). Jet, p.37.

Boguslaw, R. (1971). The Design Perspective in Sociology. In Bell, W & Mau, J.A. (eds.) Sociology of the Future. New York: Russell Sage Foundation, pp. 240-258.

Bonazzi, R. (1997) Man in the Mirror: John Howard Griffin. Orbis books: Maryknoll, New York.

Boorstin, D.J. (1961). The image: a guide to pseudo-events in America. New York: Harper and Row Publishers.

Boworth Jr., C. Tapes detail violent plans of hate group, U.S. says. (1998, May 6), St. Louis Post Dispatch, P. 1

Boyd, H. (2004, February 20). Unarmed Black teen killed in New York. SACOSERVER.COM WIRE SERVICES.

Boyle, S.P. (1962) The Desegregated Heart: A Virginian stand in time of transition. New York: Morrow and Co.

Breggin, P. R. & Breggin, G. R. (1994). The War Against Children: How the drugs, programs, and theories of the psychiatric establishment are threatening America's children with a medical 'cure" for violence. New York: St. Martin's Press.

Brown. B.S. (1972) Solutions to sickle cell: resource and responsibilities. A Paper Presented to the National Conference on the Mental Health Aspects of Sickle Cell Anemia, Meharry Medical College, Nashville, Tennessee, June 27, 1972.

Brown, C. S. (2002). Refusing Racism: white allies and the struggle for civil rights. New York: Teachers college Press.

Browning, D. Jury gives life term in killing. (1998, May 8) St. Louis Post Dispatch. P???

Brutality in Bridgeport. (1997, April 4). St. Louis Post Dispatch, p. 6B.

Byran, B. (1999, December 30). Report cites simple error with Valor Award. St. Louis Post Dispatch, p. B 1.

Bryan, B. (2004a, April 8). Chief fires rookie in shooting. St. Louis Post Dispatch, Pp.1 &A 12.

Byran, B. (2004b, April 15). Police union defends shooting. St. Louis Post Dispatch, c. 2.

Byrant, T. (1998a, May 9). Black fire captains allege bias in promotions. St. Louis Post Dispatch, P. 13.

Bryant, T. (1998b, June 18). GM settles racial bias suit at Hazelwood plant. St. Louis Post Dispatch, p. 1.

Buffalo, NY finally settles for $2.5 million in suit charging woman's death was due to racism at a mall. (1999, December 6). Jet, p. 16.

Bullard, R. Environmental racism in Alabama. (2000, October 9). The Challenger p. 1.

Bullard, D. How to handle racism. (2002, July 29). Jet, 102, 5. Pp. 15-18.

Butcher, N. (1996) Undoing the smile, in Reddy, M.E (ed.) Everyday acts against racism: raising children in a multicultural world. Seattle: Seal Press.

Butler, D. & Stokes, D. (1969) Political Change in Britain. New York: St. Martin's Press

Byron De La Beckwith. (1998, Feb 9). Jet, 93, 11, p. 20.

Camille Cosby says man found guilty of killing her son was taught racism and prejudice. (1998, July 27). Jet, 94, 9, p 26.

Carmichael, S. & Hamilton, V. (1967) Black Power: the politics of black liberation. New York: Vintage Books.

Carnahan signs law barring racial profiling by police. (2000, June 6) St. Louis Post Dispatch, p. B 1

Cater, D. & Strickland, S. (1975) TV violence and the child: the evolution and fate of the Surgeon's General Report.

Cesar, D. (1997, April 22). Zoeller apologizes for "joke" about Woods. St.Louis Post Dispatch, p. 2c.

Chaples, E.A., Sedlacek, W.E., & Miyares, J. (1978) The Attitudes of Urban Tertiary Students to Aborigines and New Australians. Politics, 13, 167-174.

Cincinnati police kill black man wielding a BB gun they thought was real: 17th shooting in past six years. (2001, December 17). Jet, 101, p. 1.

Cincinnati settles 2001 riot lawsuit. (2003, June 9). Jet, 103, 24, p. 11.

Civil Rights Commission cites improper use of racial profiling by New York City Police. (2000, July 3). Jet, 98, 4, pp.4-5.

Civil Rights Commission to probe hanging of Florida man after inquest calls death a suicide. (2002, August 18). Jet, 104, 8 p. 49-50.

Clark, K.B. (1955). Prejudice and Your Child. Boston: Beacon Press.

Clinton advisers weigh creating council on race. (1998, June 19). St. Louis Post Dispatch, P. A 5

Clinton pushes Congress to pass hate crimes legislation. (2000, September 14). St. Louis Post Dispatch, p. A 9.

Clinton suggests Americans can overcome racism by learning about how it developed. (1998, September 19). St. Louis Post Dispatch, p. 4.

Clinton wrestles with solution to racial profiling. (2000, November 8). St Louis Post Dispatch, p. A.25.

Cloud, J. (1999, July 19). Is hate on the rise? TIME, p. 33

Coca-Cola racial bias settlement nears end. (2001, June 25). Jet, 100, 2 p.19.

Coke will pay 192.5 million to settle suit alleging racial bias. (2000, November 17). St. Louis Post Dispatch. Pp. A 1.& A10.

Cole, J.B. (1990). What if We Made Racism a Woman's Issue.... McCall's October, 59.

Comer, J.P. White Racism: its roots, form and function. The American Journal of Psychiatry, 1969, 126, 802-806.

Connecticut newspaper apologizes for running slave Ads in 1700's and 1800's. (2000, July 24). 98, 7, p.19.

Conservatives, Clinton agree-cordially—to disagree on race. St. Louis Post Dispatch, (1997, December 20), p. 23.

Controversy Continues Despite Lott's Apology. (2002, December 11) Columbia Daily Tribune. P. 5A

Conversations on race relations today. (1997, June 15, p. 12). St. Louis Post Dispatch, P.12.

Cosby, C. America taught my son's killer to hate Blacks. (1998, July 8). USA Today, p. 15a.

Crawford, S. A. Black Mayor in Selma: new leader seeks reconciliation in a city divided by hatred. (2000, September 26), St. Louis Post Dispatch, p. A 6.

Cross-burning ban backed by Supreme Court (2003, April 20). Jet, 103, 18, p. 10

Cross, W. E. (1991). Shades of Black: Diversity in African-American Identity. Philadelphia: Temple University Press.

Curry, G. (2000, December 13). Racism costs corporate America. The challenger. P. 2.

Darwin, C. (1958) The Origin of the species: by means of natural selection of the favored races in the struggle for life. New York: New American Library of world Literature, Inc.

Davey, A. (1983). Learning to be prejudiced: Growing up in multi-ethnic Britain. Bedford Square, London: Edward Arnold (Publishers) Ltd.

Davidson, H.X. (1991). Somebody's Trying to Kill You: The Psychodynamics of White Racism and Black Pathology. Kansas City: M0, Ethos Growth and Development Publications.

Daytime TV's first interracial marriage set for "General Hospital" (1988, February 29) Jet, 73, 22 Pp. 58-60.

Debate continues over Affirmative Action (1998, May 11). St. Louis Post Dispatch, p. 4

Decade long hunt a boon for medical researchers. (2000, June 27). Miami Herald, p. 6a.

Delaney, L.T. (1968) The American white psyche: exploration of racism. In Schwartz, B.N. & Disch, R. (eds.) (1970) White Racism: its history, pathology and practice. New York: Dell Publishing co. Inc., pp. 155-166.

Delaney, L.T. (1980). The other bodies in the River, in Jones, R. (Ed.). Black Psychology (2nd. Ed.). New York: Harper and Row Publishers, pp. 376-382.

Department fires Inglewood officer caught beating teen. (2002, November 11) 102, 21, p. 4

Detroit police officer is charged in killing, (2000, September 28), St. Louis Post Dispatch, p. A 15

Dine, P. (2000, May 1) Contractor tries to improve relations in wake of workers' accusations. St. Louis Post Dispatch, P. A 4.

Diverse panelists share stories of racism, sexism in St. Louis. (2001, July 24). St. Louis Post Dispatch, p. B4.

D' Souza, D. (1995). The End of Racism: principles of a multiracial society. New York: Free Press.

DuBois, W.E.B. (1903) Souls of Black Folk. Chicago: A.C. McClurg and Company

Economics, History as important as race, President's Critics say. (1997, June 15). St. Louis Post Dispatch, p. A13,

Edney, H. T. (2002, October 24-October 30) A life sentence: denying ex-felons the right to vote. The Challenger, P. 1.

EEOC Files Discrimination lawsuit against Victoria's Secret (2002, September 9). Jet, 102, 12 pp. 10-11.

EEOC complaints up 200%. (2003, September 4-10) Jackson Advocate, p. 1

Encarta World English Dictionary, (1999), New York: St. Martin's Press.

Ending the never-ending story. (2000, February 28). St. Louis Post Dispatch, p. B 6.

Enterprise Leasing to pay $2.3 Mil to Settle Bias Suit. (2002, May 27). Jet, 101, 23, p .8.

Ervin Scholars program guidelines to be revised. (2004, April 2). RECORD, pp. 1 & 7.

Ex-Klansman gets life sentence for '63 Birmingham church bombing. (2002, June 10). Jet, 101, 25 pp. 4-7.

Ex-cop sentenced to 30 years in Prison for torturing Haitian Immigrant in New York with broomstick, Jet January 19, 2000, vol. 97, No. 5, p. 28-29.

Ex-Sorority housemother at Univ. of Alabama says racism was reason for her dismissal. (1998, Feb. 9). Jet, 93, 11, p. 28.

Ex US Marine Marshall wins $4million in a 13-year job bias battle. (1998)

Fairchild, H. (2001). Can blacks be racists? Psych. Discourse, September 2001, p. 2.

Fairchild, H. Modern day racism masks its ugly head. (2000, September 11) Los Angeles Times, p. B7

Family of Amadou Diallo gets $3 million settlement, Jet, (2004 January 26), vol 105, no. 4, p. 22.

Fanon, F. (1967) The Wretched of the Earth. New York: Grove Press

Father of accused Texas hate-crime killer apologizes. (1998, June 12), St. Louis Post Dispatch, p. A12.

FBI study: Blacks most frequent victims of hate crimes. (2001, March 5). Jet, 99, 12, p. 40.

Feagin, J. R. & O'Brien, E. ((2003). White Men on Race: power, privilege, and the shaping of cultural consciousness. Boston: Beacon Press.

Feagin, J. R. & Sikes, M. P. (1994). Living With Racism; the black middle-class experience. Boston: Beacon Press.

Feagin, J.R., Hernan, V. & Batur, P. , (2001) White Racism: the basics. New York: Routledge.

Feagin, J. R., Vera, H. & Imani, N. (1996). The Agony of Education: Black students at white colleges and universities. New York: Routledge.

Feagin, J.R. and Vera, H. (1995) White Racism:the basics. New York: Routledge.

Feldstein, M.J. (2004, February 29) Minorities still face workplace discrimination, experts say. St. Louis Post Dispatch, pp. B1 and B5.

Festinger, L. (1957). A Theory of Cognitive Dissonance. Evanston, Illinois: Row Peterson.

Fewer Black students enter University of Florida. (2001, September 3). Jet, 100, 12, p. 4.

Fineman, H. Ghosts of the Past. (2002, December 23) Newsweek, p. 23.

Fired white sports caster apologize for remark about Venus and Serena Williams; gets re-hired. (2001, July 9). Jet, 100, 4, p.32

Fitzgerald, J. Texaco settles race lawsuit. (1996 November 25). Orange County Register, p. A 1.

Fitzpatrick, T. (1998) Biological difference among races does not exist, Washington University research shows. THE RECORD, pp. 1&5.

Five white officers indicted on civil rights charges in torture case (1998, March 16) Jet, 93, 16, p. 52.

Five Whites Face Charges in Attack on Black Men at Denny's Restaurant, Jet, February 23, 2004. p. 5.

Florida President John Lombardi referred to Dr. Adam Herbert Jr. The new Black Chancellor of the State of Florida University System as an "Oreo" meaning black on the outside, white on the inside. (1998, Feb 2) Jet, 93, 10 pp.8-9.

Follman, C. & Edwards, R., Talking about race can make a difference. (2000, April 28), St. Louis Post Dispatch, p. B 7.

Four men shot by New Jersey white Troopers. (1999, May 17) Jet. P. 37

Four whites arrested in Texas in connection with beating of mentally disabled black man. (2002, October 27). Jet, 104, 18, p. 14

Franklin, D. (2000, September 17). Troy, Ill. man is charged with hate crime, St. Louis Post Dispatch. p. C 7.

Freeman, G. (1999, December 20). Letter from a white man. St. Louis Post Dispatch, pp. B1 and B4.

Freeman, G. (2000, April 27). Asking me to forgo writing as a black man isn't realistic. St. Louis Post Dispatch, p. B1

Freivogel, W. H. (1989, June 13). Court sets back Affirmative Action. St. Louis Post Dispatch, pp. 1 & 7.

Fuller, N. (1967). The United Independent Compensatory Code/ System/Concept: A textbook/workbook for thought, speech and/or action for victims of racism (white supremacy).

Fuzzy thinking. (1997, April 28). St. Louis Post Dispatch, p. 6 B.

Gallagher, J. (2000a, August 23). Reliable is accused of discrimination lawsuit. St. Louis Post Dispatch, p. 1.

Gallagher, J. (2000b, November 1). Majority of blacks pay high-interest rates, group charges. St. Louis Post Dispatch, pp. b1 and b4.

Gallagher, J. (2000c, November 7). St. Louis Post Dispatch, p. 1

Gallup Poll shows gaps in racial understanding. (2004, April 15-21), S. Louis American, pp. 1 & 6.

Galton, F. (1869). Hereditary Genius: an enquiry into its laws and consequences. London: Macmillan.

Gellert, L. (1933) Negro Songs of Protest. Somerville, Massachusetts; Rounder Records.

Georgia Insurance Company Agrees To Pay $55 Million to Settle Bias Lawsuit, (2002, March 11) Jet, p 7.

Georgia Power Co. hit with discrimination suit. (2000, August 14). Jet, 98, 10, p.16.

Getlin, J. Cops trial to move roils New York. (1999, December 22). Los Angeles Times, p. 1.

Gibson, L. (2002). It all started with my parents, in Singley, B. (ed). When race becomes real: Black and white writers confront their personal histories. Chicago, Illinois: Lawrence Hill Books, pp. 82-98.

Glazer, N. & Moynihan, D.P. (1963) Beyond the Melting Pot. Cambridge: MIT Press.

Goodman, M.E (1964) Race awareness in young children: a cultural anthropologist's study of how racial attitudes begin among four-year olds. New York: Collier Books.

"Good Morning America" TV show producer suspended for calling blacks 'spades". (1998, January 12). 93, 7, p. 52.

Goodrich, R. 'This is not a hate crime,' says lawyer for one of 3 suspects (1998, June 18), St. Louis Post Dispatch, p. A 8.

Goodyear apologizes for racially offensive ad. (1998, January 12). Jet, 93, 7, p. 57.

Grant, J. (1968). Black Protest: History, Documents and Analyses (1619 to Present). Greenwich, Con.: Fawcett Publications, Inc.

Guinier, L& Torres, G (2002) The Miner's Canary: enlisting race, resisting power, transforming democracy. Cambridge, Massachusetts: Harvard University Press.

Gurman, S. (2004, April 16). Student offers 'white scholarship'. The Maneater, p. 1.

Guthrie, Robert V. (1976) Even the Rat Was White: A Historical View of Psychology, 1976, New York: Harper and Row.

Gutterman, S.S (ed.) (1972) Black Psyche: the modal personality: Patterns of Black Americans. Berkeley, California: The Glendessary Press, Inc.

Halsey, M. (1946). Color blind: a white woman looks at the Negro. New York: Simon and Schuster

Hampel, P. (2004, February 28) Woman says police entered home without warrant, hurt her son. St. Louis Post Dispatch, p. 16.

Hanging in Mississippi. (2000, July 13), St. Louis Post Dispatch, P. A 8

Helms, J. (1993). Black and white racial identity: theory, research and practice. Wesport, CT: Praeger.

Hernton, C. (1965). Sex and Racism. New York: Doubleday and Company p. 3-4

Herrnstein, R. J. & Murray, C. (1994) The bell curve: intelligence and class structure in American life. New York: Free Press.

Holiday Inn in Oak lawn, IL. To pay $ 1 million to settle bias suit. (1998, June 15). 94,3, p. 7

Holmes, M. (1973) Nobody Else Will Listen: A Girl's Conversation With God, Garden City New York: Doubleday and Co. Inc, in a piece entitled "I'm so glad they're not prejudiced: a Prayer.

Hopson, D.P. & Hopson, D. S. (1993). Raising rainbow Children: teaching your children to be successful in a multiracial society: New York: Simon & Schuster.

Hornblum, A. M. (1998) Acres of Skin: Human experiments at Holmesburg prison: A true story of abuse and exploitation in the name of medical science. New York: Routledge.

Hornung regrets (2004, St. Louis Post Dispatch, p. D9.

Horowitz, D. (1999). Hating Whitey and Other Progressive Causes. Dallas: Spencer Publishing.

Hotel chain settles bias suit for record $1.1 million. (2001, Dec. 24-31). Jet, 101, 2, p. 27-28.

Howlett, D. (1998, March 13). To keep Klan away, Ill. Town helps it out. USA TODAY, p. 3a

Hutchinson, E. O. (2000a, September 28 to October 4). Clinton and Congress Should Get The Feds Out of the Death Penalty Business.), The Challenger, p. 2.

Hutchinson, E.O. (2003b, July 11). Nailing a cop takes more than a tape. Los Angeles Times, p. B 15.

Illinois Racing Board official resigns over racial remark about track worker. (1998, July 2). St. Louis Post Dispatch, p. 1

In Philadelphia, reactions to police beating vary, (2000, July 16), St. Louis Post Dispatch, p. A 11.

Jackson, A. and Smith B., Racism: polarization's costs cited. (1989, November 22), St. Louis Post Dispatch, p. 1.

Jacobs, B. (1999). Race Matters: navigating the minefields between black and white America. Boston: Arcade Publishers.

Jensen, A.R. (1980). Bias in Mental Testing. New York: The Free Press.

Jensen, A.R. (1969) How much can we boost IQ and scholastic achievement? Harvard Educational Review, 39, 1-123.

Jensen, R. White privilege shapes the U.S. (1998, July 19) Baltimore Sun, p. C-1

Johnson, G.C. (2002, November 7-November 13). Inglewood fires cop in videotape beating. The Challenger, p. 1.

Johnson, Michelle (2004). Working While Black: the Black person's guide to success in the white workplace. Chicago; Lawrence Hill Books.

Jones, C., Racist guilty in dragging death. ((1999, February 24), USA TODAY, p. 1.

Jones, C. Balancing act for California Students: anti-affirmative action law makes college choice harder. (1998, April 28), USA TODAY, p. 1.

Jones, C. (1998, April 28). Balancing Act for Calif. Students: those accepted fear isolation, guilt if they don't. USA TODAY, p. 1 a.

Jones, J. H. (1981). Bad Blood; The Tuskeege Experiment. New York: Free Press. London: Collier Macmillan Publishers.

Jones, J. M. (1972) Prejudice and Racism. New York: McGraw-Hill

Jones, R. (1973). Is God a White Racist? A preamble to black theology. Garden city, New York: Anchor Books.

Jonsson, G., Nursing home operator settles racial suitcase. (2001, July 3), St. Louis Post Dispatch, pp B 1 & B3.

Judge rejects criminal charges against New Jersey Troopers. (2000, November 1). St. Louis Post Dispatch, p. A 9.

Judge rejects shielding Jurors in Cosby slaying. ((1998, June 17). St. Louis Post Dispatch, P. A 8

Jury convicts three New York city cops of conspiracy in Abner Louima torture case, (2000, Jet, March 20), p. 32

Kamin, L. (1977). The Science and Politics of IQ. Harmondsworth: Penquin Books.

Kardiner, A. & Ovesey, L. (1951). The Mark of Oppression: explorations in personality of the American Negro. New York: The World Publishing Co.

Karenga, M. (1991). Introduction to Black Studies. Los Angeles, California: University of Sankore Press.

Karon, B.T. (1975) Black Scars. New York: Springer Publishing Company.

Kelly, E. (1998, July 9). Victim's daughter pleads for stronger hate-crime laws. St. Louis Post Dispatch, p. 6A.

Kennedy, A. (2000, July 1) Prosecute the Cop Who Killed Murray and Beasley. St. Louse American. P. 6.

Killing of gay black man puts West Virginia town in spotlight. (2000, July 21). St. Louis Post Dispatch, P. A7.

King, J. (2000, February 4). Driving while Black, then and now. USA TODAY, p. 15a.

Kivel, P. (1996), Uprooting Racism: how white people can work for racial justice. Gabriola Island, British Columbia: New Society. P. 73.

Krauthamer, C. (1997, May 25) St. Louis Post Dispatch, p. 3b.

Labov, W. (1994). Principles of linguistic change. Cambridge, Massachusetts: Blackwell.

Ladner, J. (1971). Tomorrow's Tomorrow: the Black woman. New York: Doubleday and Company, Inc.

Lamprich, E. & Beauchamp, C. (2004, April 20). White scholarship misses point entirely. The Maneater, p 20.

Lantigua, J. Environmental racism threatens minority communities. (2000, September 14) The Challenger, p. 2.

Lasker, B. (1929) Race Attitudes in Children. New York: H. Holt and Company

Las Vegas NAACP calls for resignation of official who made derogatory remarks about King Day. (1998, February 23). Jet, 93, 13, p. 38

L. A. will retry assault case against white Inglewood Cop after 1st trial ends in hung jury. (2002, August 18). Jet 104, 8, p. 48-49.

Lemon, C. (2004, February 13) A Travesty in Columbus, Georgia. AOL Internet

Lee, M (1993) Essence, (April 1993) p. 48

Levinson, A. Man's burning, beheading blamed on outsider, (1997, August 14). St. Louis Post Dispatch, p. 3A.

Lewin, T. (2002, July 18) Police caught on tape beating suspects often are not prosecuted. St. Louis Post Dispatch, P. A 4.

Lhotka, W. (1999, December, 31). St. Louis Post Dispatch, p. B 2.

Lhotka, W. (2000, June 15) Army officer mistakenly accused of rape says his race was a factor in the charges against him. St.Louis Post Dispatch, pp. B1 & B3.

Lippman, W. (1922). Public Opinion. New York: Harcourt Brace.

Litwack, F. (1961). North of Slavery: The Negro in the Free South: 1790-1860. Chicago: Unversity of Chicago Press.

Louima receives $9 Million in NYC Police brutality settlement (2001, April 11). The Challenger, P.1

Macy, R. Killer pleads for forgiveness before getting life sentence. (1998, October 15), USA TODAY, p. 9 A.

Man confesses slaying of Bill Cosby's son, Ennis and drops appeal. (2001, Feb. 26). Jet, 99, 11 p. 16.

Man dragged by vehicle may be hate crime victim. (2002, June 13-19) Jackson Advocate, vol. 64, p. 1 and 12 A.

Man who killed girl, 7, says he's sorry, gets life term. (1998, October 14). St. Louis Post Dispatch. P. A 4.

Marosi, R. & Wride, N. (2003, July 30). The Inglewood Police trial: Mistrial declared in Inglewood police case. USA TODAY, p c2

Mayor wants video in police cars in wake of incident. (2002, July 14). St. Louis Post Dispatch, p. A 4.

McCall, N. (1994) Makes M e Wanna Holler: a young black man in America. New York: Random House.

McDermott, K., Illinois racing board official resigns over racial remark about track worker,   (1998, July 28), St. Louis Post Dispatch, p. B1.

McDermott, k. Illinois House approves bill aimed at "racial profiling" by State Police. (2000, March 4). St.Louis Post Dispatch p. 11.

McGurk, F. (1956, September 21). Psychological Tests: A Scientist's Report. U.S. and World Report, Pp. 92-96

McIntosh, P. (1995). White Privilege and Male Privilege: A Personal Account of Coming to see Correspondences Through Work in Women Studies. In Andersen M. & Collins, P.H. (Eds.) , Race, Class and Gender: An Anthology, (2nd ed.) (Pp 76-87), Belmont, CA: Wadsworth, 1995.

McIntosh, P. (1989). White Privilege: Unpacking the Invisible Knapsack. In Peace and Freedom, July/August. Pp. 10-12

McMahon, P. Affirmative action fight hits Wash. State. (1998, October 21), USA TODAY, P. 3A

McWhorter, D., Texas killing recalls racism in the past, (1998, June 16), USA TODAY, P. 15 A.

Meacham, J. A. Man Out of Time (2002, December 23) Newsweek, P. 27.

Michigan Judge who allegedly made racial comments removed from bench. (1998, August 17). 94, 12, p. 14.

Mississippi hanging of black teen raises questions. (2000, July 17). Jet, 98, 6 P.12-16.

Missouri children are faring better, report says. (1999, December 20). Pp. B1 and B4.

Moore, D. (2002, September 2). HUD Lawsuit accuses Belleville landlord of racial discrimination, St. Louis Post Dispatch, p. 11 A.

Moore, M.T. Jasper, Texas tries to breathe again. (1998, June 29), USA TODAY, P. 5 A

Mozambican's widow testifies in Neo-Nazi's trial. (2000, August 24). St. Louis Post Dispatch, P. A 10.

Mulligan, T. & Kraul, C. Texaco settles race bias suit for 176 million (1996, November 16). Los Angeles Times, pp. A 1, A21.

Murray, C. & Smith, J.O. (1995). White privilege: the rhetoric and the facts. In D.A Harris (Ed.), Multiculturalism from the Margins: non-dominant voices on differences and diversity. (pp. 139-153). Westport: Bergin and Garvey

Myrdal, G. (1962-1944). An American dilemma: The Negro problem and American democracy. New York: Pantheon. (Original work published in 1944).

Mydans, S. (1991, March 21). Friend relives night of police beating. The New York Times, p. B1.

NAACP calls for federal probe of Cincinnati police. (2003, December 4-10). Jackson Advocate, p. 1.

NAACP Kweisi Mfume says Merriam-Webster decision to use racial slurs is "unacceptable". (1998, May 25,) jet 93, 26 p. 12.

NAACP, we Won the Hate Crime Vote in the House of Representatives Last Week!!! (2000, September 28 to October 4), The Challenger, p. 3.

Nationally 49% of African Americans were rejected for conventional mortgage loans whereas whites were rejected at 25%. (2000, August 23), St. Louis Post Dispatch, p. C 1 and C 2.

New Jersey Governor signs bill requiring Black History in all schools. (2002, September 23). Jet, 102, 14, p. 6.

New Jersey to pay $12.9 million to four racial profiling victims (2001, February 19), Jet, 99, 10, p.8.

New York Brokerage House Settles Sexual and Racial Abuse case for $ 1.75 million. (1998, May 4). Jet, 93, 23, p 48.

New York City Settles Bias Suit; Agrees to Pay Minority Cops 26.8 Million, Jet, February 23, p. 4.

"Nice Lunch" gets Woods and Zoeller face to face. (1997, May 21) St. Louis Post Dispatch, p. 8d.

N J. State Police Supt. apologizes for Trooper's 'conduct'. (2001, January 22). Jet, 99, 6 P. 56.

Notre Dame Alum Hornung regrets saying it needs to lower standards to 'get the Black Athlete' (2004, April 19). Jet, 105,6, pp. 50-51.

O'Connor, P. (2001, January 4). Class-action suit is filed against Adam's Mark. St. Louis Post Dispatch, p. c 1 & c7.

Officer Indicted in Taped Arrest. (2002, July 18, AOL Internet.

Officer in Texas quits, is accused of racial remark (2000, October 24). St. Louis Post Dispatch, P. A 5

O'Neil, D. (1998, April 11). Woods-Zoeller pairing was no big deal. St. Louis Post Dispatch, p. 6.

On Line poll (2004, April 20). The Maneater, p. 3.

Page, C. Kerner follow-up: good news and bad news. (1988, March 12), St. Louis Post Dispatch, p. B 10.

Page, C. The problem is social, not just mental, (1999, September 7), St. Louis Post Dispatch, p. B 17.

Parker, L. & Fields, G., In Texas town, a 'deep wound". (1998, June 15), USA TODAY, p. 3A.

Pastor wants to help teens. (2004, April 13). St. Louis Post Dispatch, p. A4.

Police beating tarnishes Philadelphia's aim to polish image before convention (2000, July 15), St, Louis Post Dispatch, p. 24.

Police shooting of a mentally disabled Denver teen draws outrage, investigation. (2003, August 11). Jet, 104, 7, p. 5-6.

Police search for suspects in fight. (2000, May 2). St. Louis Post Dispatch, P. B2.

Poll: Americans believe color is basis of most bias in U.S. (2000, January 10). Jet, p. 21

Porter, J. D. R. (1971). Black child: white child: the development of racial attitudes. Cambridge, Mass: Harvard University Press.

Poussaint, A. (1968). The Confessions of Nat Turner and the Dilemma of William Stryon. In Clark, J.H. (ed.). William Stryon's Nat Turner: Ten Black Writers Respond, Boston: Beacon Press.

Powell, R. (2001). Straight Talk: growing as multicultural educators. New York: Peter Lang Publishing, Inc.

Pressley, S.A. (1998, June 10). Disabled man dragged to death: three whites charged with murder; FBI probes for racial motive. The Washington Post, June 10, p. A3.

Pringle, P. (2003, January 6). Deal considered with fired officers; fatal police shooting in a divided Riverside. Los Angeles Times, p. B 1.

Prof. Sues University of Texas: says she wasn't promoted due to bias (2002, September 16). Jet, 102, 13, p .20.

Race and lending: The problem behind the numbers. (2000, August 26), St. Louis Post Dispatch, p. 30.

Race and Opportunity. (2004, April 16). St. Louis Post Dispatch, B 8.

Race, DNA and Police. (2000, June 19). St. Louis Post Dispatch p. B 6.

Racist flyers circulated throughout town of Kobe Bryant case. (2003, September 1). Jet, 104, 10, p. 48

Racist guilty in dragging death. (1999, February 24), USA Today, p. 1.

Racists try to get views "into the mainstream". (1999, July 8). St. Louis Post Dispatch, p. A 9.

Radke-Yarrow, M., Trager, H. G. and Miller, J. (1952). The role of parents in the development of children's ethnic attitudes. Child Development, 23, 13-53.

Raspberry, W. Death and incivility. (1998, May 27), St. Louis Post Dispatch, P. B7.

Raspberry, W. Law and Racism A Fuzzy Distinction. (1997, April 28), St. Louis Post Dispatch, P. B 7.

Raspberry, W. Minorities play role similar to miner's canary. (1998, May 17), St. Louis Post Dispatch, P. B 3

Raspberry, W. Town seeks racial healing after killing, (1998, June 19), St. Louis Post Dispatch, p, 19.

Ray, J.J. (1978) Determinants of racial attitudes. Patterns of Prejudice, 12, (5) pp. 27-32.

Raybon, P. The case of severe bias. (1989, October 2), Newsweek, P. 11.

Reddy, M.T. (Ed.). (1996). Everyday Acts Against Racism: Raising Children in A Multiracial World. Seattle: Seal Press.

Reep, J. T. (2000, July 13-July 19). Cornell West speaks at the Sorbonne. The Challenger, p. 1.

Reeves, T.A. Killing of a gay black man puts West Virginia in spotlight. (2000, July 21), St. Louis Post Dispatch, P. A 7,

Renouncing and denouncing the use of the "N" word. (2002, November 14-November 20). The Challenger, P. 6.

Report of the National Advisory Commission on Civil Disorders (1968) New York: Bantam Books.

Rice, P. Beating of 3 black teens prompts service on racism. (2000, May 20), St. Louis, Post Dispatch, P. 25.

Richardson enacts safeguards against racial profiling within Energy Department. (2000, October 10). St. Louis Post Dispatch, p. A 2.

Richard Williams laments his tennis daughters are subjected to racial slurs; denies rigging their matches. (2001, April 9). Jet, 99, No 17, p. 51.

Riesman, F. (1962). The Culturally Deprived Child. New York: Harper and Row.

Riggs, M. Producer/Director. (1986, Ethnic Notions [Video]. San Francisco, CA: Resolution/California Newsreel.

Riley, M. (2002, October 3). Blacks are more likely denied loans more often, study says. St. Louis Post Dispatch, Pp. c1 and c4.

Ritchie, J. Carnahan speaks at launching of effort to open dialogue, fight against racism, (1998, May 3), St. Louis Post Dispatch, P. C 4.

Robbins, K. Patrolman Receives Belated Medal of Honor (1999, December 16), St. Louis Post Dispatch, Pp. A1 and A11.

Robertson, T. Racist preacher is building audience for TV show one station at a time. (2000, September 7), St. Louis Post Dispatch, P. A 9.

Rowden, T. (2000a, June 7). Inquiry nears end in attack on black teens. St. Louis Post Dispatch, p. B 3.

Rowden, T. (2000b, June 17). Man pleads guilty in attack on three black teen-agers. St. Louis Post Dispatch, p 7.

Ryan, W. (1976) Blaming the Victim. New York: Vintage Books.

Samuel, T. Carnahan will participate in nationwide effort to improve race relations. (1998a, May 1). St. Louis Post Dispatch, P. A 16.

Samuel, T. (1998b, May 11). Debate continues over affirmative action. St. Louis Post Dispatch, P. A 4.

Samuel, T. When white supremacists gather, their talks can get very detailed. (2000, April 6). St. Louis Post Dispatch, P. A 6.

Scharnberg, K. Racist church uses Nazi salute as greeting. (1999, July 15) S. Louis Post Dispatch, P. A 6.

Schmalz, J. (1989, January 24). Officer arrested in Miami death that began riot. New York Times, p. 1.

Schremp, V. & Bell, B. (2000, June 17). FBI says it will investigate killings outside fast-food restaurant. St. Louis Post Dispatch, p. 3.

Schwartz, B. N. & Disch, R. (1970). White racism: its history, pathology and practice. New York: Dell Publishing Co., Inc.

Segregation: Belleville faces its racism. (1998, May 14), St. Louis Post Dispatch, P. B 6.

$7.5 million High School racial bias case settled in Washington State. (2002, October 14), Jet, 102, 17. p. 24.

Settlement reached in fatal shooting of Black California motorist. (2000, August 14). Jet, 98, 10, p.17.

Shlachter, B. (1988, June 12). Black man's torture-killing forces town to examine image. St. Louis Post Dispatch, P. A 1.

Singley, B. (2002). Why Race Becomes Real: Black and white writers confront their personal histories. Chicago, Illinois: Lawrence Hill Books.

$60 million wrongful death suit. (2000, July 3), Jet, 98, 4, p.8.

Slater, J. (1972) Sterilization: newest threat to the poor. Ebony, 150-156.

Slavery but he rules out paying compensation to Blacks. (1997, June 17). St. Louis Post Dispatch, p. 27

Smith, B. and Jackson, A. (1989, November 22). Summary of proposals by Racism Task force. St. Louis Post Dispatch, 4A.

Smith, L. (1961). Killers of the Dream. New York: Norton.

Social Security Administration will pay $7.75 mil. to settle employment bias suit. (2002, February 4). Jet, 101, 7 p. 6.

South Carolina Senator asked to apologize for slur against NAACP. (2000, January 31). Jet, 97, 8, p. 30

Southern Poverty Law Center. (2000,Summer). Intelligence Report, 99.

Standing up to prejudice (1998, May 4,). St. Louis Post Dispatch, p. B. 6.

Stanton, W. (1960). The Leopard Spots: Scientific Attitudes Toward Race in America, 1815-1859, Chicago: University of Chicago Press.

Steiner, C. M. (1974). Scripts People Live; transactional analysis of life scripts. New York: Grove Press.

St. Jean, Y. & Feagin, J. R. (1998). Double Burden: Black women and everyday racism. Armonk, New York: M.E. Sharpe, Inc.

St. Petersburg, Fl Police Chief fired for saying Black suspect acted 'like an orangutan.' (2002, January 14). Jet, 101, 4, p 5.

Study reveals hate crime epidemic: Conyers backs new law to track violence. (1988, February 29) Jet 73, 22 p. 55

Study shows geographic and racial disparities in U.S. death penalty cases. (2000, September 13) St. Louis Post Dispatch, P. A 5.

Styron, W. (1966) The Confessions of Nat Turner. New York: Signet Books

Sullivan, H.S. (1953). The Interpersonal Theory of Psychiatry. New York: W.W. Norton.

Supremacist's speech draws demonstrators. (2002, January 13), St. Louis Post Dispatch, P. A 2

Tangonan, S., Slurs to be labeled as such in dictionary, but not deleted. (1998, May 7), USA TODAY, P. 2A.

Tatum, B.D. (1994,Summer). Teaching white students about racism: The search for white allies and the restoration of hope. Teachers College Record, 95, 463-476.

Tatum, B. D. (1997). "Why are all the Black Kids sitting together in the cafeteria?": And other conversations about race. New York: Basic Books.

Terman, L. (1916) in Nobles, W.W. (1986) African Psychology: towards its reclamation, reascension and revitalization. Oakland: The Institute for the Advanced Study of Black Family Life and Culture. P.p. 11-12.

Texas Health Exec quits after making racial slurs. (2000, November 13). Jet, 98, 23, pp. 9-10.

Texas officials probe alleged attempted lynching. (2002, November 14-to November 20), The Challenger, P. 1.

The Fight Against Racism: Economics, History as Important as Race, President's Critics Say. (1997, June 15), St. Louis Post Dispatch, P. 13 a.

This is not a hate crime says lawyer for one of three teens suspects. (1998, June 18) St. Louis Post Dispatch, P. A 8.

Thomas, C. W. (1970) Different Strokes for Different folks. Psychology Today. Pp. 49-53 and 80.

Time to erase inequality. (1989, January 14). St. Louis Post Dispatch, p.2 B.

Thornton, J. Whitman, D. & Friedman, D. (1990, November 9) Whites Myths About Blacks, U.S. News and World Report, Pp. 41-44.

Tillman, D. (2000, May 15), Jet, p. 37

Three white men accused of dragging black man to death in Jasper, TX (1998, June 29). 94, 5, pp. 10-18.

Three years after discrimination lawsuit, Texaco improves its record. (1997, August 24-August 40). P. 1.

Tiger Woods says death threats continue. (1997, November). Jet, 93, 1 p. 56.

Tuft, C. (1998, June 20). Tension is high in Belleville after racial dragging charges. St. Louis Post Dispatch, p. 3

Tuft, C. (1999, July 8). Fatal hate crimes have been rare in the St. Louis area-misleadingly so, some say. St. Louis Post Dispatch, p. A 8.

Tuft, C. (2000, November 25). Ad to sell gun is actually a link to supremacist group. St. Louis Post Dispatch, P. 8.

25 years later: is white racism still dividing America into black and white races-separate and unequal? (1993, May 31). Jet, Pp. 12-17.

Twaecap (1998) White supremacy. AOL Internet

Two South Carolina insurers ordered to pay millions to overcharged Blacks (2002, January 14). 101. 4 p12.

2 White House aides say they were victims of racial profiling. (2000, September 28). St. Louis Post Dispatch, p. A 12.

Uhlenbrock, T., Bias Crime Widespread in Missouri, Experts Say. (1989, September 21), St. Louis Post Dispatch. P. 9.

Ukrainian Immigrant Mikail Markahsev found guilty of murdering. Ennis Cosby (1998, July 27)) Jet 94, 9, pp. 24-26.

Unitrin Inc. Insurance Company to Repay Millions in discrimination Suit. (2002, May 27) Jet, P. 39.

Urban America, Inc. and the Urban Coalition (1969). One Year later: an assessment of the nation's response to the crisis described by the National Advisory Commission on Civil Disorders. New York: Frederic A. Praeger, Publishers.

Urban League Chief asks groups not to use Adam's Mark Hotel until lawsuit is settled. (2000, February 24). St. Louis Post Dispatch, p. A 1.

U.S. Civil Rights Commission says NY Police use racial profiling against blacks, Hispanics. (2000, June 17). St. Louis Post Dispatch, P. 20.

US President Thomas Jefferson fathered child with slave. DNA study shows (1998, November 16). Jet, 94, 25, p. 25.

Victim shot on ground, medical examiner says. (2000, February 9). St. Louis Post Dispatch, p. 4A.

WABC (1992). Bob Grant Radio Talk Show Host.

Washington State Senator Apologizes for Slur: Many Blacks Want Him to Resign. Jet, February 23, 2004, p. 12.

Watson, J. (2004, Almost half of African American Men in New York City unemployed. (2004, March 4-11). Jackson Advocate, p. 2a

Welsing, F. C. (1991) The Isis Papers: the keys to the colors. Chicago: Third World Press.

What can cities do to ease the racial tension? (2001, May 28). Jet, 99, 24, pp. 4-6.

White Cincinnati officer acquitted. 2001, Jet 10, 15, p. 46.

White ex-cop sentenced to 7-15 years for 1992 death of black motorist Malice Green in Detroit. (2000, June 25). Jet, p. 25.

White Hampton, VA man sentenced to three years for cross burning (1998, February 23). Jet, 93, 12 p.40.

White, J. (1972) Toward a Black Psychology, in R.L. Jones (ed.) Black Psychology, New York: Harper and Row, 43-50.

White man imprisoned for attack on black Trooper who danced with white woman. (2002, April 15). Jet, pp. 38-39.

White man sentenced to life in prison for killing Black girl in casino bathroom. (1998, November 2). Jet, 94, 23, pp. 6-7.

White Muslim woman donates kidney to Black Christian man. (2001, October 29). Jet, 100, 20, pp10-12.

White New York cops shoot 41 times. (1999, February24). Jet p. 15.

White officer kills armed black man in 1st fatal shooting in Cincinnati since riots. (2001, July 25). St. Louis Post Dispatch, B 4.

White Polygram Records Exec. makes racist comments leaves company. (1998, March 23). Jet, P. 64.

White President of University of Florida apologizes for racist remarks about Black Chancellor of State University. (1998, February 2) Jet, 93, 10, Pp. 8-9.

White supremacist on death row convicted of double murder in Ohio (1998, November 16). Jet, 94, 25, p. 47.

White Virginia man found guilty of burning and beheading black man. (1998, November 23). Jet, 90, 26, p. 53.

White Virginia man gets life for burning, be-heading a black man. (1998, June 15) Jet, 94, 3, p.12.

William sisters victims of racism, says Father. (2001, April 11) The Challenger, P. 1

Wilson, M. Missouri law on racial profiling in fast lane. (2001, May 31). St. Louis American, P. A 9.

Wilson, W.J. (1978) The declining significance of race. Society, Jan./Feb.pp.125-132.

Wilson, W. J. (1978) The Declining Significance of Race: Blacks and Changing American Institutions. Chicago: University of Chicago Press.

Woods to Zoeller: apology accepted. (1997, April 25). St. Louis Post Dispatch, p. D 3.

Woodson, C.G. (1933) The Mis-Education of the Negro. Washington, DC: Associated

Wright, B. (1954) The Psychopathic Racial Personality: And Other Essays. Chicago: Third World Press.

Zoeller, Black Golfer Joke on 'Touchy Subject'. (1997, April 29), St. Louis Post Dispatch, 1997. p. 3c

Zoeller Pulls Out Of Tournament. (1997, April 27), St. Louis Post Dispatch, p. D 1 and D 6.

ABOUT THE AUTHOR

A retired Washington University professor, Robert L. Williams in 1973 coined the term "Ebonics" which came into use as controversy grew around the linguistic status of Black language. He has been a steadfast critic of racial and cultural inequities in standardized IQ testing of African American schoolchildren.

Developer of the Black Intelligence Test of Cultural Homogeneity he published more than 60 professional articles and two books including Ebonics: theTrue Language of Black Folks and The Collective Black Mind: Toward an Afrocentric Theory of the Black Personality.

Dr. Williams has been a guest on several national televisions programs relating to IQ testing, including CBS's "IQ Myth" with Dan Rather, Prime Time Saturday Night, The Phil Donohue Show and The Montel Williams Show. Most recently he appeared on Black Entertainment Television (BET) and NBC News to discuss the controversial topic "EBONICS".. His works were, also, used for one of the "Good Times" TV programs.

Dr. Williams has been employed as Staff Psychologist, Arkansas State Hospital (Little Rock, Arkansas); Chief Psychologist, VA Hospital (St. Louis, Missouri) Director of a Hospital Improvement Project (Spokane, Washington) and Consultant for the National Institute of Mental Health (San Francisco, California). From 1970 -1992 he was employed as Full Professor of Psychology and African and African –American Studies at Washington University. He developed the Black Studies at Washington University and served as its first Director. He retired from Washington University and is now Professor Emeritus. Dr. Williams returned to the academy (2001-2004) as The Distinguished Visiting Professor of Black Studies at the University of Missouri-Columbia and served as the University's Interim Director of Black Studies for the academic year 2002-2003.

Robert L. Williams earned a BA degree (cum laude and Distinction in Field) from Philander Smith College (Little Rock, Arkansas); M.Ed. from Wayne State University (Detroit, Michigan); Ph.D. in 1961 from Washington University (St. Louis, Missouri) with a major in Clinical Psychology.

CPSIA information can be obtained
at www.ICGtesting.com
Printed in the USA
FFOW04n0332121015
17608FF

9 781425 9259